CARCERAL APARTHEID

Justice, Power, and Politics

Heather Ann Thompson and Rhonda Y. Williams, editors

EDITORIAL ADVISORY BOARD

Dan Berger
Peniel E. Joseph
Daryl Maeda
Barbara Ransby
Vicki L. Ruiz
Marc Stein

The Justice, Power, and Politics series publishes new works in history that explore the myriad struggles for justice, battles for power, and shifts in politics that have shaped the United States over time. Through the lenses of justice, power, and politics, the series seeks to broaden scholarly debates about America's past as well as to inform public discussions about its future.

A complete list of books published in Justice, Power, and Politics is available at https://uncpress.org/series/justice-power-politics.

CARCERAL APARTHEID

HOW LIES AND WHITE SUPREMACISTS RUN OUR PRISONS

Brittany Friedman

The University of North Carolina Press | Chapel Hill

© 2025 Brittany Michelle Friedman
All rights reserved

Designed by April Leidig
Set in Arnhem by Copperline Book Services, Inc.

Manufactured in the United States of America

Cover art: *An American Target* by Adam Niklewicz.
Courtesy of Adobe Stock.

Complete Cataloging-in-Publication Data for this title is available from the Library of Congress at https://lccn.loc.gov/2024033128.

ISBN 978-1-4696-8339-3 (cloth: alk. paper)
ISBN 978-1-4696-8340-9 (pbk.: alk. paper)
ISBN 978-1-4696-8306-5 (epub)
ISBN 978-1-4696-8341-6 (pdf)

> I'd rather go down in history as one lone Negro who dared to tell the government that it had done a dastardly thing than to save my skin by taking back what I said.
>
> —IDA B. WELLS

CONTENTS

List of Illustrations ix

Prologue xi

Acknowledgments xv

Chronology. Carceral Apartheid: US Edition xvii

Chronology. Carceral Apartheid: World Edition xxi

Introduction to Fate 1

PART I
Carceral Apartheid

1. Carceral Apartheid as Governance 19

PART II
Obey

2. Adjusting Problem Inmates 37

3. White Above All 67

PART III
Rebel

4. The Dragon 93

5. Live Free or Die Trying 109

PART IV
Aftermath

6. Adapt to Survive 135

7. Guerilla 149

Conclusion. Invitation to Awaken 163

Appendix. Truth-Telling as Method 165

Notes 171

Index 197

ILLUSTRATIONS

Figures

My grandmother holding my aunt xii

Exterior of Building 22, San Quentin State Prison xxiv

Great Mosque of Gaza 18

Warden Clinton T. Duffy with two incarcerated men at San Quentin State Prison 36

One of many similar signs strung along the fence enclosing San Quentin penitentiary grounds 43

Exterior of Building A, San Quentin State Prison 56

Ku Klux Klan parade in Washington, DC 68

March on Washington 95

Interior of Building E, San Quentin State Prison 110

Interior of Building B, San Quentin State Prison 136

Tables

1.1. Levels of analysis in the governance regime of carceral apartheid 25

A.1. Primary documents from public and private archives 167

A.2. Memoirs 169

PROLOGUE

> There is a reason, after all, that some people
> wish to colonize the moon, and others dance
> before it as before an ancient friend.
>
> —JAMES BALDWIN

My family comes from all throughout the Deep South, but I grew up in Missouri. Born in 1914, Early Ida Marie Coffee Wilderness Avery, my maternal grandmother, was once a sharecropper and young mother evicted from her home. My mother's family found a photograph of grandma holding my aunt surrounded by their belongings on the side of a highway in Southeast Missouri. It is held in the Library of Congress. The archive labeled the photograph "Evicted sharecropper," but when I see the image, I see my family, our hopes and dreams, and a world that has forced us to be resilient. In 1939 my grandma was a part of a major protest staged by 1,500 evicted sharecroppers and the Southern Tenant Farmers' Union, who lined up along Highways 60 and 61 in New Madrid County, Missouri, otherwise known as the "Bootheel." All their belongings lay strewn along the roadside for passersby to see their desperate conditions. Though mostly Black sharecroppers, a group of poor white sharecroppers also joined the protest, signaling a moment of cross-racial consciousness against division and exploitation, which terrified the state. Highway patrolmen were sent by white landlords to intimidate the protesters to leave and eventually, the local police forcibly relocated several hundred people evicted from their homes to dire circumstances in the nearby swampland.[1]

Born in the 1950s, my mother and father grew up in small rural towns in the Bootheel, an area of my home state I frequently visited as a child. Driving down to grandma's house, my dad would point out the swamplands where rice was grown, the fields where he picked cotton as a small child after school, the Hayti Negro School where he received a segregated education even after the 1954 Supreme Court *Brown v. Board of Education* decision, and the tiny house in the "projects" where my grandma raised my mom and her eleven siblings.

My grandmother holding my aunt after being evicted as a sharecropper, 1939. She was a part of a protest against this injustice. Farm Security Administration—Office of War Information Photograph Collection, Prints and Photographs Division, Library of Congress, Washington, DC.

Strong and unstoppable, grandma taught me that in this family we speak the truth.

I remember the many conversations around the table and at family functions about interactions people had with police and their experiences inside jails and prisons. One memory I will never forget because the experience remained etched in my mind for years. I remember as a child on a road trip through "Klansville" in Missouri and my parents—Black and visibly nervous—advised my younger sister and me to stay in the car. Unfortunately, we needed to stop in a region that all Black people in our state know to avoid. Our car required gasoline and we could not wait until we were closer to home.

When my dad tried to pump the gas, the attendant deliberately turned the pump off and smirked through the window as dad was frustratingly forced to put the nozzle back on the pump holder. My sister and I needed to stretch our legs, but my mom advised us to get out quickly, move some and then get back in the car as my dad went inside to speak to the station attendant. When I stepped out of the car (I was an elementary school kid), I remember the white people at the gas station staring at us, shooting hateful darts with their eyes at the audacity of a "colored" family stopping in their little white town. I remember a white woman's anger and confusion at the sight of my mom, sister, and me—our skin tones ranging from caramel to yellow to light brown. Racist and confused, she did not know that Black people, thanks to legacies of colonialism, genocide, and rape, could come in many shades, even in one family. The woman continued to stare in disgust as my dad returned to the pump, his head down to the point I could not tell whether he was ashamed or angry. Looking back, I suspect he was likely both.

The white crowd continued to stare.

Keep in mind that all these white people did not know each other personally, but even still, they all knew what team they were on, and they all knew they were white, together, and that we were not. They psychically and then socially agreed, almost like a program, that we did not deserve to exist freely without their collective punishment. It was cultural instinct.

Dominance enacted by white supremacist civilians, often empowered by their status adjacent to law enforcement, forms a web of white solidarity predicated on the assumption of Black inferiority. Black people know this well from an embodied rather than a descriptive place. What you will read in this book are examples of white civilians who, emboldened by their whiteness, collectively berate, humiliate, and degrade Black people. Through their actions they contribute to a government-sponsored project, present since the inception of colonial America, to isolate, target, and ultimately declare a domestic war on Blackness, mobilizing carceral systems such as police, prisons, and jails in order to win a doomed game.

To experience this form of governance both personally and intergenerationally produces a simple but dislocating question: *Whose governance?* We continually witness the power of white solidarity across class, law enforcement status, and personal boundaries—even if the actors are complete strangers—in support of the collective decimation of Black people.

Unfortunately, sometimes my memories of this reality move beyond episodes of shaming, such as that experienced at the gas station, and into the anxious realm of impending doom. Like that one time in the Mississippi Delta—not too far from where Emmett Till's body was beaten, tortured, and mutilated—a fact I was well aware of riding in the back of a modest car, while my college friend's father drove-while-Black. We were young Black women, recounting to her parents the latest tea from our Southern university campus; our joyous conversation and laughter ceased when we all noticed the police lights behind us. The flashing red and blue mimicking the American flag glimmered against the sunlit particles dancing in the air.

I felt my shoulders tighten, lifting like small mountains I wanted to crawl up and hide within, as the thickness of our fear overtook the car. Her father's contagious smile immediately fell to the floor, and he swiftly pulled the car onto the right shoulder, the abrupt stop causing red dust to pool on the front dash. We heard feet slowly approaching, and I was too afraid to move or turn around to see who was coming. The crunch of the gravel and leaves warned us with every new step. The middle-aged white officer slowly waved his baton at the car and commanded my friend's father to roll the window down, placing the baton on the glass as if to push it down faster.

We were alone on that road with him.

To feel his cool blue gaze and smell his hot breath as he leaned into the window and smirked, a smile filled with intention—for you and he both know: he wields total power over you and could make your body exit the car should it please him. He slowly licked his lips and moved the baton across the top of the window, seeming satisfied for the moment and bent on pointing the baton at my friend's father. "Seems like you have some young women in the backseat," he sneered, grinning as he gestured backward, turning his lower body to face us. My friend and I locked eyes, forgetting to breathe, holding still as if that might help us disappear—our light feeling momentarily dimmed.

These memories are part and parcel of a broader web of white supremacist assumptions, behaviors, and solidarity among white civilians and with state actors that serve as a touchstone. I am telling you about them because while this book draws examples from prisons, this book also underscores themes that are, in fact, related to a Black grandmother forcibly evicted, a Black family harassed at a gas station, and two Black girls in the back seat of a car being gawked at by a white police officer. We cannot separate examples of the collective humiliation and degradation of Black people in the service of white supremacy no matter where they occur.

This book unveils an underlying racialized governance structure that encourages, profits from, and celebrates Black degradation and the labeling of an entire demographic of people as targets for genocide on American soil.

What you will read in *Carceral Apartheid* will stretch your mind beyond the case of prisons, white supremacists, and lies. This is ultimately a book about racist intent, its enduring legacies and manifestations, and the carceral foundation of US empire.

ACKNOWLEDGMENTS

During the decade it took me to research and write this book, my life saw many significant changes. I celebrated several triumphs and endured profound traumas. I gave birth to two beautiful children whom I love with all my heart. I survived two emergency C-sections, and with the birth of my youngest, she and I almost died on the table. Not too soon after, I got divorced (née Jenkins).

My daughters and I caught COVID-19 in 2020, landing me in the emergency room only a year after my cousin was murdered and a close relative was sentenced to several decades in prison for the slaying—a trauma that shook our entire family to its core.

And just as it seemed like things were getting brighter, a few years later my oldest and I were in a serious car accident that made me feel as though I would never be in the right place at the right time to finish this book. Even still, I pushed on, and just when I thought daylight might break, I had to pull from the core of my being to survive a sexual assault.

But I believe in the wisdom of divine protection and divine timing.

I am tremendously grateful to my ancestors, angels, God/Goddess, spirit team, devas, family, friends, mentors, editorial and fact-checking team, and everyone who has ever held me in their hearts, prayers, and thoughts.

I will be forever grateful to the people who opened their doors to me and allowed me to hear their stories and spend time in community.

This book is here because of the communal support I received. I wrote this for all of us.

We did it.

CHRONOLOGY

CARCERAL APARTHEID: US EDITION*

1819: Indian boarding school era begins
March 3, 1819: Civilization Fund Act
July 1852: San Quentin State Prison opens
April 12, 1861: Start of Civil War
January 31, 1865: Thirteenth Amendment to the US Constitution abolished slavery expect for those imprisoned
April 9, 1865: End of Civil War
April 15, 1865: President Abraham Lincoln murdered
1860–1880: Black Reconstruction
July 1880: Folsom State Prison opens
1892: Ida B. Wells publishes *Southern Horrors: Lynch Law in All Its Phases*
February 20, 1895: Frederick Douglass dies
July 26, 1908: FBI established
March 10, 1913: Harriet Tubman dies
1919: J. Edgar Hoover becomes head of FBI General Intelligence Division
Jan. 17, 1920: Prohibition begins
September 17, 1922: Founding of Nationalist Party of Puerto Rico
June 1923: Marcus Garvey imprisoned in federal prison after FBI investigation
May 10, 1924: J. Edgar Hoover becomes director of the FBI
November 1927: Marcus Garvey deported from the United States to Jamaica
August 1929: Great Depression begins
1932: Tehachapi State Prison opens as California Institution for Women
December 5, 1933: Prohibition ends
June 18, 1934: Indian Reorganization Act
1939: Great Depression ends
June 21, 1941: California Institution for Men (Chino) opens
June 22, 1944: Servicemen's Readjustment Act (GI Bill)
1946: Correctional Training Facility (Soledad) opens
1950: *Siegel v. Ragen* court case
1951: "We Charge Genocide" presented by Civil Rights Congress to United Nations

*This is not an exhaustive list.

1952: California Institution for Women (Chino) opens
1953: Deuel Vocational Institution (Tracy) opens
1953: CDC Committee on Intensive Treatment of Problem Cases established
1954: *Brown v. Board of Education* US Supreme Court case
1954: CDC Final Protocol on Adjustment Centers
1955: Black Americans represent 20.6 percent of California's imprisoned population
December 1, 1955: Rosa Parks arrested in Montgomery, Alabama
December 5, 1955: Montgomery Bus Boycott begins
1956: Indictment of Montgomery Bus Boycott leaders
1956: FBI initiates COINTELPRO
December 20, 1956: Montgomery Bus Boycott ends
1957: Mexican Mafia established in Tracy, California
1958: CDC Administrative Bulletin 58/16: Special Procedures for Muslim Inmates
1960: Black Americans five times as likely as white Americans to be incarcerated in the United States
1961: CDC Administrative Bulletin 58/16 Revised: Inflammatory Inmate Groups
1961: George Jackson sentenced to one year to life for stealing seventy dollars
1961: *Ferguson v. California* court case
April 12, 1963: Dr. Martin Luther King Jr. and Rev. Ralph Abernathy jailed in Birmingham, Alabama
August 28, 1963: Dr. Martin Luther King Jr. delivers "I Have a Dream" speech at the March on Washington, DC
September 15, 1963: 16th Street Baptist Church bombing
November 22, 1963: President John F. Kennedy murdered
April 12, 1964: Malcolm X delivers "The Ballot or the Bullet" speech
1964: Aryan Brotherhood established in San Quentin
February 21, 1965: Malcolm X murdered
1965: Black Americans represent 26.9 percent of California's imprisoned population
1965: Selma to Montgomery Marches
1965: Watts Riots in Los Angeles
1966: Black Panther Party founded in Oakland, California
1967: 159 Race Riots in the United States and FBI initiates COINTELPRO-BLACKHATE
April 4, 1968: Dr. Martin Luther King Jr. murdered
June 6, 1968: Robert F. Kennedy murdered

Chronology

June 30, 1968: Huey Newton indicted for murder of Oakland, California, police officer
1968: Aryan Brotherhood aligns with Mexican Mafia
1968: Nuestra Familia established in Tracy and aligns with Black militants
January 17, 1969: Bunchy Carter and John Huggins murdered at University of California, Los Angeles
December 4, 1969: Fred Hampton murdered by police in Chicago
December 9, 1969: 41st and Central Shootout between Los Angeles Police Department and Black Panthers
1969: Anthony transferred from Soledad State Prison to San Quentin
January 13, 1970: Soledad Incident
January 16, 1970: Officer Opie Miller acquitted in Soledad Incident and Officer John Mills killed in revenge
February 14, 1970: Soledad Brothers charged with killing Officer John Mills
1970: George Jackson and Hugo Pinell transferred to San Quentin
1970: Black Guerilla Family established in San Quentin and continues allyship with Nuestra Familia
August 7, 1970: Jonathan Jackson killed during Marin County Courthouse incident
August 14, 1970: FBI initiate national manhunt for Angela Davis
October 13, 1970: Angela Davis captured in New York City
October 15, 1970: RICO Act
August 21, 1971: Black Guerilla Family attempt to free George Jackson, and he is murdered
September 9, 1971: Attica Prison Uprising and massacre of protestors by New York State
June 4, 1972: Angela Davis acquitted
July 28, 1972: Geronimo Pratt wrongfully convicted
1973: Fay Stender steps away from the prisoners' rights movement
1974: Aryan Brotherhood and Mexican Mafia declare war on Black Guerilla Family
1974: Black Guerilla Family summit to vote on United Guerilla Front split
August 9, 1974: President Nixon resigns after Watergate scandal and impeachment proceedings
1976: *Spain v. Procunier* court case
August 12, 1976: San Quentin Six verdict stemming from incident on August 21, 1971
1978: National Security Council report on Black movements
May 28, 1979: Fay Stender shot and paralyzed
November 2, 1979: Assata Shakur escape

1983: *Spain v. Rushen* court case
1983: First D.A.R.E. program founded in Los Angeles, CA
1984: Sentencing Reform Act
1988: George H. W. Bush's dog-whistle "Willie Horton" ad
1988: Anti-Drug Abuse Act
1989: Pelican Bay Supermax Prison opens
1994: Violent Crime Control and Law Enforcement Act
1994: California Three Strikes Law
October 16, 1995: Million Man March in Washington, DC
1997: Geronimo Pratt conviction vacated
September 11, 2001: 9/11 attacks
October 26, 2001: USA Patriot Act
2011: California Security Housing Unit (SHU) hunger strikes begin
2011: Occupy Wall Street
February 26, 2012: Murder of Trayvon Martin
May 31, 2012: *Ashker v. California* court case filed
August 12, 2012: Agreement to End Hostilities
November 6, 2012: Prop 36 revises Three Strikes Law
2013: Black Lives Matter established
August 12, 2015: Hugo Pinell murdered by Aryan Brotherhood in New Folsom Prison
September 1, 2015: *Ashker v. California* court case settled
2017: SB 394 abolishes juvenile life without parole in California
August 21, 2018: National prison strike against prison slavery begins
December 21, 2018: First Step Act
December 18, 2019: President Trump impeached first time
March 13, 2020: Murder of Breonna Taylor
May 25, 2020: Murder of George Floyd
2020: Summer Racial Uprisings: Largest social movement in history
January 6, 2021: Capitol riot
January 13, 2021: President Trump impeached second time
2021: Atlanta Cop City protests begin
January 18, 2023: Manuel "Tortuguita" Terán (environmental and Atlanta Cop City activist) murdered by Georgia State Patrol
2015–2023: Dispute over California Department of Corrections and Rehabilitation not upholding terms of Ashker Settlement Agreement
August 2023: Atlanta Cop City protestors indicted in RICO criminal case
2024: Pro-Palestinian protest encampments rise across US college campuses and face police repression

CHRONOLOGY

CARCERAL APARTHEID: WORLD EDITION*

1870–1914: "Scramble for Africa" by European imperialism

1884–1885: Berlin Conference to divide African colonies for European control

December 1898: United States gains Puerto Rico in Treaty of Paris

July 28, 1914: Start of World War I

August 15, 1914: Completion of Panama Canal

1917: United States purchases what becomes US Virgin Islands

March 8, 1917: Start of Russian Revolution

November 11, 1918: End of World War I

September 16, 1919: Adolf Hitler issues comment on "Jewish Question" in Germany

1919–1921: Irish War of Independence

February 24, 1920: Adolf Hitler presents twenty-five-point plan at a Nazi Party Meeting in Germany

June 16, 1923: End of Russian Revolution

February 27, 1925: Adolf Hitler declares reformulation of Nazi Party and declared leader in Germany

1933: Nazi Germany Holocaust begins

September 1, 1939: Start of World War II

September 2, 1945: End of World War II

1945: End of Nazi Germany Holocaust

May 14, 1948: Founding of Israeli nation-state

1948: Palestinian "Nakba" and expulsion to form Israel by Zionist paramilitary groups

1948: South Africa's Nationalist Party touts apartheid as national governing strategy

1949: Chinese Communist Revolution

1952: Mau Mau Rebellion begins

November 1, 1955: Start of Vietnam War

1960: Republic of Congo Independence

1960: Mau Mau Rebellion ends

1960–1961: Nigerian Independence

*This is not an exhaustive list.

1968–1998: "The Troubles" in Northern Ireland
April 30, 1975: End of Vietnam War
1990: Namibian Independence
1990–1994: Negotiations to end apartheid in South Africa
1994: Rwandan Genocide
May 10, 1994: Election of President Nelson Mandela in South Africa
1996: Start of the First Congo War
1997: End of the First Congo War
1998: Start of the Second Congo War
October 7, 2001: Post-9/11 War in Afghanistan starts
2002: Construction starts on Guantánamo Bay detention camp
2003: End of the Second Congo War
2010: Haitian earthquake
2011: Arab Spring
February 20, 2014: Russian invasion of Crimea and Revolution of Dignity
2016: Brexit
August 30, 2021: War in Afghanistan ends
February 24, 2022: Russian invasion of Ukraine
October 7, 2023: Start of Israeli genocide of Palestinians in Gaza
December 28, 2023: South Africa files application charging Israel with genocide in International Court of Justice
2023–2024: United Nations agencies sound alarm over ongoing genocide in Congo
January 26, 2024: International Court of Justice orders Israel to stop any attacks on Palestinian civilians
2024: Pro-Palestinian protest encampments rise across global college campuses and face police repression
May 2024: Israel and United States threaten members of International Criminal Court amidst talks of warrants for war crimes in Gaza

CARCERAL APARTHEID

Exterior of Building 22, San Quentin State Prison, 1933. Photo by Robert A. Hicks. Historic American Buildings Survey Collection, Prints and Photographs Division, Library of Congress, Washington, DC.

INTRODUCTION TO FATE

> Life is tragic simply because the earth turns and
> the sun inexorably rises and sets, and one day for each of us,
> the sun will go down for the last, last time.
>
> —JAMES BALDWIN

Most major institutions in our lives are built on lies. And for this, we are all haunted. One way or another, the ghosts find us. It is easier for them to uncover our whereabouts when we live in a cage, when there is nowhere else to be. In 1965, Hugo "Yogi Bear" Pinell was sentenced to three years to life. Ghosts surrounded him. He did not know he would spend a lifetime in darkness. No one imagines they will live for forty-five years in solitary confinement. Because if you knew, if they warned you, the panic might set in. Soon after, either hopeless paralysis or survival could follow, and the authorities wouldn't want to take a chance on the latter.

The gates at San Quentin State Prison brought the sea breeze closer, though the facility was and continues to be "little more than a warehouse of human flesh."[1] The frigid water did not appear welcoming. It did not look like home. But where was home, anyhow?

Hugo knew the dark waters owned him and that now was not the time to feel. Now was not the time to fear. But he couldn't contain the surge as he arrived, the crisis brewing, raging.[2] Even adults are afraid of the dark. As many at San Quentin will tell you, you should be.

If you are not afraid, then you are naive. Naivete won't save you. Maybe nothing will, but at least you know it. San Quentin is a gladiator school, a model of a successful social order.[3] And you might wonder who you should be afraid of. Movies, television, and even academic experts will tell you it is the other people incarcerated beside you . . . but as Hugo's life shows, it is not the incarcerated who wield total control over life and death.

We like to think that incarcerated people find God in prison and redeem themselves—but there is a more nefarious exercise at work, a game of death work where agents of the state play God by wielding power over human life and deciding fate.

The correctional officers, who allegedly placed bets on Hugo's life during the final weeks of his incarceration, would have reveled in this knowledge. If even a fraction of the claim is true, then the officers were drunk with power.[4] A dead Hugo would serve justice for white power, or that's what many imprisoned white supremacists, correctional officers, and prison officials long believed. After all, to them he symbolized the "worst of the worst," which meant that he "did not come out of his cell without many chains and a choke chain installed."[5] One could say he was nothing more than a black animal, it seems, in the eyes of the officers. But alternative explanations remain, because "if you put men in cages, and treat them like animals, how do you expect them to behave?"[6] For even the naivest of correctional officers should know, "injustice heaped upon injustice inevitably produces rage, and then retaliation."[7]

Hugo discovered this early on, and in isolation, it became even more true. He tried to fight it, but now, uncertain shadows were all he could see. Years passed, with even his fingers becoming imaginary friends. Their loyalty was tested as they grazed the cold cement floors, reminding him that yes, these walls were real. *Will I ever see the light?* he wondered. When you cannot see the floor beneath your feet, you see the past, the ones you'll never really touch again. His mother's face visited him often. Each time she came, arms open, Hugo lifted his gaze and reached out. But when he went to embrace her, the love evaporated, and her body floated away.

"It could be that the sun and the moon have collided to spark the obscure eclipse one would imagine," Hugo pondered. "Yet in mind and spirit I see your flame of love. No need for electricity nor elements from above when there's you to cherish, to adore . . . to think of. I have written you two letters and can't understand why my letters have not reached you. This stench is something like a beautiful feeling—to be hated."[8]

His daughter's budding eyes appeared sometimes, always yearning. Her eyes brought him calm, willed him to stay put in the dark. He became afraid that if he stood, she too, might disappear. And he needed her to stay. Even if only for a second in time. That might make the darkness ease its grip—for just one more day. "I'd rather feel healthy, strong, alive, and human . . . got to keep on pushing, moving, running to the next day, next moment, next stage of living," Hugo professed.[9]

He dreamed of touching the light, and wondered, would resistance be worth it?[10]

Before the darkness, Hugo lived skies away from the cement he came to call home. Born in 1945, young Hugo once dreamt of America. *Morenos* could make it there, he knew.

At only twelve years old, he felt the manifest reach, pulling his family from the eastern shores of Nicaragua to the sunniest destiny on earth: California. A new life, his mother promised. We will labor, long and hard, just like they told us, and the dream will be ours. But when Hugo reached out, the dream ran farther away. Catching it proved an impossible strain. He soon discovered meritocracy is a structural fallacy and survival by any means necessary a reality.

California was not heaven, and the fantasy was a trap. Promoting it as such secured non-white labor and funneled it into a system of racial capitalist dreams, where financial capture loomed immanently.[11] The trouble was, only those traveling the journey toward a better life ever stopped to look at the trail of broken bodies. The furtive endpoint, the elusive American dream, would all be worth it, they hoped, if only they worked harder.[12]

"Yet that wasn't the beginning, nor the end of things. . . . If he knew then the hell he would face in America, would he have left the land of his birth? We'll never know. He came . . ."[13] A journey led Hugo from one colonial master to another. But this time, migration could not provide escape. This time, physical captivity was swift, certain, and severe.

Rape is a serious charge. A Black man standing accused of kidnapping and raping a white woman is a cardinal sin in the United States, both in California and the South. Nothing more than a Black man in the eyes of the court, nineteen-year-old Hugo had simultaneously taken her purity and wounded the white man's patriarchal, entitled spirit. And for this he would pay. To white men, social order is predicated on the inferiority of black flesh, disgusting flesh that requires a lesson in piety. Hugo must writhe and pant, pleading like a broken dog.

In custody, Hugo attempted to assert his innocence. But who truly cares when the allegations personally offend one's sense and sensibility? Regardless of his guilt or innocence, this was a matter of performative justice—a fact Hugo swiftly felt. Police officers, always ready for the symbolic policing of this order, began with round one, breaking a sweat as the blows flew, insisting that Hugo admit his guilt. Hugo begged, auditioning for trust from an audience that would not care if he lived or died.

Cuffs held Hugo, pulling his arms tight. *Don't look, or they might keep seeing me. If I can just hold my breath, maybe I will disappear.* But the blows from the officers continued, and the lights flickered. A smiling audience grew.

Can't they see me hurting? Can't they see me? I know my body rings of guilt, but I am innocent. Hugo professed his innocence. But the sweat began to taste saltier, a familiar flavor. Red droplets touched his crumpled pants as he knelt, keeping his head low. *If I speak, they will see me. If I speak, I might be free one day.* But Hugo was not fully convinced, so he stayed quiet while the fists continued to fly. *Where is my mother? Have they gotten to her?*[14]

Racist patriarchy made it easy for them to admire Hugo's mother. She looked like a good one in her attempts to speak English. An actual ma'am and not a girl like the others. Perched high above, they were eager to assure her that all Hugo needed to do was admit guilt. Tell your son to admit guilt, and he will not die the slow, painful death of the gas chamber.

Unsure of Hugo's fate but aware of his current anguish, she did not need much convincing. Certain death. Even his public defender agreed this was the best way to avoid such an ending. Hugo would only serve six months, they promised, and parole would be his quick escape. Given the choice between quick time versus certain demise, many mothers would agree to choose the former, even more so when your son is Blackened, bloodied, and broken. A new land with ripe dreams, America still held possibilities for them, and she believed this would not be the end for her son. Soon this would all be over, and Hugo could begin anew with better choices.[15]

But Hugo couldn't really see anymore. His sockets could not open as the dark called, the pain seething effortlessly. Too much energy required to fight, he reasoned. The insistence to admit guilt pulled from each angle, each person presenting their own reasons. Nothing seemed real anymore. Only the possibility of release seemed reasonable. Pleading guilty was not an admission of guilt, and their promises just might end the pain, Hugo hoped.[16]

"The deputies beat me several times because the alleged victim was white, and the public defender and judge influenced my mother into believing that I would be sentenced to death unless I pled guilty," Hugo recounted. "At their insistence and despite my innocence, I pled guilty to the charge of rape, with the understanding that I would be eligible for parole after six months. [But] when I arrived at the California Department of Corrections, I was informed that I had been sentenced to three years to life."[17]

But Hugo did not know the true level of indifference that awaited him. San Quentin's aged white walls, the gates a dusty, rust-engulfed black: those wouldn't be the only ones he'd cross. Hugo would end up calling many California prisons his cage, emphasizing their passing nature by refusing to accept his prisoner status and the replacement of his name with a number.[18] He preached survival by any means necessary and lived by this creed. This dogma was routinely tested. Rage brewed inside him against the system and all who represented it. The Department of Corrections eventually deemed Hugo a threat to correctional officers and public safety, and he was often confined to Adjustment Centers (restricted housing units) rather than the general population as a result.[19]

On January 13, 1970, now caged in Soledad State Prison and only five years after the start of Hugo's incarceration, conflict erupted into an explosive freight train that continues to haunt how people survive prisons today. Years of cyclical racist violence between imprisoned Black and white people, intentionally sown by white correctional officers, laid the groundwork for the murder of three of Hugo's closest associates.

Their deaths pushed Hugo to a breaking point: live free or die trying.

W. L. Nolen, Cleveland Edwards, and Alvin Miller were shot and executed in broad daylight by Opie G. Miller, a white correctional officer with a history of racist violence against imprisoned Black people, especially those marked by the Department of Corrections in secret files for alleged participation in Black movement groups. The three men were murdered after self-identified white supremacists deliberately initiated a fight on the yard. Acting as agents of the state and the strategic pawns of white correctional officers, the fight they started gave officers the excuse to shoot Hugo's comrades.

The dust settled, and a familiar sight haunted the yard.[20] Three Black people lay dead, caged people who self-identified as Black militants and were outspoken about their belief in the human right to Black freedom in the United States and around the world.[21]

Convinced they were next—and that the only solution to certain death was solidarity—once transferred to San Quentin, Hugo and approximately nine others founded the Black Guerilla Family in 1970. They believed this merging of Black movement groups into a single unified organization would give all incarcerated Black people the best chance of surviving the California Department of Corrections.[22]

The Black Guerilla Family became the consolidated prison arm of the Black Freedom Movement.[23] The founders knew revolutionary fervor could spread like wildfire across California prisons and beyond. Revolutions born in blood would resonate in other penal systems worldwide and the intimately networked Black revolutionaries surviving on the outside. The Black Guerilla Family's founders pledged to fight the same regime from the inside that led to the degradation of their communities in society and the subsequent mass incarceration of Black people.

To do this, the founders accepted the most important truth of all.

Lasting Black freedom could only come to pass across the world if liberation movements challenged what I term in this book as carceral apartheid, the carceral foundation of US empire domestically and internationally. I define carceral apartheid as the following:

State governing through the deployment of official carceral apparatuses (i.e., police, military, courts, jails, prisons, detention, probation and parole, and surveillance technology) to achieve the imperial management, division, and decimation of racialized, target populations. These carceral apparatuses rely on their official capacity to engage in legal controls (surveillance, arrest, conviction, imprisonment, and supervision). However, their success in this endeavor is only made possible by their willingness to engage in clandestine controls that are at times extralegal (i.e., disappearances, torture, gladiator fights, lynching, sexual assault, murder, planting evidence, and corrupt alliances between civilians and law enforcement)—to ensure a white supremacist victory in war over their opponents and the maintenance of sovereignty over how all populations live and die.

For generations, civil rights movement leaders and Black Freedom fighters like the founders of the Black Guerilla Family dissected the validity of this governance regime using social and political theory. They advanced their ideas in reading groups, preaching to any incarcerated person who would listen. The Black Guerilla Family emphasized the material validity of a "prisoner class," challenging penal actors that purposefully sowed division among racial and ethnic groups—seeing them as a clear continuation of the colonial master who instrumentally fostered racial and ethnic division between white workers and the Black people enslaved, and who further split enslaved Black people by enforcing skin color hierarchies. For penal actors this was a proven cultural template for control. The end goal was to maintain the structure of chattel slavery within prison and, ultimately, ensure Black demise.

Though the Black Guerilla Family chiefly attempted to save imprisoned Black people from this fate, the founders knew the key to their success lay not only in a Black revolution. They also needed to convince imprisoned white people and non-white people alike, that on a material level, we are all prisoners and that the very same tactics they use on us, they will someday use on you. They envisioned a future world of solidary cultures.[24]

Months went by since the January 13, 1970, Soledad Incident and the white supremacist murders of three Black militants. The founders of the Black Guerilla Family diligently planned their next move, starting with San Quentin. They felt the darkness hovering—waiting and watching them patiently. True omnipotence thrives in the shadows, they realized. And if nothing else, reaching for the light might set an example for others of what could be.

Hugo knew this and the time had come to live and die on his own terms. Hugo entered the world stage on August 21, 1971, when he attempted to free George Jackson from San Quentin to save him from certain death. Like the other founders, Hugo heard word that George was next. His song was ending, and the dance with the dark was almost over. But on that fateful day, the escape plan to free George failed, and George was indeed shot dead.[25] Prison officials, white correctional officers, and imprisoned white supremacists all hated George Jackson, and his demise was celebrated as a ritual of white group solidarity—death by carceral apartheid, with another Black militant successfully exterminated. George was treated by the Department of Corrections like a hunted prize. A bronze plaque hangs today in San Quentin Museum commemorating the weapon used for the kill.[26]

For his participation in the escape plot, Hugo would spend the rest of his life in darkness. His dance with death continued, unabashedly growing bolder with each passing decade. In the 1980s, Hugo even survived a noxious gift from the Aryan Brotherhood—a homemade bomb thrown directly at him. If this wasn't enough, Hugo continued living, somehow managing to survive being figuratively and literally stabbed in the back by one of his own comrades. Even so, Hugo could not fight the dark forever. He was only human. Hugo knew this truth but resisted its reach for as long as possible. Correctional officers, wardens, and parole boards labeled him a beast, and he responded, "I've found myself pushing and working so hard, going through time spaces, resisting, transcending, acting like 'I'll show you, Monster, I'll be the most extraordinary beautiful human being.'"[27]

He wanted to touch the light, to feel its grace. To escape the cold cement he had learned to accept as home. But his mind couldn't shake this feeling of darkness. "To push so hard that I've flown away from my own humanity because being a whole human in here is so much work. It's too complex. Too bizarre." He wondered incessantly, "Who can understand me? Really see me, feel me? Haven't had a contact visit in 42 years! Under such extreme inhumane treatment and condition I'm trying to scream, hey I am human. Am I really? Or simply an energy who created a big fantasy to escape this horrible reality?"[28] Losing oneself in the dark is the intention of carceral apartheid, and in Hugo's case, officers cheered as the dark devoured his light, like a vampire in the night. Hugo came to accept that the dark has many meanings, owns many spaces, and contains many ghosts.

But energy cannot be destroyed, only transferred, siphoned, or alchemized.

Hugo's flame held on until one day the gates of fate opened to swallow him whole.

The reality of Black life flickering within this precarious state of being finally ended Hugo on August 12, 2015, in New Folsom Prison.[29] Jayson Weaver and Waylon Pitchford, two associates of the Aryan Brotherhood, pierced Hugo's body with their weapons, anointed in their fulfillment of a near fifty-year prophecy. California prison officials were keenly aware of this decades-long threat on Hugo's life.[30] Feeling the darkness rise and permanently engulf his spirit, Hugo lay there living the moment he always knew would come. He told his family that one day, *they* would finish what they started.[31] His "eyes were wide open as he took his last breath."[32] Chocolate eyes that held memories, dreams, and patiently waiting demons coming to collect his soul. Sometimes, we know when they will come knocking, eager to devour what remains of us. Sometimes, only ghosts can comfort us.

The Aryan Brotherhood lay in wait, having issued a death notice for Hugo on that fateful day of August 21, 1971, when two of their associates perished while attempting to prevent George Jackson's escape from San Quentin. Some claimed prison officials knew this prophecy because it was in Hugo's file. Others claimed they knew it because they had helped issue it.[33] Some explicitly called Weaver and Pitchford white supremacist "agents of the state" with the Department of Corrections being "the real monster."[34] In a letter to the *San Francisco Bay View*, a longstanding national Black newspaper, a witness who knew Hugo and saw him murdered described Hugo as the victim of a routine pattern endemic to how lies and white supremacists run our prisons, rather than a tragic one-time occurrence.

"There is so much that the brothers and sisters don't know. However, make no mistake that this was a plot, a setup between the administration and staff, also the Aryan Brotherhood that carried out this racist assassination on Yogi—so much so the white AB knew about this assassination on Yogi Pinell's life, dating back as far as 1971 when two of their beloved generals were killed, John Lynn, 29, and Ronald L. Kane, 28, along with three correctional officers (COs), COs Paul E. Krasenes, 52, Frank DeLeon, 44, and Jere P. Graham, 34."[35]

The circumstances surrounding Hugo's death reveal how imprisoned people alternate between phases of demise and the terms of fate are ultimately in the hands of the state. Herein lies the state's sovereign right, the power to dance with people as they please. A reaper, but without a conscious.

For more than 150 years, local, state, and federal law enforcement has empowered white supremacist organizations, such as the Ku Klux Klan, and more recently the Oath Keepers and Proud Boys, to help the state govern through carceral apartheid, both as public spectacle and hooded secrecy.[36] I suggest the extent of this connection in jails and prisons in the United States remains deliberately in the dark. To this day, for example, California prison officials refuse to publicly comment, particularly on correctional officer alliances with the Aryan Brotherhood.[37] If we look at the social order wrought by carceral apartheid in a supposed free society (e.g., the Ku Klux Klan's connections to police officers), imagine what has occurred for years within our prisons, which are conveniently tucked away from a critical gaze.

Carceral apartheid allows officers and officials to lurk in the dark and brandish unbridled control over how those caged survive or fail to survive captivity.

One thing is certain. The history of nation-building in the United States foretells that the state has always needed white supremacists to do its bidding in the daylight and shadows, in free society and within its cages. One must watch out for the puppet strings attached to the state's hands, where white supremacy as carceral power rests on lies and seeking almost total autonomy over each fate.

As a captive of carceral apartheid, they want you to believe that if you touch the light, you will be killed.

Lies Rule the World

In *Carceral Apartheid*, I place racist intent at the crux of my analysis. I focus on the state's arming of white supremacists as a key institutional entanglement structuring our society. Through this analysis I argue our societal social order is created through carceral apartheid as governance—to maintain white supremacy as carceral power at all costs. Excavating the roots of this social order uncovers death work as the true nature of law enforcement and centers carceral apartheid as an intentionally racist structure dually governing confined and free society. Imperialism and the necessary cultural logics of white supremacy, racial capitalism, and division encase the creation of official, clandestine, and at times extralegal controls. These serve as death-dealing routine practices available for adoption and replication across institutional, organizational, and individual contexts, both domestically and abroad. Prisons then, and their interior social organization, mirror US societal and global race-relations and invite a catacomb of knowledge for exploration, which I offer in this book. To ensure our eradication, we see the longstanding systemic formation of white supremacist alliances across law enforcement and the white civilian populace to solidify white supremacy over class consciousness.

Centering racist intent invites us to reimagine several cases as throughlines across time, space, and place. For example, the 1921 Tulsa race massacre, where city officials armed white residents and let them loose to kill and maim Black residents, is not an anomaly, but a historical, sociological pattern. White racists can be empowered officially and extralegally to weaponize their whiteness in the service of carceral apartheid, dealing death as white supremacists with or without the KKK hood or a swastika emblem. They enjoy a pattern of the state regularly arming them to do its bidding, in the broad daylight of US streets, in the shadows of its prisons, and in the lands of its global enemies.

Shining a light on the darkness that is racist intent allows us to claim this intent as instrumental. Racist intent is not solely rooted in the racist ideas of an institution or the individual purview of a few. Instead, I view racist intent as lasting institutional entanglements and the organization of resources designed to inflict genocide against a racialized people socially, politically, economically, and spiritually. Racist intent manifests because of who we are as racial subjects, the lost property we represent, and jealousy of the creative genius we embody.

I offer the term carceral apartheid as a theoretical scaffold and tell the story of carceral apartheid through the lens of our prisons, with the Black Guerilla Family and the California Department of Corrections as an instructive example. I invite future writers to explore other instances of carceral apartheid across time, space, and place—to continue to teach us.

For the beneficiaries of this governance regime, acts of comradery and celebration abound, some private but some that are very much public and brazen—much like the 2019 incident where police officers in Washington, DC, fist-bumped a member of the white supremacist sect Proud Boys after a Proud Boys political rally in front of the White House. A year later, the events of 2020 further reveal that death is the endgame. I proposed and crafted this book's arguments before 2020, after what now amounts to over a decade of research. But now the words flow to heavier, yet hopefully more open minds. The world reads my words from the ashes of an era that provided us with even more evidence that our society is built to kill. The racist intent of carceral apartheid remains an open secret within law enforcement, from corrections and police to migrant detention and counterterrorism. This evidence is drenched with our blood. Death is not relegated to history as this state is actively killing Black people to deny Black Lives Matter.

We watched George Floyd—a Black man—gasp for help on Minnesota cement and cry for his mother while a smirking white police officer knelt on his neck and squeezed his life away like it was just another Monday.

We witnessed Ahmaud Arbery—a Black man—beaten and dying alone on a quiet Georgia road while a former police detective and two fellow white supremacists watched on, one calling him a "fucking n——" before issuing their final murderous gunshot.

We wait for justice, after Breonna Taylor—a Black woman—while resting in her home, was startled by unannounced police officers and shot six times without reason or thought. For yet another Black woman, we wait.

The public murders of Breonna Taylor, George Floyd, and Ahmaud Arbery, amidst the sea of deaths at the hands of law enforcement and white vigilantes across history, violently bring the reality of carceral apartheid as governance to the forefront of our minds, as the throughline producer of societal order writ large.

Oh, the joy this violence brings to some.

A correctional officer in New Jersey reenacted George Floyd's murder for laughs while posing in front of a President Donald Trump banner, unmarked federal agents snatched Black Lives Matter protestors off the streets of Portland, Oregon, and correctional officers in West Virginia performed the "Heil Hitler" for an official basic training graduation photo.

Carceral Apartheid clarifies this nonsense as perfect white-sense.

In the wake of 2020, some looked to 2021 for a new dawn. Instead, we embarked on a familiar historical namesake when a US president once again signaled to his followers that it was open season for white supremacy as carceral power. Republican president Trump was impeached a second time for openly fanning the flames that led to the January 6, 2021, Capitol riot, during which his protestors—many of whom were active and former law enforcement from across the United States—carried Confederate and Nazi-affiliated symbols while storming the US Capitol.

His followers subsequently claimed temporary control of the building, cheering as members of Congress and the vice president fled in fear of their lives. As many as thirty-five members of the Capitol Police Department have been potentially implicated in the riot. In all, 120 House GOP members were found to have posted incendiary social media content challenging the 2020 presidential election results leading up to the attack, aiding President Trump in inciting organized white supremacist violence. These are the same 120 House GOP members who voted to overturn the election.[38]

A government official's redacted email to Paul Abbate, then Associate Deputy Director of the Federal Bureau of Investigation, admits that sympathy to white supremacist goals is widespread within the highest levels of the state: "There's no good way to say it, so I'll just be direct: from my first-hand and second-hand information from conversations since January 6th there is, at best, a sizable percentage of the employee population that felt sympathetic to the group that stormed the Capitol. . . . Several also lamented that the only reason this violent activity is getting more attention is because of political correctness."[39]

The 2021 Capitol riot once again brings to the forefront how not only our prisons, but our nation, is run by lies and white supremacists with the expressed goal of preventing Black freedom. Carceral apartheid has long ushered in the genocide of those in free society and those we disappear into the belly of the beast. Resilience and resistance are the only ways to survive. When people awaken, they want "to live free or die trying," but also create joy and lasting love in this world too.

And then in 2023, we witnessed a ramping up of our country's continued exportation of genocide abroad under Democratic president Joe Biden, with the latest government atrocity being the United States supporting the Israeli nation in its extermination of the Palestinian people in Gaza. Carceral apartheid is operating in tried-and-true fashion. We see the labeling of an entire demographic of people as undesirable political targets and the mobilization of official carceral tools through the military and police, imprisonment, and chemical weapons, and are still yet to know the full extent of clandestine and extralegal tools such as torture, starvation, and rape. An entire people in real time are being wiped from the earth to uphold carceral apartheid. And to be expected, politicians and public figures around the world continue to lie about the full extent of the intentional death and carnage taking place in the Gaza Strip to try and subdue certain segments of the public. The truth is that January 19, 2024, was day 105 of the Israeli genocide in the Gaza Strip, marking at least 29,720 Palestinian civilians killed—estimating 12,660 of them children—since the October 7, 2023, Hamas attacks on Israeli civilians.

Targeting children and people who give birth is an age-old tactic deployed to wipe out whole generations—its genocide. Our country supports this because we also do the same at home through carceral means—for example, in the United States we continue to see some of the highest world rates of children detained in migrant camps and incarcerated in jails and prisons, and we have witnessed some of the highest world rates of Indigenous children stolen from their homes and held in boarding schools.

During this same snapshot in time, an additional 2,350 Palestinian people, likely an underestimate, are reported as forcibly disappeared or detained in Israeli prisons and this number is steadily climbing. The Israeli military continues to intentionally execute Palestinian civilians to exterminate the populace. One Israeli general described this moment with joy as the final "Nakba," referencing the 1948 Zionist expulsion of over 750,000 Palestinians from their homes.[40] As the perpetrator of genocide at home against Indigenous, Black, and Latinx communities, the United States will never acknowledge that it also supports genocide abroad with money, weapons, and military intelligence.

Refusing to use the term genocide is a strategic choice and remains a foundational lie structuring America's legacy at home and abroad.

Once again, the mind, body, and spirit of an entire people continue to be erased before our very eyes as journalists on the ground try to tell the truth in the face of being murdered for it.[41]

While the United States remains complicit, South Africa, a predominantly Black Indigenous country that survived European-imposed apartheid for over half a century, stood up for Palestinian lives on the international stage and filed on December 28, 2023, an Application Instituting Proceedings at the International Court of Justice (ICJ) against Israel for the ongoing genocide in Gaza, documenting the horrors in their statement: "Including intentionally directing attacks against the civilian population, civilian objects and buildings dedicated to religion, education, art, science, historic monuments, hospitals, and places where the sick and wounded are collected; torture; the starvation of civilians as a method of warfare; and other war crimes and crimes against humanity."[42]

The ICJ responded January 26, 2024, by court-ordering Israel to try and prevent civilian deaths in Gaza but stopped short of calling for a permanent ceasefire.[43]

Sociologist W. E. B. Du Bois, a Black founder of the discipline, dissected the ills of US empire in his writings at the turn of the twentieth century, arguing that the expansion of European colonial imperialism was bent on creating "slums of the world" and justified it through the "doctrine of the natural inferiority of most men to the few."[44] He saw a direct link between empire at home and abroad, naming "the race problem in America, the problem of the people of Africa and Asia, and the political development of Europe as one."[45] Du Bois linked ongoing struggles for civil rights and Black freedom in the United States to anticolonial struggles in Africa and Asia, writing: "The history of our day ... may be epitomized in one word—Empire; the domination of white Europe of Black Africa and yellow Asia, through political power built on the economic control of labor, income, and ideas."[46] Importantly, however, Du Bois's understanding of imperialism and linked-fate was still limited, as evidenced by his rejection of Palestinian sovereignty and his full support for the Zionist movement no matter the human cost.[47] Every theorist has their faults and blind spots, yet committing exceptionalism is quite consequential as it ultimately induces the normalization of carceral apartheid.

Carceral apartheid is the carceral arm of empire and manifests domestically and internationally as warfare against any population deemed problematic and in need of social adjustment—whether this is accomplished through extermination or propaganda—the use of carceral techniques to achieve success is foundational. Lies remain a key means of maintaining this governing structure, with white supremacy being the first lie. Often the second lie is that violence is not taking place in its name. Facilitating disinformation is a millennia-old tactic of war used to confuse, disillusion, decimate, destroy, and divide. Disrupting and hiding the truth undergirds racist intent, providing the ability to tell a story how one wants it to be seen to ensure your opponent's demise. Domestically, this is how our society is run. Globally, this is how we control the world. This book tells but one of these stories, but in doing so, I hope to illuminate the many stories that are waiting to see the light: the millions of people here and the billions abroad who deserve to live free of America's carceral grasp.

Building a Rebel Archive

It soon became apparent to me while researching and writing this book that rebel archives are a necessity of truth-telling. In her book *City of Inmates*, historian Kelly Lytle Hernández gifts us the term "rebel archive" to highlight the remaining artifacts, narratives, and pieces of history that governments and their operatives have attempted to hide and destroy, and the active work of rebels, revolutionaries, and abolitionists to discover and reinstate these narratives through a multitude of sources.[48] The emphasis is on the need to rewrite the story. As Hernández describes in an interview, "The rebel archive is . . . the records that have been authored by the people who have fought policing and incarceration across centuries [including court records]. . . . Even cases that make it all the way up to the United States Supreme Court. It's also records that—by the grace of God—have somehow evaded destruction by law enforcement authorities over the centuries. And so it's a rebel archive because it has survived to tell the tale of what happened, and how it happened, and why."[49]

On September 24, 2018, I learned a valuable lesson, one many historians and historical sociologists already know to be true: archives disappear. That day, a scholar emailed me, distressed, regarding what could be described as a failed public records request. After learning of my work from a radio interview I gave in 2018, they felt the archival materials I cited could be useful for their upcoming book. Much to their dismay, the California State Archives gave them the following story regarding files I have in my possession: "This summer I requested these files, specifically File F3717:378 'Muslim Correspondence, 1961–1968' and File 3717:379 'Muslim Assassination Plot, 1963.' I was told these were being processed and were 84 and 63 pages each, but then abruptly had my check voided and was contacted by a California State

Attorney who told me all these materials were embargoed for 75 years from date of creation. She sent along 5 pages of 'disclosable' materials, which I've attached here. One is the Administrative Bulletin No. 58/16 that you cite."[50]

Since that radio interview, many more researchers have contacted me asking for more information and requesting to see these and other files.

Little did I know, when I stumbled upon these collections at the California State Archives, what secrets lay in wait. I invested my time in the fall of 2013 preparing for an upcoming summer research trip to California, and, in the spring of 2014, I submitted the necessary paperwork to view any collections pertaining to the Department of Corrections, many of which were restricted. After passing through their checks and providing my university's Institutional Review Board approval, I was assured access to anything I asked for.

When I arrived in Sacramento in the summer of 2014, I was told in a stern but kind tone by an archivist that I needed to sit up front, put away my phone and camera, and, most importantly, only copy restricted information by hand rather than photocopy it. It was easy to tell what was restricted to hand copying, both for the archivists closely watching and the anxious researchers trying to follow the rules, because those folders had a red stamp on them that everyone could see. So, I played by their exact rules. I sat and copied by hand archival material detailing the Department of Corrections' investigations into incarcerated Black militants and their control strategies for subduing them.

The following year, I returned to the archive and copied more.

After a couple of years combing through what I had uncovered, in 2017, I began scrolling through the archive's online catalog and noticed I had overlooked a collection on solitary confinement during my visits. I promptly emailed one of their archivists, using the same email thread I had started a couple of years before in the hopes they would remember me, and asked if she would be willing to scan an entire collection (for a fee) and mail it to me—which much to my surprise, she did. Upon opening the box, I quickly realized I had just received the final clue in my quest to uncover obscure information.

The archivist sent me the complete copy of the Adjustment Center Collection, which outlines how the Department of Corrections planned, constructed, and evaluated the first specialized solitary confinement units in the state of California beginning in 1953.[51] This is decades earlier than the current starting point listed in the prominent historical literature on the rise of systematic solitary confinement, which focuses on the 1989 opening of California's supermax facility, Pelican Bay State Prison, also known simply as Pelican Bay.[52]

Carceral Apartheid's empirical contribution is further substantiated by additional collections from public and private archives, which together create a dataset of several hundred primary documents, including letters by imprisoned Black militants, underground prisoner newspapers, court case transcripts, and prison incident reports.

I built an extensive archival database, but it does not stand alone.

Over the course of roughly four and a half years, I managed to build trust with key members of the original Black Panther Party in Oakland and Los Angeles, US Foundation, and Black Liberation Army in California and New York, who generously facilitated introductions to founders and early members of the Black Guerilla Family, all of whom have worked for decades to keep their identities a secret. Their greatest fear is re-incarceration, more surveillance for them and their families, and security threat group validation (placement in a gang database), which would effectively sentence them to death by incarceration in Pelican Bay. As a result, I have taken great care throughout this book to use pseudonyms and otherwise disguise their identities; however, those who are deceased are identified in the book by name.[53] All of these choices to disguise identities are in line with sociological methods and ethics for interview research. In total I conducted forty-one interviews with men who were founders or members of various prison organizations during their years incarcerated in California, and with political activists of the Black Freedom Movement and those advocating for prisoners' rights. My interviews with formerly incarcerated founders and early members of the Black Guerilla Family ranged from spending the day talking for several hours to sustained contact and many conversations over years. It took me over a decade of research to produce and analyze this original "rebel archive" of life history interviews and archival documents that I draw from as the empirical foundation for this book.[54]

Start the journey but hold tight, as you will have no choice but to finish.

CARCERAL APARTHEID

But what on earth is whiteness that one should so desire it?
Then always, somehow, some way, silently but clearly,
I am given to understand that whiteness is ownership
of the earth forever and ever, Amen!

—W. E. B. DU BOIS

Great Mosque of Gaza photographed between 1867 and 1899 by Maison Bonfils. A multireligious holy site since biblical times, the landmark was destroyed on December 7, 2023, by an Israeli airstrike amid the ongoing Palestinian genocide. Library of Congress, Prints and Photographs Division, Washington, DC.

CARCERAL APARTHEID AS GOVERNANCE

> Racism will disappear when it's no longer profitable
> and no longer psychologically useful.
>
> —TONI MORRISON

In Afrikaans apartheid translates to "apartness." The term is most often used to describe South Africa's twentieth-century regime established through racial segregation, land dispossession, and economic extraction to preserve centuries of white European settler colonial rule over the majority Indigenous Black population.[1] Famed Black freedom fighter President Nelson Mandela recognized apartheid as a quintessential governance structure necessary for the emergence and maintenance of racial capitalism. He understood apartheid as inescapably cultivated and reinforced through racial terror, with whiteness functioning as the ability to name and claim property, both in the form of land and Black people.[2]

A series of colonial policies solidified apartheid in the region prior to the rise of the white-ruled Nationalist Party. However, their political ascension in 1948 ushered in years of increased segregation laws, genocide, torture, Black cultural erasure, and an exponential rise in the mass incarceration of Black South Africans. International and continental calls to end white European colonial rule across Africa, which peaked in the mid-twentieth century and spurred the rise of several independent African nations, reignited the minority white settlers' need to maintain a firm grip on power over an ethnically diverse Black majority in South Africa.

Black survivors of South African apartheid recount the everyday violence perpetrated by white people with and without law enforcement badges, committed to terrorize Black communities and provide amusement for white ones. White people without a badge could drive into the outskirts—where

Black people were forced to live—and commit a variety of crimes against Black residents with impunity, such as beatings, rape, and property theft. White people with a badge could do the same and more, firing shots into Black neighborhoods, snatching Black people from their homes while they slept, and arresting and torturing Black people within official law enforcement premises, such as jails, prisons, and police stations.[3]

Anytime Black communities asserted their right to freedom, state-sanctioned "death squads" composed of multiple levels of law enforcement collaborated to intensify their repression of Black resistance. This was done to ensure the continuation of white power, routinely using torture, sexual violence, physical death, or disappearance in jails and prisons. Prisons in South Africa during this era were especially brutal, with the imprisoned routinely subjected to assaults and isolation. In the words of Historian Natacha Filippi, "prisons [in South Africa] were used to a significant extent to protect the white minority against a contagion by pathological colonized populations, to ensure the economic exploitation of colonial subjects, and to assimilate 'seditious activity' with 'indigenous crime.'"[4]

President Nelson Mandela himself, South Africa's first Black president elected in 1994, survived twenty-seven years imprisoned for his Black militancy and resistance against apartheid. He spent many of these years in solitary confinement.[5] In a letter from prison, he wrote "I am convinced that floods of personal disaster can never drown a determined revolutionary nor can the cumulus of misery that accompanies tragedy suffocate him."[6] When prison authorities tried to prevent him from writing letters, President Mandela remarked that this represented "a deliberate intention and policy on the part of the authorities to cut me off and isolate me from all external contacts, to frustrate and demoralize me, to make me despair and lose all hope and eventually break me."[7]

A comparative understanding of social structures across nations reveals that apartheid consists of patterns of social behavior that are trans-contextual and paralleled across superficially disparate settings. This means there are fundamental patterns endemic to apartheid found across time, place, and space.[8] South Africa is by far the most common incidence referenced, but not the only case when considering the rise and consequences of apartheid as governance.[9]

Other prominent cases to consider that illuminate common social patterns endemic to apartheid as governance include the German-Belgian occupation of Rwanda and Congo Wars, the Armenian Genocide, Nazi Germany, the Israeli occupation of Palestine, the Rohingya expulsion from Myanmar, and slavery and enduring racial segregation in the United States.[10] Apartheid and its consequences can be viewed as broader ideal types to understand commonalities among nation state regimes rooted in settler colonial methods such as racialization, land extraction, segregation, ethnic cleansing, and genocide.

For example, some urban sociologists have also used the term apartheid to understand how the instrumental use of de jure and de facto racial segregation in the United States led to the creation of what they refer to as the "Black ghetto" and produced intergenerational socioeconomic dispossession for Black communities.[11] This argument suggests that racial segregation and land extraction remain a constant force in the United States, manufactured by white communities, law enforcement, and incarceration to ensure domination over Black communities through creating concentrated poverty.[12]

Carceral Apartheid—Underscoring and Centering the Carcerality in Apartheid

governance
: the act or process of governing or overseeing the control and direction of something (such as a country or an organization)[13]

Why do we need a new term?
Governance is how states "see" so they may create legible subjects that are under their control and behave according to desired ends.[14] Apartheid is impossible as governance without the deployment of carceral controls designed to foster this obedience and ensure victory over political opponents. Thus, carcerality must scaffold all analyses seeking to understand the logics and methods of apartheid across time, place, and space, before the severity and longevity of the socioeconomic and cultural consequences can be fully understood.

The underscoring and centering of carcerality explains the organized violence and warfare of apartheid as necessary for its emergence and maintenance. Carcerality is not a consequence of apartheid but instead its life force, structuring the process by which extraction, discipline, and social control successfully transform political opponents into undesirable populations and thus suitable carceral subjects. This lens prioritizes seeing apartheid as rooted in fundamental patterns of punishment and social control, legitimated by the state's sovereign right to criminalize populations labeled as undesirable, thus requiring discipline, incarceration, and ultimately extermination.[15]

Apartheid as governance always has and always will be a carceral endeavor, whether structuring life within or outside of prisons. It is thus more accurately termed what I call "carceral apartheid," highlighting the prescription of carcerality, in terms of its blueprint, operating structure, strategies of decimation, and intentionally racist consequences. I center the field of corrections and its constituting penal organizations such as prisons because they are the darkest corners of our social world, where the existence of this governance structure can operate in the shadows away from public scrutiny. After careful empirical investigation, prisons as a microcosm of society remain one of the starkest examples of carceral apartheid in action that I could identify, and upon which I base my broader conceptual claims.

Centering Carcerality, Warfare, and Racist Intent

As a concept, carceral apartheid unveils carcerality and warfare as throughlines that are key to understanding racist intent in the past and present. Apartheid is where warfare and social engineering meet to adjust carceral subjects—a process that ensures their racial subjugation and chained existence as vital to enduring state sovereignty.

Racism refers to the alleged supremacy of certain racial groups over others based on notions of biological and cultural dominance, which then justifies the material and social stratification of racial groups rooted in these presumptions. Racism is a dogma of oppression and division that seeks to secure control over property, resources, and people, and is rooted in the violent histories of white European colonization and warfare within Europe and between North Africa, and its export and reconfiguration across the Americas, Asia, and the rest of the African continent. Racist intent is the strategic foundation of warfare unleashed to generate carceral apartheid. For example, Europe declared war on the peoples indigenous to the "new worlds" it sought to conquer, and once settled, the resulting rising colonial states worked to eradicate that which was undesirable from the old to forge a new socioeconomic and cultural order. A sizable percentage of the population became considered disposable and ripe for eradication, while the remaining populace underwent a violent transformation of the self so they could produce for their settler captors.

The infamous words of General Richard Henry Pratt reflect this strategic foundation: "A great general has said that the only good Indian is a dead one. In a sense, I agree with the sentiment, but only in this: that all the Indian there is in the race should be dead. Kill the Indian in him, and save the man."[16] Pratt founded Carlisle Indian Industrial School in 1879, a vicious example of an off-reservation boarding school that forcibly removed Indigenous children from their families in the United States. Social theorist Frantz Fanon described this same imperial process with regard to Black descendants of chattel slavery surviving in settler colonial states in his work

Black Skin, White Masks.[17] For Fanon, racism underscores the physical and psychological warfare deployed to nation build.[18]

Though sociologists have documented how racism is expressed both overtly and covertly, by individuals, organizations, and institutions, the issue of racist intention has remained elusive and taboo among those who claim it is difficult to prove.[19] Carceral apartheid as a concept argues racist intentionality is the overarching root of each level, where acts of warfare mobilize carcerality to defeat a racialized opponent to achieve a political end. Societal institutions such as education and healthcare, for example, are designed to create and maintain anti-Black racial hierarchies that usher in our demise. There is a push and pull between these institutions and the legal, political, and cultural structures that satisfactorily aid this racist purpose. Organizations such as prisons, for instance, are nested and operate within these institutions. As a conceptual and structural shift, carceral apartheid pushes us to see a bigger and broader visionary scaffolding the warmongering origins and strategic intentions of racism at multiple levels.

Black feminists, activists, revolutionaries, and imprisoned intellectuals have long argued that the United States has from its inception until the present declared war on Black people.[20] Black survivors of genocide and exploitation all over the world have already provided ample proof of racist intent and been at the forefront of publicly condemning the United States and its white supremacist allies for the atrocities used to maintain carceral apartheid. The writings and advocacy of those imprisoned and on the outside reveal a centuries-long fight for domestic and global freedom from the decimation inherent to this oppression. For example, in 1951 in Paris, France, William L. Patterson on behalf of the Civil Rights Congress presented to the United Nations "We Charge Genocide: The Historic Petition to the United Nations for Relief from a Crime of the United States Government Against the Negro People."[21] Simultaneously, it was presented in New York City by Paul Robeson. This document exposed the United States for the genocide of Black Americans through racial violence and lynching, enacted using white supremacist civilian and law enforcement alliances.

The US criminal legal system has historically operated as the domestic enforcement arm of our imperial settler colonial state as seen through the police, jails, prisons, and courts.[22] The resulting violence is legitimated based on the ability to officially label and then dehumanize entire populations of people and then disappear them within cages or string them up in trees across the country. Prisons are settler colonial tools of displacement, dismemberment, and disappearance and we must understand them as such to grasp their connection to racism and racist intent. The United States readily exports this carceral apartheid model abroad, as seen not only in aiding Israel's genocide of Palestinians, but in the US support of England over Ireland's sovereignty, the construction of Guantánamo Bay in Cuba, the suppression of the Puerto Rican Nationalist Movement, and the torture of prisoners of war in the Middle East, to name a few from a long list of bloody examples.

Levels of Analysis

Carceral apartheid is an applicable governing approach found within a variety of organizational types (e.g., bureaucracies), nation types (e.g., democratic republics), and economic types (e.g., capitalism), given its utility and resonance. Carceral apartheid, as a conceptual paradigm, adeptly outlines the governing structure which creates and perpetuates societies as carceral containers, where no facet of life is left un-surveilled, unracialized, and, for the undesirables, unmarked. I propose that carceral apartheid as governance operates and influences society at nested levels, including the macro, meso, and micro levels, that directly interact with and influence each other.[23] The macro level provides the overarching platform for the meso and micro levels, while at the same time, the micro and meso levels "influence up," meaning, for instance, that changes within and enacted by social movements at the micro level can directly shift the representative features of and conflict existing at the meso and macro levels.

Institutional Level (Macro)

At the macro level, for example, in alleged democratic republics with histories of colonialism and racial capitalism, carceral apartheid is often sustained through routine tools of violence that secure the decimation and genocide of peoples who are racialized as non-white for the purpose of revenue generation and settler communal enrichment. We see this example in the United States through Indigenous erasure, chattel slavery, convict leasing, Jim Crow, continued racial segregation, and consecutive waves of mass incarceration for minoritized communities. By looking at carceral apartheid as governance at the macro level, I suggest carceral apartheid is a nation-building enterprise that continues to propel and protect the rise of the United States as a racial capitalist empire, and any revolution attempted against carceral apartheid is born in blood.

The dispossession and killing of subjugated populations, particularly Black and Indigenous peoples, to fund empire is a sociological pattern. Disrupting coalitions and sowing division across racial and ethnic boundaries is the number-one tool of destruction. Death is an inevitable outcome, and racist intent makes it so, whether the death is slow or quick, obvious,

Table 1.1. Levels of analysis in the governance regime of carceral apartheid

Levels of analysis	Analytic frames	Representative features	Conflict over	Racialized intention
Institutional (macro level)	The racial state	State racial categorization	Group membership	Genocide
	Racial projects	Racial legal codes	State resources	Exploitation
	White supremacy and anti-Blackness	Racial segregation	National inclusion	Assimilation
	Divide and conquer	DEI/CRT restrictions		
	Settler colonialism	Extractive revenue generation		
	Whiteness as property	Surveillance technology		
	Racial capitalism			
Organizational (meso level)	Military	Official controls (surveillance, arrest, conviction, imprisonment, probation, and parole)	Group sovereignty	Spatial domination
	Corrections	Clandestine and extralegal controls (murder, disappearances, lynching, sexual assault, planting evidence, gladiator fights, civilian alliances)		Containment
	Law enforcement			Disillusionment
	Courts			

Table 1.1 *(continued)*

Levels of analysis	Analytic frames	Representative features	Conflict over	Racialized intention
Individual (micro level)	Social movements (rebel groups, gangs, religious groups)	In-group favoritism	Capital (economic, social, political)	Survival
		Racial mobilization		Revolution
		Racist intergroup and intragroup violence		Alliances

Source: Table contents are original to *Carceral Apartheid*. Table headings adapted from Victor Ray, "A Theory of Racialized Organizations," *American Sociological Review* 84, no. 1 (2019): 26–53, table 1. Ray's work inspired me to revise and update his table according to my theory of carceral apartheid.

or hidden, the work of white liberals or card-carrying Nazis. The travesty of white supremacists acting as agents of the state to kill non-white people with impunity is not confined to single historical events or to singular types of white people.

For instance, the blood of Black people flows far and wide across the shores of enslaved voyages, through the fields of stolen, settled land, and from within and around prison walls. Systematic killings are not one-off periodic narratives but a part of a durable governing blueprint which institutionalizes sadistic abuse as part and parcel of a penal approach to nation building. This is the true nation-state, stretching far beyond the bars of penal organizations such as jails and prisons. We must question the lengths to which society will go to rationalize the official, clandestine, and extralegal weapons of violence used to eradicate populations labeled as undesirable.

Organizational Level (Meso)

I focus on corrections at the meso level as a critical locus of carceral apartheid, representing but one organized enforcement arm of the governance regime, which is protected through incessant funding, correctional officer unions, and bi-partisan tough-on-crime political lobbies. The Black and non-white communities targeted for death in the streets by law enforcement are the same people targeted within our prisons. As of 2023, Black people alone constitute roughly 37 percent of people in jail or prison in the United States, despite comprising only 13 percent of the general population.[24] And the linkages do not stop there. Courts, corrections, policing, the military, counterterrorism, border patrol, and immigration enforcement—these are all heads on an imperial hydra, sharing intelligence to act cooperatively to the same white supremacist tune. Where one goes, the other is close behind. All seek to kill, steal, and destroy the life force of the "underclasses" by way of official, clandestine, and extralegal means, learning from the colonial predecessors before them.

Individual Level (Micro)

I suggest that the macro and meso levels directly influence in-group favoritism and conflict over capital at the micro level. They also form the foundation of the corresponding emergence of racial and class-based mobilization and inter/intra group racist violence. For example, the racialized social movements emerging within penal organizations such as prisons (e.g., rebel groups and religious sects) are an example of how carceral apartheid spurs consequences at the micro level. Specifically, in later chapters I focus on collective mobilization endemic to prisons, such as groups traditionally identified by the state using gang labels or security threat group identification (e.g., Black Guerilla Family and Aryan Brotherhood), and religious sects (e.g., Nation of Islam) that are often categorized using similar surveillance labels.

I focus my empirical analysis on social order within prisons to ultimately make a broader conceptual claim that carceral apartheid as governance flows within and beyond confined walls. Penal organizations, such as prisons, are but a microcosm of society, a mirror that illuminates how social order is maintained in what we ironically term "free society." I reveal this linkage through analyzing the durable governance structure (i.e., carceral apartheid) and resulting social conditions that led to the rise of mobilizing groups such as the Black Guerilla Family and Aryan Brotherhood.

Durability

I suggest that carceral apartheid is both a throughline and socially durable governance structure in that it continues to evolve during moments of perceived heightened threat within a given period of institutional (macro) and organizational (meso) memory. In these moments we witness nuance and contingency in how carceral apartheid necessarily expands organizational capacity to maintain social order at the individual level (micro).

In other words, general time and place differences across carceral apartheid regimes, or variability in the look and scope of carceral apartheid, can be traced to moments when perceived threats to social order are identified by the state and corresponding crisis management approaches are developed and implemented to neutralize these threats.

Perceived threats are most notably populations identified as problematic, and thus criminally deviant, because their behavior visibly subverts norms and requires official, clandestine, and extralegal remedies. Groups who also visibly demonstrate a disdain for white supremacist subordination are considered the most threatening (e.g., Black militants being targeted by prison officials while Nazis are left to their own devices). It is when the state and its organizational arms identify perceived threats that we witness their expansion through funding and updated policies.

For example, when Black militants became public enemy number one to the state at the macro level, directives were sent to corrections officials at the meso level, who also shared information back to the state regarding their prerogatives, with both influencing the legitimation of their needs to expand official, clandestine, and extralegal capacities for control to maintain the structure of carceral apartheid.

Carceral Apartheid in Action: Official, Clandestine, and Extralegal Controls

Pioneering Sociologist Ida B. Wells argued long ago that there are two justice systems in the United States, one for white people and the other for Black people.[25] I take this to mean that Black people and other populations labeled as undesirable are often subjected to three types of control simultaneously. We should define and operationalize how these levels operate as official, versus that which is clandestine and at times, extralegal, in the service of carceral apartheid as governance. To operate in a clandestine manner refers to something "marked by, held in, or conducted with secrecy."[26] Official controls meaning formal policies, procedures, and rules as sanctioned by administrative mandates and laws.[27] For example, official controls operate using regulated carceral power in the form of organizational protocols, such as classification schemes and housing placements that are often enforced through administrative and officer discretion, with the expressed goal of identification and subduing problem populations.

Official controls are unsustainable to maintain complete sovereignty over fate. Further, operating in a clandestine manner is key to employing what are often extralegal controls. Extralegal controls, meaning unregulated actions existing outside of the law and not sanctioned through these formal means, are still deemed culturally legitimate and thus appropriate to a particular organizational setting. Extralegal controls are explicitly outside the official designation of carceral power, such as arranging gladiator fights, but are highly effective in instilling terror in and achieving the annihilation of problem populations. The legality or extralegality of these controls can shift in accordance with cultural, political, and social movements that have pushed governments on the legality of certain carceral techniques. This contentious history of what constitutes extralegal is ongoing and could be described as a push and pull dynamic rather than a linear one.

The state strategically allows penal actors to employ extralegal controls, often in secret alongside official controls to ensure carceral apartheid as governance is successful in fostering spatial domination over the penal environment. This gives penal actors godlike status to deal death in all its forms and play games with people's lives. This approach to governing and maintaining order is embedded within every square inch of the prison and can be found in all social relations.

The Case of California Prisons

My research draws from the case of California prisons during the civil rights and Black Freedom Movement eras to illuminate the history of governance through carceral apartheid, the durability of carceral apartheid to expand the structural capacity of penal organizations during heightened moments of perceived threat, and the resulting consequences for social organization among the incarcerated. I zero in on the significance of the 1950s as a starting point, with the steady considerable influx of Black people into California prisons, especially those aligned with the Black Freedom Movement and self-identified as Black militants.

Official controls that I identify and trace as significant include the following: racial categorization and sorting, expanded threat categorization schemes, isolation and behavioral modification using Adjustment Centers/Units, and the expansion and diversification of solitary confinement (e.g., supermax). Extralegal controls that I identify and trace as significant include the following: spreading false rumors among the incarcerated of impending violence, beatings and abuse, snitch jacketing, gladiator fights, creating higher-status "prisoners" or "prisoner elites," and arming with weapons those with higher-status markers (e.g., white people in the US context). All of these controls are typically used in a clandestine fashion at strategic moments during the ongoing war against imprisoned Black people.

I uncover how penal organizations at the meso level drew from longstanding control tactics at the macro level to weaponize race and eradicate Black protest. These produce profound effects on the micro-level interactions among the incarcerated and between prison staff. For example, white correctional officers came into the penal environment with identities and belief systems that influenced them to try and replicate alliances with white supremacist incarcerated people to silence Black protest, which directly parallels the alliances seen in society between the Ku Klux Klan, police officers, and white supremacist civilians.

This alliance works to support white supremacist solidarity and create conditions akin to what sociologist Nicole Gonzalez Van Cleve calls ceremonies of "racial degradation" in her work on courts and the solidarity among judges, prosecutors, and law enforcement to humiliate, berate, and ultimately convict those labeled as society's undesirables.[28] Similarly in prison, *Carceral Apartheid* shows how officers and those labeled as "prisoners" find solidarity around their whiteness and the joint racial degradation of Black people even though officers and the imprisoned are not of the same powerful status in the governance regime. Importantly, I showcase this behavior as an intended strategy of carceral apartheid and its goal of division, decimation, and ultimately, domination.

Racialization and Penal Organizations

Prior sociological research has demonstrated that penal organizations are racialized spaces, and that official policies and procedures play a predominant role in the racialization of the environment. When someone becomes incarcerated and is labeled a prisoner, the penal organization strips them of their personal belongings, replaces their name with a number, and questions them about their criminal history. Official organizational rituals designed to transform human beings into prisoners—all aspects of life conducted in the same place, rigid schedules, enforced distinction between staff and the confined, stigmatization of confined status—are compounded by informal negotiations at reception centers between newly created prisoners, officers, and correctional administrators.[29]

Sociologist Philip Goodman's research on California shows how these negotiations determine a new prisoner's racial and ethnic category and threat classification for the purpose of official housing assignments. Choices mainly include Black, White, Hispanic, or Other, with some reception centers offering Asian and Native American as options.[30] Becoming transformed into a prisoner means being subjected to racial projects alongside the widely recognized "pains of imprisonment" such as restriction of liberty, deprivation of goods and services, loss of autonomy and security, and lack of choice in sexual expression.[31] The category "prisoner" is a political tool, after all, with incarcerated people inhabiting a particular racialized and gendered space.[32]

Sociologist Michael Walker's research on contemporary jails advances our understanding of racialization because he shows how societal racial projects and risk management are foundational to how penal organizations sort by race and ethnicity in California.[33] He suggests the requisite racial projects can be understood as "an interpretation, representation, or explanation of

Carceral Apartheid as Governance 31

racial dynamics, and an effort to reorganize and redistribute resources along particular racial lines. Racial projects connect what race 'means' in a particular discursive practice and the ways in which both social structures and everyday experiences are racially 'organized,' based upon that meaning."[34]

As Walker explains, racial projects first emerge by linking the ideologies of perceived biological difference to sentiments about human worth. Second, they are perpetuated by putting this link into action through organizing bodies, space, and resources to reflect hierarchies of worth. It is "the perception that race is real [that] has real consequences."[35]

Applying Walker's logic to prisons, I suggest we can expect to find that racial projects coalesce with risk management protocols to produce an organizational racial project that maintains racial segregation through categorizing and sorting, effectively structuring the everyday experience of incarcerated populations. Walker uses the term "institutional racial project" and "institutional sorting"; however, I use organizational racial project and organizational sorting because I make an analytical distinction between institutions at the macro level (e.g., state) and penal organizations (e.g., prisons) that reside at the meso level.

A prison's organizational racial project officially maintains racial divisions, which structures boundaries among incarcerated individuals in their everyday micro-level interactions. They are forced by prison administrators and staff to buy into the racial project first at the organizational level, even if it means an increased likelihood of violence and no official guarantee of opportunities for protection. The main point here is that the penal organization only provides choice within a set of prespecified parameters that have corresponding consequences at the micro level. This point is true even for those who happily choose a category from the penal organization's preordained list.

Significantly, organizational racial sorting leads to violence and contention rather than preventing it. Sociologist Patrick Lopez-Aguado's work on contemporary California penal organizations shows how officially categorizing and then sorting newly created prisoners according to predetermined racial and ethnic categories effectively exposes people to violence. This consequence occurs despite organizational claims that threat classification combined with racial segregation reduces violence. For example, categorizing a person as Hispanic in a northern California prison automatically forces them to contend with the associated politics endemic to the prison system, where the category Hispanic splits allegiances across northern and southern regions of the state (e.g., Norteños vs. Sureños).[36]

Whether or not a person desires to participate in the politics, the organizational racial project maintains the political status quo by evoking official racial and ethnic categories and forcibly sorting all new prisoners accordingly. The micro-interactional consequences of organizational racial projects are well represented in how people remember their first lesson in racial sorting.

For example, upon entering Calipatria State Prison, a formerly incarcerated man described his experience with quickly being educated by a person also categorized as Hispanic who warned him not to fraternize with Black people: "Hey, homie, we don't associate with *llantas* (tires) around here. The *animales* (animals) have their own rules. We follow ours. Don't talk to them too much because someone might feel disrespected, and you're going to get dealt with."[37] This example showcases how forced adherence to the organizational racial project coerces newcomers to exhibit compliance with the existing carceral apartheid regime. The incarcerated maintain this project as an act of survival and did not create it. But rather, I advise that it is the product of historical organizational processes perpetuated through carceral apartheid to succeed in what amounts to a state-sanctioned war on the Black community.

Strategic Racialization:
Weaponizing Racial Categories through Carceral Apartheid

I extend the contributions of previous sociological research to suggest that the official categorization and racial sorting described by scholars are insufficient on their own to induce widespread, cyclical violence and maintain racial and ethnic divisions. Instead, other mechanisms are also at work. I claim it is the *weaponization* of racial categories that produces this outcome through the employment of official, clandestine, and extralegal controls. Carceral apartheid is realized through routine practices that weaponize racial categories to directly control the micro-interactional racial projects between the incarcerated, where racist intentionality and ritualized in-group solidarity around whiteness are pervasive fuel. I contend these are first and foremost state weapons at the macro level, which materialize as organizational purpose at the meso level, structuring the organizational desire to institute a state of precarity at the micro level by 1) isolating incarcerated people and 2) causing discord among the incarcerated based on race and ethnicity.

Official, clandestine, and extralegal control practices minimize incarcerated populations' risk to penal actors by preventing sociopolitical solidarity within and across racial and ethnic groups that might challenge the organization's sovereignty. Penal organizations engage in what I term *strategic racialization*. This occurs when maintaining white supremacy among the incarcerated is paramount because it is key to organizational sovereignty over spatial domination within the penal environment. Strategic racialization mirrors macro-level prerogatives defined by the state in free society that seek to create and sustain empire.

I argue that carceral apartheid as governance creates a triangle of division, where the sovereign resides at the top, in the middle the white faction of the incarcerated underclass is granted contingent inclusion in exchange for their loyalty, and the lowest incarcerated underclass faction is annihilated because their existence challenges the sovereign's claim to power (e.g., Black militants). For instance, within penal organizations when white incarcerated people fail to remember their place (e.g., fraternize with a Black person), their precarious position in this social structure is revealed. White incarcerated individuals must remember white supremacy is key to maintaining organizational sovereignty and that cruelty and degradation against Black people is the backbone of in-group solidarity.

If not, they are quickly reminded by prison administrators and staff using the same control strategies revised and further adopted by the organization to eradicate Black incarcerated people and Black militants especially. For example, it is a heinous violation of carceral apartheid when white incarcerated people and organized groups eventually forget to show deference to penal organizations and attempt to take over. This specifically occurs when we see things such as escape attempts or the perpetuation of violence against prison staff. In sum, when white incarcerated people resist carceral apartheid too strongly and do not show deference to penal controls, they are reminded of their contingent status in the organizational hierarchy and face repression. When these pressure points occur, the warning from Black militants that they will someday use on you the very same tactics they use on us becomes quite real, as I detail in the chapters ahead.

Importantly, at the micro-level incarcerated individuals also innovate against complete penal control and come to claim a level of power within this social order. In fact, the organizational intensification of carceral apartheid in the 1950s and 1960s sparked the rise of sophisticated movement groups among the incarcerated, which eventually became categorized by penal actors as security threat groups (e.g., prison gangs). Even so, white incarcerated people maintained a privileged position in proximity to penal actors because they were instrumental as allies of repression, fulfilling the original organizational desire to disproportionately expose Black incarcerated people—especially those who self-identified and were coded as militants—to physical extraction, injury, alienation, and death.

I identify the micro-level intended consequences of weaponizing racial categories at the meso level, including the following: strict self-policing of racial and ethnic boundaries among the incarcerated, blurred social boundaries between penal actors and incarcerated individuals to promote strategic in-group solidarity, and a dialectic of prison-wide repression and resistance among the incarcerated and between incarcerated individuals and penal actors.

The cycle of repression and resistance generates penal innovation within the organizational racial project and ultimately further entrenchment of official, clandestine, and extralegal controls, rather than a dismantling of the social order produced through carceral apartheid. Racial projects emerge within a history that flows cyclically through free society and from within penal organizations. This history typically points to an identified problematic threat that the state feels it needs to subdue by administering slow rational poison in the form of incapacitation.

My operationalization of carceral apartheid necessarily uses the case of California to historicize my conceptual contribution and trace the consequential organizational conditions that intentionally cultivate structurally violent outcomes. For example, my work clarifies the conditions that created the very same racialized movement groups the California Department of Corrections and Rehabilitation (renamed to add "rehabilitation" in 2004) currently uses to justify forcibly sorting incarcerated individuals by race and ethnicity. This rationalization further gives grounds for maintaining widespread draconian conditions including supermax confinement, two significant contemporary consequences that disproportionately harm racial and ethnic minorities.[38]

A theory of carceral apartheid as governance opens a variety of questions about how institutions and organizations decide whom to label and target as undesirable in a society. It puts up for analysis the means through which they decide to employ varying types of controlled violence as solutions. Governance is essentially a problem-solving enterprise designed to mobilize these solutions to produce intentional, hoped for outcomes. Social problems ultimately germinate from "a process of collective definition," which determines whether they arise, if they become legitimated, how they are molded in discussion, how they are contemplated in official policy, and how they are reconstructed into a plan for organized action.[39] Social problems are not the result of objective indicators. When states render things or people legible as a social problem, they use carcerality as the preferred approach to solving it.[40]

Thus, it is important to interrogate when and how states decide to label populations as an undesirable social problem as a precursor to declaring war on them. Who is the problem and how are they "solved"? How does the problem become one requiring adjusting? How is carceral apartheid as governance wielded across time to disproportionately target these "problem" populations and force them to obey?

OBEY

Slaves, obey your earthly masters with respect and fear,
and with sincerity of heart, just as you would obey Christ.

—EPHESIANS 6:5*

*A scripture routinely taught to enslaved Africans to justify their
bondage in the United States. Indicative of the perverse use of
cultural norms to control and coerce non-white populations.

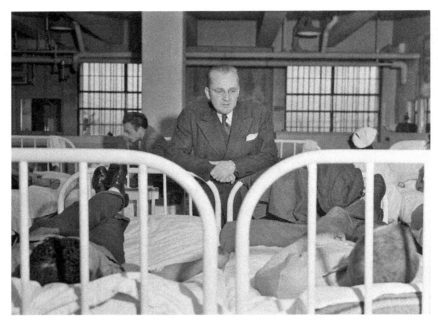

Warden Clinton T. Duffy with two incarcerated men at San Quentin State Prison who had just given blood to the Red Cross for World War II. Photograph by Ann Rosener, 1943. Farm Security Administration—Office of War Information Photograph Collection, Prints and Photographs Division, Library of Congress, Washington, DC.

ADJUSTING PROBLEM INMATES

Those who commit the murders write the reports.
—IDA B. WELLS

The doctor's white office is always a confessional. The prison doctor's office is the confessional of the damned. For twenty-seven years I have served as Chief Surgeon of San Quentin, the largest penal institution in the world. During those years forty thousand men have entered its iron gates to come, sooner or later, under my personal care. Forty thousand history charts in my office files hold the life stories of as many men. Ill, despondent, broken, they have come before me, stripped not only of body but of their secret and most terrible thoughts. Men—at their worst.[1]

When Dr. Leo Stanley wrote these words in his memoir, he knew he could cure the imprisoned with the right medicine. Physicians, he championed, could serve as a viable "crime deterrent."[2] It was 1940, at the heyday of the modern rehabilitative ideal: a belief that the primary purpose of confinement is to effect a social change in character and to treat deviant afflictions, ultimately strengthening the welfare of the individual and social cohesion among the community.

Chief Surgeon of San Quentin since 1913, as a medical doctor Dr. Stanley once viewed nature as the primary driver of a person's criminality. Criminality, which was understood as deviant behavior and condemned by society as a violation of criminal law, was thus punishable through penal organizations.

In line with the shifting times, Dr. Stanley began to change his mind on the nature vs. nurture debate. He now advocated against lingering calls for a predominantly biological understanding of criminal behavior in favor of combining the modern rehabilitative ideal with his biological training.

Dr. Stanley felt that he could take the modern rehabilitative ideal a step further by pushing the boundaries of science. He saw himself as a leading innovator among a two centuries-long list of natural and social scientists researching the determinants of criminality.

By 1940, Dr. Stanley's shifting views were becoming mainstream among the scientific community, rather than a strictly radical proposition touted by religious reformists. Like many penologists of the time, working in penal organizations such as asylums, reformatories, jails, and prisons, Dr. Stanley believed that overall, "crime, then, is a social disease in that it disturbs the normal action of organized society" and that it was his duty to send the incarcerated back out into society "better than when they came in, [a key step] toward rehabilitation."[3]

Treating the Once Untreatable Problem Populations

Populations labeled as a "problem" have always been of the utmost concern for societies, as, to be a problem is to be deviant, which elicits fear.

In the words of sociologist Howard Becker, "Social groups create deviance by making the rules whose infraction constitute [sic] deviance, and by applying those rules to particular people and labeling them as outsiders. From this point of view, deviance is not a quality of the act the person commits, but rather a consequence of the application by others of rules and sanctions to an 'offender.' The deviant is one to whom that label has successfully been applied; deviant behavior is behavior that people so label."[4]

Dating to the Early Modern Era of history, Western societies have long positioned macro-level institutions such as nation-states and meso-level organizations such as prisons as the legitimate definer and governor of what constitutes normal behavior.[5] The state-level institutionalization of the ideas of normality versus deviance has long prevented us from questioning such definitions of normality.

We have yet to adequately flip the gaze back to societal organizations, and, instead treat them as powerful social machinations that perpetrate the most deviance in society even when measured against their own definitions of deviance. For example, in many societies law enforcement continues to commit the most violence within national borders and exports these warmongering techniques around the world, yet we fail to label them as abnormal.[6]

People labeled as abnormal and thus problematic, rather than problematic societal organizations, unfortunately remain the centuries-long dominant subject of criminological inquiry across the natural sciences, such as biology and neuroscience; and the social sciences, such as sociology, political science, and economics; and the interdisciplinary fields of criminology and criminal justice.[7]

Instead of taking a critical view of society and examining the dark side of the state, prior research on the determinants of criminality overwhelmingly employs an essentialist vantage point that privileges penal organizations such as prisons as self-justifying, legitimate sources of governance. This distorted view asserts that criminality is centered on the alleged problematic individual and social group, while the justice system solely exists to solve these problems through regulation.[8]

Norms or regulations of human behavior have always been critical matters in all societies. However, specific intellectual energy dedicated to understanding criminality or the legal breaking of these norms and regulations did not surge until the latter part of the eighteenth century. Prior to that time, criminality was solely attributed to religious interpretations of supernatural forces such as the devil, demons, witches, and, in general, those conceived of as evil entities, which were thought to be acting through the person who committed the offense, due, in part, to some flaw in that person's moral character and familial "bloodline." Patriarchal and racist theological explanations of reality were supreme, and to question such explanations was considered heresy, triggering the wrath of the Christian church and their nation-state pawns across Europe and the Americas.

The pious state viewed society as hanging in the balance at the constant mercy of the supernatural, with mortal sins, also known as felonies, viewed as manifestations of people's supposed evil dispositions. Societal organizations subsequently developed procedures according to the logic that criminality reflects sin and just damnation by otherworldly forces and thus was only treatable by the church and the king. For example, only those anointed by God could interpret human behavior and its presumed relationship to the supernatural, giving authoritative power to a few select white men, who wielded complete control over society.[9]

Significantly, this worldview perceived human behavior as determined by forces beyond the individual's control, and thus, retribution against these forces was a major logic for developing practices to control populations labeled as problematic and formally administer punishment. Retribution operationalized as penal logic often took the form of public humiliation; torture; tests of guilt or innocence, such as forcing people to walk on fire; and public ceremonial death penalties, such as burning at the stake, quartering, or hanging. This societal orientation for punishing the body reigned for centuries and those in positions of authority did not begin shifting their views until the latter half of the seventeenth and early eighteenth centuries, largely due to the social and intellectual upheavals that defined the Enlightenment Era.[10]

The Enlightenment had a profound effect on the development of the scientific method to seek and categorize knowledge. This era brought us the ideals of free will and rationality as opposed to appealing to the Christian divine and theological explanations of societal events. Emerging liberal philosophies espoused by political thinkers such as Locke, Hobbes, and Rousseau advocated for the natural rights of white men as a guide to regulating human behavior. Importantly, they also questioned how a few among the clergy and aristocracy could maintain a stronghold over the state and societal organizations. Out of this era came the belief that the source of criminality does not reside outside of an individual's control and in the realm of the supernatural, but instead, the individual has free will and rationally partakes in deviance, should it be to their benefit. The state should thus also target punishment of the individual's mind rather than focus on the body.[11]

It is from this decidedly enlightened place that prominent white men emerged as scholars, such as Cesare Beccaria and Jeremy Bentham, whose ideas eventually structured penal organizations around the globe for centuries to come.[12] Our society still, for example, uses both scholars as the basis for contemporary sentencing guidelines that purport to instill rational deterrence to crime, despite ample research that deterrence is at best a nuanced, mixed bag (and that is a generous assertion).[13]

Cesare Beccaria famously argued that those in authority should let the punishment fit the crime in his 1764 long-form essay *On Crimes and Punishments*, which, in time, significantly impacted the foundation of European and American criminal legal systems and their deterrent approach to problem solving. The Catholic Church condemned his essay in 1777 for its rationalistic ideals and placed it on the church's *Index of Forbidden Books* for more than 200 years.[14] Beccaria argued against what he saw as the arbitrary nature of the criminal legal system of his time. He believed it to be unpredictably violent—especially the practice of extracting confessions by means of torture—and completely subject to the whims of religious and aristocratic authorities. Beccaria argued that, as rational actors, if people could instead anticipate the accompanying penalty for a criminal offense, it would deter them from committing that action in the first place.

He also argued that authorities should have limited discretion and employ rational, predictable procedures for distributing proportional punishment through penal organizations. For Beccaria, these guidelines were key to bureaucratizing justice and thus institutionalizing efficient, official controls governing human behavior, with the ultimate goal of achieving stable order in society.[15]

Jeremy Bentham believed these types of deterrence-based guidelines could be operationalized to officially control behavior through the precise regulation of time and space. He argued that people were not only motivated by free will but by hedonism, seeking rational means to satisfy their desires. Bentham espoused treatment in the form of penal architecture and repetitive discipline, arguing the regular minimization of pleasure and maximization of pain within a controlled setting could deter people from these impulses. He invented the infamous panopticon as the ideal architecture for penal organizations and, in 1791, published *Panopticon: Or The Inspection House*.[16]

Sociologist Ashley Rubin's exemplary work on Eastern State Penitentiary, established in 1829, details how the panopticon model and routine solitary confinement attempted to root out the purported evils endemic to incarcerated populations.[17] At this time in history, society was experiencing a transition from remoralization techniques, such as workhouses, to those specifically focused on rehabilitation of the mind, predominantly through isolation. This focus would continue to intensify into the late nineteenth century and early twentieth, forming what scholars describe as the early rehabilitative ideal.[18]

This approach remained heavily influenced by positivism, the Enlightenment, and biological determinism in its desire to treat populations labeled as socially problematic and, thus, at risk of being codified as criminally deviant. It was not until the late nineteenth and early twentieth century canonization and rise of the social sciences as valid disciplines that scientists began to distinguish social discoveries from biological ones. At this point in time, we begin to see the refinement of the early rehabilitative ideal into what we now consider the modern rehabilitative ideal. This shift did not completely discount biological determinants, but differed in that it placed a much stronger emphasis on the social causes of what was considered problematic behavior.[19]

The modern rehabilitative ideal had its heyday from the post–World War I era until the 1960s and was driven by the belief that experts could use knowledge in order to scientifically diagnose and treat the deviance within problem populations. This logic placed the responsibility of criminal reform in the hands of social and scientific elites rather than solely on the shoulders of state bureaucrats without scientific training. Social scientists were tasked with discovering preexisting conditions and diagnosing the problematic person with predictive disorders that contribute to their criminal behavior.

This approach differs widely from the notion that undesirable human behavior is based on individual sin or on the need to introduce morals to a "bad" person. Instead, it is assumed that deviance and criminality can be controlled if social scientists can determine what conditions cause it. Upon determining these conditions and diagnosing the issue, experts, such as Dr. Leo Stanley, believed they could then prescribe therapies to effect changes in behavior, and cure "men at their worst."[20]

Architects of Death, 1913–1951

We must understand Dr. Leo Stanley and his 1913 start as the Chief Surgeon of San Quentin State Prison through the lens of this historical arch. Dr. Stanley combined his belief in the modern rehabilitative ideal with his medical training in the natural sciences, leading him to blend medical and social experimentation to treat the minds and bodies of imprisoned people.

Dr. Stanley saw himself as a true pioneer on the brink of discovery, someone who could seamlessly bridge the old and new worlds of thinking within his laboratory to find cutting edge behavioral modification remedies for problematic populations.

His mixed expertise guided him in treating those categorized as problem inmates, the ones he called "undesirables," delivering his version of eugenics medicine for their persistent physical and social ailments.[21] For example, healing problem inmates of their masculinity deficits was one of his foremost cures and Dr. Stanley believed this could be done through a combination of Lombrosian, eugenics-based criminological techniques and psychiatric and psychological treatments.[22]

Keep in mind that Cesare Lombroso, the father of criminology, was a staunch proponent of positivism and put forth the idea of the "born criminal" who could be cured through physical interventions.[23] Lombroso infamously created the phrenological skull charts that now hang in many contemporary museums and were once used to justify the European colonization, genocide, and imprisonment of non-white peoples here in the United States and globally, who were diagnosed, using these charts, as naturally deviant or predestined to become so.

To Dr. Stanley, incarcerated individuals embodied "men at their worst" but he was determined to find both a medical and social cure.[24] As the lead medical provider within California's oldest functioning prison, during his tenure from 1913 to 1951 Dr. Stanley performed over 10,000 human experiments on people imprisoned within San Quentin.[25] Dr. Stanley maimed thousands, inflicting irreparable effects of criminality treatments such as sterilization,

One of many similar signs strung along the fence enclosing San Quentin penitentiary grounds. Photograph by Ann Rosener, 1943. Prints and Photographs Division, Library of Congress, Washington, DC.

castration, and injecting foreign animal and human substances into incarcerated test subjects' bodies.

"He believed that the decline of white, masculine vigor would lead to a degrading of the moral values of the country" and focused his treatments on "sterilizing people with less desirable traits" and implanting others "with 'testicular substances' from executed prisoners or, in some cases livestock."[26]

In describing his racist, classist "treatments" that blended medical and social science, Dr. Stanley wrote the following passages in his book *Men at Their Worst*:

> There is a growing theory that criminals and crime should be treated by surgeons and physicians instead of by wardens and courts. Much as I would like to believe that possible, I do not think we can as yet predict through medicine the end of crime. But it is certainly possible that a long and thorough study of disease and its relationship to the crime problem may serve as an opening wedge in the doorway leading to the solution of that problem.

> The prison surgeon learns what brings men into prison. It is his ambition to prevent their return. By sending men out in better shape than they were when they came in is one move, and an important one, toward rehabilitation. In this way the physician serves as a crime deterrent.
> Crime, to speak simply, is the inability to resist.
> Any physical weakness or abnormality lowers the ability to resist.
> Crime may be defined as any act which makes the doer liable to legal punishment. Disease is defined as a disturbed or abnormal physiological action in the living organism. Crime, then, is a social disease in that it disturbs the normal action of organized society.
> Disease as a "crime-contributer" may be divided into three classifications: moral disease, which has to do with character; physical disease, which applies to abnormalities; and mental disease, which pertains to the brain....
> Physical disease is largely a matter of surroundings and environment. ... Moral disease is influenced by early training and environment. ... Mental disease may be hereditary or environmental or brought on by a disregard of the physical laws of health.[27]

Dr. Stanley worked with a team of medical assistants, dental assistants, psychiatrists, and psychologists who aided him in his research and treatments.[28] His tenure with the California Department of Corrections is emblematic of how the early and modern rehabilitative ideals structured the diagnosis, labeling, and treatment of incarcerated individuals deemed problematic by the state—populations the state needed to deal with.

Penal organizations, such as San Quentin, allowed scientific experts such as Dr. Stanley to architect official policies and protocols designed to control and reconfigure the body and minds of those labeled as problem inmates. Dr. Stanley's agenda-setting legacy structurally induced states of death, meaning that problem inmates were violently coerced to die psychically, socially, and in some cases, physically. In contrast to physical death, social death denotes the dehumanization of a person, while psychic death is the coerced fundamental renovation of the cognitive self to produce a desired behavioral outcome.

The history of treating the once untreatable problem populations documents how the state's power rests on dealing such death(s) first through the official use of penal organizations. No longer placing severed heads on pikes or tarring and feathering in the town square, the state instead publicly employs the power of rationally-administered containment to produce a civic and humanitarian death, incapacitating those subjects deemed as external to the body politic. The ugly truth is that official, formally acknowledged controls are only the beginning. Dr. Stanley's work shows how the state began to place a particular focus on targeting the individual's mind as well as their body to shape the constitution of their soul into a docile specimen.[29]

The desire is to produce inmates who are no longer problems but instead defer to the penal organization, with repeat exposure to death(s) that hopefully fosters a renewed commitment to their degraded social status. Though Dr. Stanley retired from the prison in 1951, San Quentin and the California Department of Corrections inherited his legacy. Dr. Stanley built the structure of official control strategies that, rather than being tossed aside with his retirement, were folded into the architecture of the carceral apartheid governance structure moving forward.

During Dr. Stanley's reign, when questions emerged about his approach, the *San Francisco Examiner* published an article titled "San Quentin's Valuable Work for Science Should Continue," lauding Dr. Stanley for his contributions to penology:

> The layman cannot realize the extent to which the medical skill of California's physicians and surgeons, and hence the health of the whole public, has been advanced and benefitted, through the cooperation extended by Dr. Stanley, all during the years of his services as a prison physician. The prisoners themselves have had the advantage of treatment, by their own consent, administered by the best and most progressive medical men in the state. Remarkable cures have been made, curative technic [sic] has been advanced, and San Quentin has become famous for contributing, much as the army did, to the progress of medical science all along the line . . . must be recorded the many years of remarkable work done at San Quentin for the alleviation of human suffering.[30]

To this day, the California Department of Corrections, with "Rehabilitation" now added to its name, spreads disinformation about Dr. Stanley's legacy by outright lying and watering down the story of his violent impact on the penal system.

In a 2018 article on their official website titled "Early San Quentin doctor pushes prison medicine into 20th century," they proudly commemorate Dr. Stanley for innovating the penal system, saving the life of San Quentin warden James B. Holohan, and improving the conditions at San Quentin. They only included one tiny subsection glossing over his eugenic treatment protocols, titled "Experiments tarnish San Quentin doctor's legacy."[31] However, their attempt to paint a picture of a genius doctor with a complicated past falls short and, instead, is a vile attempt to gaslight the public regarding the reality of Dr. Stanley's role in the annihilation of imprisoned people as routine, official policy.

Rise of the Adjustment Center, est. 1953

adjust
a: to bring to a more satisfactory state:
    (1): settle, resolve | ways of *adjusting* conflicts
    (2): rectify | *adjust* an error
b: to make correspondent or conformable: adapt | had to *adjust* our approach
c: to bring the parts of to a true or more effective relative position | *adjust* a carburetor[32]

Notably, after the retirement of their beloved chief architect of death Dr. Leo Stanley in 1951, the California Department of Corrections built upon his life's work to shift how it labeled problem inmates. Now relying on an interdisciplinary committee of scientific experts, in 1953, California prison officials devised an official definition for the term "problem inmate," to be adopted within all its facilities. Problem inmates were officially considered those who needed extensive psychological treatment for "intractable psychopathic" behavior.

However, given there was only one Dr. Stanley and a shortage of available treatments across penal organizations, solitary confinement thrived as a key treatment of choice within California prisons. But prison officials were unsettled by this fact that, prior to the 1950s, most problem inmates were kept "for long periods of idleness and in isolation or segregation."[33]

Richard McGee, the Director of Corrections in California, proposed to wardens and superintendents an alternative to extended isolation, which instead would attempt to rehabilitate problem inmates within separate "Adjustment Units" also known as "Adjustment Centers" that would be constructed at each prison. He suggested consulting with social and psychological therapists to design an effective treatment regime that could be scaled across the Department of Corrections and would successfully "readjust" problem inmates back into the general prison population and, eventually, society.

McGee created the Committee on Intensive Treatment of Problem Cases, and, in November 1953, the committee released a preliminary statement outlining the policies and procedures for Adjustment Centers within California prisons. The committee proposed an official transition from current methods to a focus on treatment more squarely aligned with the social causes of criminality paradigm of the modern rehabilitative ideal. They explicitly cautioned wardens, however, that this change could be difficult to enforce among staff considering "the need to punish prisoners, while feeling righteous indignation or some other emotional satisfaction seems to be deep in the attitudes and habits of prison workers."[34]

The committee felt this desire to punish was inherent in human nature and endemic to corrections, fearing that "not all prison officials are capable in their own hearts of the full acceptance of the program of treatment." For example, the committee identified this disposition as a flaw of the Disciplinary Court, which they still put in charge of Adjustment Center sentencing, of displaying "anger and the self-righteous compulsion to punish the irritating problem cases which appear before them."[35] Their reservations about these pervasive punitive attitudes particularly involved how the Disciplinary Court approached "those who cause disturbances in prison."[36] Regardless, when the committee moved forward to finalize their Adjustment Center recommendations, they gave the Disciplinary Committee complete control over identifying and sentencing problem inmates to Adjustment Centers.

In October 1954, the committee released their final protocol on Adjustment Centers, defining in considerable detail the centers in the following manner:

> An area of the institution set aside and designed for the intensive treatment of problem inmates with the objective of returning them to the rehabilitation program of the institution proper. It replaces the older concepts of isolation and segregation and is not a punishment unit. The Unit shall consist of individual cells or rooms and facilities for dining, recreation, and work. It is designated by the Warden or Superintendent, with the approval of the Central Office, for inmates who are removed from the general population of the institution because of emotional disturbances, behavioral disorders, or other maladjustments. In general, the individual cells or rooms shall be similar in furnishings to those regularly in use by the institution.
>
> For the very seriously disturbed inmates, there may be provided quiet or stripped cells, which contain none of the usual furnishings. If necessary these may be soundproofed. Inmates placed therein are prevented thereby from harming themselves or destroying State property, or by their noise and destructiveness interfering with the routine activities, treatment, or sleep of other inmates housed in the Adjustment Unit or

in the vicinity thereof. Although ordinarily the inmates are sent to the Adjustment Unit on a temporary basis, in some cases inmates may be assigned there with the approval of the Central Office for a longer period of constructive treatment. Experience has shown that conventional methods of handling these serious problem cases in prison are inadequate. Costly, riotous incidents offer evidence of the failure of present procedures. So likewise does the recidivism among the prison problem cases, who return time after time to the isolation unit . . . it is a fundamental policy of the proposed program that the Adjustment Unit shall be planned for treatment rather than punishment.[37]

Anxieties about disturbances among the incarcerated drove the push for a therapeutic approach to those deemed problem inmates. The concern was that traditional methods, which amounted to idle isolation, seemed to exacerbate the issue and cause higher levels of aggression and antisocial behavior. The Adjustment Center became the treatment center for incarcerated people who were diagnosed as mentally disturbed or unable to cope with the deprivations of prison life—which the committee claimed led them to assault other inmates or officers, destroy property, "daydream and try to escape reality," or simply revolt in other ways against penal authority.[38]

Because of the emphasis on treatment, corporal punishment was officially banned, and the committee laid out extensive policies in an effort to create an environment where in theory, excessive physical assault would be frowned upon, and social and psychological therapy would be paramount.

In practice, this was far from the case.

In leaving room for the "forceful control . . . of riotous" problem inmates, the committee's protocol overlooked the reality that certain racial and ethnic minorities, such as incarcerated Black people, were thought to be especially prone to participate in disturbances and antisocial behavior. Further, the allowance of indeterminate sentences in the Adjustment Center would soon support the argument that these "treatment" units were in fact solitary confinement by another name, despite the committee claiming it hoped people would only need short stints in the units.

In particular, though its final protocol referenced the preferred temporary nature of Adjustment Center sentencing on page four, only a few pages later, the committee contradicted this stance in outlining its official inmate admission procedures. On page sixteen, the committee established the use of indeterminate sentences as a standard policy, advising "the principle of the indeterminate sentence shall govern the assignment of an inmate by the Disciplinary Committee to the Adjustment Unit . . . determination of readiness for release is also a function of the same group on the basis of clinical and other observations."[39]

As a result, the admission and release of problem inmates was left up to the discretion of the Disciplinary Committee, leaving room for the racist and classist intentions of those in authority to impact how many Black incarcerated people entered Adjustment Centers and the length of their sentences. The Disciplinary Committee based its release recommendation on subjective reports generated by Adjustment Center staff, who used a five-point rating system to record their opinions on problem inmate adjustment.

Despite being ordained by the committee as a treatment facility, the vast majority of Adjustment Center staff were not therapists but instead "selected correctional officers to be assigned there who are able to learn how to use information of a clinical character."[40] Wardens and superintendents were instructed to use "care" and only choose, if possible, "officers capable of accepting the point of view of treatment."[41] These officers were given considerable discretion to decide when counseling by clinicians and outside social agencies was necessary, creating an environment where the lead sergeant and his officers maintained majority control over treatment within—and release from—the Adjustment Center, as opposed to the few number of clinical staff.

The rise of California's Adjustment Centers marks a period when penologists believed that curated isolation, coupled with medical, psychiatric, and psychological experiments under the direction of scientific experts, could once again become the crown jewel of the modern rehabilitative ideal. However, in practice, the Department of Corrections used science to justify the intensification and expansion of a violent governance structure that wielded considerable control over how people entered and left Adjustment Center facilities.

Given the proposed treatment agenda, the committee's personnel choices were seriously flawed, considering their own earlier admission that at times correctional officers had been known to engage in "possible sadistic or vengeful practices" against imprisoned people whom they did not like or felt wronged by.[42] However, the committee naively believed special training would prepare Adjustment Center staff to understand the Centers' modern rehabilitative purposes and disregard their previous training as officers.

Officer training highlighted the need to become "familiar at first-hand with the functions of the Classification Committee," governed ultimately by the Disciplinary Committee. Officers were to account for any negative flags in an imprisoned person's file and report them directly to the Classification Committee, which at the time was in charge of categorizing newly identified problem inmates based on their alleged behavior.[43] The emphasis on classification became especially important four years later when prison officials shifted their attention from imprisoned people seen as psychologically disturbed, to any imprisoned person who displayed hostility toward authorities. This shift widened the definition of problem inmate. To prison officials, problem inmates who displayed hostility to authorities primarily consisted of Black Americans involved in political movements; they became framed as dangerous threats to the maintenance of social order within penal organizations, prompting prison officials to devise a plan to destroy them using this new tool at their disposal, the Adjustment Center.

In June 1958, the department conducted its first review of Adjustment Centers (AC), focusing their attention on three prisons—Folsom, Tracy, and Soledad. On a given day in Folsom, the average number of incarcerated individuals in the Adjustment Center was ninety-six, with eighty-five in Tracy and fifty-four in Soledad. The review praised Tracy for having "custody personnel [who] represent the best and most capable officers [and are] carefully screened for this specialized assignment," whereas Soledad and Folsom were ranked lower for using more discretionary humane criteria to select correctional staff, such as "patience, tolerance, [and] confidence."[44]

The review continued to compare the Centers, using several indicators such as inmate to personnel ratio, which was quite low in Tracy (14:96) when compared to Folsom (11.3:1) and Soledad (6:1), and other markers such as the physical structure of the units. This section was particularly revealing regarding inmate conditions. In all three ACs, the review committee recognized the need for improved sanitation, recreation, and therapeutic treatment. In Folsom, the committee went a step further, highlighting Folsom's own admission that "the lack of any semblance of treatment staff within the unit or facilities with which to conduct that treatment is certainly the greatest deficiency of our AC program."[45]

Folsom and Tracy by far had the highest average length of stay. Soledad had a three-month average, with incarcerated people in Adjustment Centers in Folsom and Tracy averaging five months in isolation. Comparing the longest recorded stays, Folsom significantly surpassed Tracy and Soledad, with an incarcerated individual in the Folsom Adjustment Center for three years and two months.[46]

On average, the Classification Committee categorized the majority of problem inmates in Adjustment Centers as Behavior Problems (Folsom: 29 percent, Soledad: 46 percent, Tracy: 32 percent), with virtually none identified as psychotic or otherwise seriously mentally impaired (Folsom: 4 percent, Soledad: None, Tracy: None). Other well-represented classification groups included Assaultive Inmates (Folsom: 6 percent, Soledad: 28 percent, Tracy: 4 percent) and Protective Cases (Folsom: 26 percent, Soledad: 35 percent, Tracy: 2 percent).[47]

Black Militants = Problem Inmates

Three months before this June 1958 internal review of Adjustment Centers, the department released an administrative bulletin zeroing in on Black militants as the most dangerous problem inmates. This bulletin contextualizes why all three Adjustment Centers report a high proportion of incarcerated individuals classified as "Behavior Problems," a common label given to Black militants sentenced to the Adjustment Center.

This emphasis on subduing a Black militant threat to state sovereignty would become the structural basis for a legacy of war against Black militants such as Hugo Pinell and his comrades.

In February 1958, prison officials released Administrative Bulletin 58/16, indicating the California Department of Corrections was shifting its views about which incarcerated individuals constituted the most significant problem inmates and, thus, deemed notable security threats requiring immediate treatment. The department was moving away from a focus on "psychotic" individuals as the most important problem inmates to isolate in Adjustment Centers and instead turned their attention to Black people, especially those validated as belonging to or displaying sympathy toward Black political movements in free society.

The bulletin, titled "Special Procedures for Muslim Inmates," was the first administrative bulletin targeting Black militants, who either self-identified as such or had that label ascribed to them. The bulletin's first target was the Nation of Islam as a Black political movement of interest and this document would later serve as a model for future movement identification schemes. The bulletin outlined a new process for identifying and classifying members of the Nation of Islam newly admitted to reception centers and those already present in the general prison population.[48]

California prison officials were heavily influenced by the US Department of Justice and its Federal Bureau of Investigation, which released secret, classified reports from investigations dating to the 1950s. These internal reports described residents identified as Black political activists, with "backgrounds of immorality, subversive activity, and criminal records."[49] Black militants were quickly identified as an official social problem requiring immediate correctional solutions, which conflated suspected or known organizational affiliation with behavioral issues.

Prison officials perceived Black militants as risky for organizational safety and thus a significant threat, adding this group to the top of their list of problem inmates. This included claims about the volatility of Black militants, with secret internal memos and administrative bulletins sent to officials at every prison to make them aware of the urgent situation.

A few months after the release of Administrative Bulletin 58/16, Milton Burdman, Chief of the Classification and Treatment Division, wrote a letter on behalf of the wardens at Tracy, Folsom, Soledad, and San Quentin. This letter was sent to officials in Sacramento, requesting more Adjustment Center staff with the following justification:

> The staffing requested above represents an emergency need and a workload factor based upon an increased accumulation of severe and violent problem behavior cases in the Department of Corrections. Without the provision of the requested treatment and custodial staff, the state prison system stands in danger of experiencing increased numbers and intensity of violent destructive episodes. . . . The Adjustment Center populations are by definition the most seriously disturbed inmates in the Department. Included in the group are incorrigible inmates with constant records of unpredictable violence; homosexual inmates whose activities have often resulted in institutional murders; men in protective custody who have had serious difficulties and are a source of potential violence from others; and severely mentally disturbed inmates. . . .
>
> Recognizing the limitations on state budget policy this year, we must nevertheless urge with all force the adoption of this program within the Department. Thus far we have been managing a tenuous situation with inadequate means. As the prison population grows, the proportion of the Adjustment Center group keeps increasing, with this situation aggravated by the fact that these men obviously serve much longer terms and remain with us as problem cases for years.[50]

Administrative Bulletin 58/16 instructed reception center and prison staff to notify the Departmental Chief Records Officer of any inmate they classified as belonging to the Nation of Islam, with proceeding memos recommending segregation in Adjustment Centers if necessary to ensure public safety.

An inter-office memo written by the Parole and Community Services Division describes these administrative bulletins and their purpose as follows:

> There have been three Administrative Bulletin's [sic] issued relative to Muslims. The first was 58/16, dated 2-25-58, titled "Special Procedures for Muslim Inmates." This A.B. described methods to be used in identifying members of this group, and forwarding of this information to Central

Office Records. The second Administration Bulletin was 58/16 (First Revision,) issued May 18, 1961, titled "Inflammatory Inmate Groups." This bulletin outlined method to identify these people, where this information is to be recorded in the Cumulative Case Summary, and established policies and procedures concerning the handling of these inmates. The third A.B. was 61/40, issued 4-4-61, titled "Islamic Literature." This bulletin outlines the Islamic Literature that will be permitted in the institutions. . . . Not one of these bulletins has a policy statement to guide the Parole Division in their contracts with this organization or its members.[51]

This memo references the first revision to Administrative Bulletin 58/16 in May 1961. The revision is significant because it expanded the notion of a Black militant threat within prisons to encompass more Black political movements that were found in free society.

With this revision California prison officials expanded their initial 1958 policies on the Nation of Islam by launching an internal investigation into the presence of all Black militants in their institutions. The revised version of Bulletin 58/16 was sent not only to wardens and superintendents, but to all offices and staff members, labeling Black militants as belonging to "inflammatory inmate groups," and citing public safety as the justification for revising the bulletin (Administrative Bulletin No. 58/16, 1961).

This bulletin conflated all Black militants with Islam and mirrored memos that used "Muslim" interchangeably with other identifiers (e.g., preacher, agitator) to describe politically active Black incarcerated people.

The revised bulletin opened with the following statement: "The policy of the Department of Corrections is to support constructive inmate activities. . . . However, the Department of Corrections is also responsible for the welfare and safety of all inmates as well as the security of the institution. The Department must, therefore, in the interest of public safety take necessary precautions in respect to activities, organizations, and communications media that may contribute to unwarranted agitation or inspire violence."

Necessary precautions included identification at reception-guidance centers prior to entering prison, with department officials calling all "staff members preparing the cumulative case summary evaluations [to be] alert to the possibility of membership by inmates. . . . Probation reports and other documents may contain evidence of such an affiliation."[52]

Staff were also directed to note any requests for militant or pro-Muslim literature as indications of interest in Black political movements. For those incarcerated individuals who were not previously identified at a reception center, as soon as correctional authorities became aware of their affiliation, they filled out a form, "a CDC 128-B chrono with a carbon copy [and] forwarded [it] to the Chief Records Officer." When a person neared parole, staff were instructed to "note membership in the paragraph Institution Activity," and, specifically, the Associate Superintendent was to inform the Departmental Chief Records Officer of the release date of any identified Black militant.[53]

The term "problem inmate" was becoming synonymous with the term "Black militant," with the Department of Corrections becoming particularly concerned with the recruitment of other Black incarcerated individuals into Black militant organizations, believing potential recruits were mentally defective and security risks: "The sect seems to attract the low IQ, socially inadequate persons. It is the writer's feelings that those individuals who become involved would, in all likelihood, present adjustmental problems in any event."[54]

Prison officials decided that in addition to systematically identifying Black militants, their next line of defense would be segregating them in Adjustment Centers and quietly spreading them throughout the prison system. The Adjustment Center, previously conceived of as a therapeutic treatment center, became a cage of indeterminate isolation for Black militants labeled as problem inmates with the potential for "riotous behavior."[55]

The California Department of Corrections' new policies reveal how prison officials lost interest in those considered to be psychologically disturbed and began to focus heavily on Black militants as the department's primary preoccupation. Officials believed that increasing numbers of Black incarcerated individuals in their prisons were sympathetic to Black militant goals in free society, regardless of their actual organizational affiliation.

Between 1955 and 1965, the percentage of Black prisoners in California prisons increased by almost 7 percent (20.6 percent to 26.9 percent), resulting in a noticeable rise in department fears, though Black militants made up no more than 5 percent of this growing population.[56] Still, the percentage of Black incarcerated individuals sympathetic to Black militant ideology was indeed growing, perhaps in part in response to prison officials' policies.[57] Black incarcerated people were especially vulnerable within California prisons, and many believed prison conditions were a continuation of the degrading racist experiences they had previously survived in free society.

The Department's Parole and Community Services Division was very concerned in particular about the number of Black Muslims within the system, writing a memo to officials in Sacramento titled "The Problem." In this 1963 memo, the Division observed that creating martyrs gave the Nation of Islam more notoriety and increased membership:

> It would appear that the professor of Philosophy and Religion who wrote *Black Muslims in America* remarks about notoriety bringing an increase

in membership is accurate. According to figures available, on January 25, 1961 there were 114 Muslims in CDC institutions and 25 Muslims on parole. On May 9, 1962, which was after the riots in Los Angeles [April 1962], there were 219 Muslims in the institutions and 49 on parole. As of March 22, 1963, there are 235 known Muslims in CDC institutions and 65 on parole.

Because the number of Muslims is increasing, the parole division insists that it is prudent to develop a policy, whether or not the increase is from Muslims becoming less secretive about their membership, whether there is an actual increase in membership, or whether the department is becoming more skilled at identifying Muslims. Regardless, they are increasing, so we need a policy to handle it for parole.[58]

Because of the intense fear surrounding any increase in Black militants among the incarcerated population, the Adjustment Center was no longer used for rehabilitative treatment, but instead as a warehouse to segregate Black militants from the general population in the name of public safety.

Prison officials were proud of their policies and seemed to believe these practices would become official policy across the country, advising other state law enforcement and penal systems through letters, such as this 1962 letter of advice to the Arkansas State Police: "we have attempted to spread these individuals out throughout our ten institutions and have identified and segregated the leaders."[59]

An almost verbatim inter-office memo within the Department of Corrections went out a few years later, adding the sentiment, "For the most part their [Black militants] recruiting is aimed at the easily lead [sic], low intelligence Negro."[60]

In a 1963 letter written by prison officials in Sacramento in response to an inquiry from the Nevada State Prison System about how to handle Black militants, the department again revealed its use of segregation in the Adjustment Center as a way to solve the problem: "We explain to him [a Black militant] very empathetically that we are not concerned particularly with his individual beliefs and that, as long as he does not attempt to recruit or agitate other members of the population, he can believe what he chooses without any interference from us; however, the minute he attempts to recruit other members of his race, or for that matter anyone ... or attempts to preach the beliefs of [his] group to others, he will be locked up immediately."[61]

The adoption of indeterminate sentencing in Adjustment Centers reinforced an emerging regime of carceral apartheid as governance, prescribing the official and clandestine use of control tactics against Black Americans labeled as politically active. The department's end goal was to neutralize their

Exterior of Building A, north facade, iron-latticed gate dungeon entrance, San Quentin State Prison (after 1933). Photo by Robert A. Hicks. Historic American Buildings Survey Collection, Prints and Photographs Division, Library of Congress, Washington, DC.

perceived threat to the sovereignty of penal organizations and, above all, to white supremacy.

The dark, secretive corners of the Adjustment Center became sites of profound psychological and physical distress, rising to the level of torture, and imposed selectively on Black militants. The Department of Corrections was aware of this pattern, but instead of addressing this, the officials instructed staff to be discreet and calculated in their handling and disappearing of Black militants, so they did not cause alarm among the general population or in free society. The department insisted in secret correspondence that it "did not wish, in any way, to create Martyrs."[62]

It took a while for prison officials to realize that Black militants regularly communicated with one another, often through the use of lawyers, who would recount narratives of abuse and torture to other imprisoned people and Black political organizations on the outside.[63]

For example, in 1962, a Black militant named Richard wrote a letter to his lawyer while in isolation in the Adjustment Center at Folsom State Prison, describing the plight of Black militants in California prisons. He instructed his lawyer to make his story known to all Black militants and African-Americans who would listen, in addition to his local community and relatives.

Instead of focusing on the content of this letter, internal department memos reveal prison officials in Sacramento were instead concerned with how this Black militant had managed to smuggle his handwritten letter into the general population so another incarcerated individual could type it and mail it on his behalf.

Richard's 1962 letter shows how carceral apartheid governed the prison population as a system of racial domination and genocide. He intimately details how his experiences, and the torture of Black militants more generally, were routinely overlooked, dismissed, and instead encouraged by prison officials as acts of war.

> In view of the many discriminatory practices, illegal beatings, etc. being inflicted upon those of the Negro general population, notwithstanding the record of the administration which will clearly show that all of the inmates who have been shot, beaten, abused, etc. in the California State Prison at Folsom, Represa, California, have been Negroes, for it is a well settled fact that although the various white inmates have gotten into many fights, etc., we can bear no personal record of any of them being shot down like dogs, as the Negroes are in and under this present administration.
>
> Moreover, the official staff of prison administrators use force, violence, coercion, and intimidation, threats and unlawful means of attacks upon the various inmates of this institution in a futile attempt to silence the witnesses of these alleged violations of the laws of the land, and are now attempting to use the same type of brute force, physical and mental torture upon the writer in question in view of the fact that my citation of the brutal, unprovoked attack of this officer who administered said physical torture of beating and kicking [of another] inmate.
>
> I was then summoned before the prison disciplinary court and given twenty-nine day isolation sentence with an additional sixty days loss of privileges, which is effective immediately. And threatened and warned

by those sitting in the court to keep my mouth shut no matter what I see or observe, for it was none of my business if the officer was beating and kicking [another] inmate. I was supposed to do my own time and pay no attention to the fellow, brother inmate.[64]

Richard's detailed account documents how racist intent fueled official, clandestine, and extralegal policies that targeted Black militants because these populations were considered a recognizable social problem within the California Department of Corrections.

Because of this label, Black militants were at risk of serious injury and death when correctional officers believed them to be threatening. Another example is the shooting of an unarmed Black militant on the recreation yard in San Quentin in February 1963. Depositions with multiple incarcerated people reveal that a small group of Black militants were jumped by white individuals, and a fight inevitably broke out among the incarcerated, prompting guards in the tower to shoot at the crowd without issuing a warning shot.

One witness stated, "It was a simple fist fight which did not warrant the use of weapons. There was no warning shot as I was standing just a few feet from the guy. I do not believe that a guy should be shot for a fist fight."[65]

Another witness remarked, "I seen the gun rail officer out of the corner of my eye and heard a lieutenant say 'shoot, shoot one of those bastards, kill him right now!'"[66]

One of the surviving Black militants explained, "White boys jumped us and I was hit in the eye. . . . My brother said, 'Don't move. I see one of the gunmen.' You officers then came out. We were walking towards you and we were attacked. . . . When [he] was shot, three of us walked toward fourteen white boys to fight."[67]

The shooting at San Quentin is one of many violent incidents described by Black militants. All of the those I interviewed remembered shootings of unarmed Black militants on various yards, indeterminate sentences in Adjustment Centers, and torture at the hands of correctional officers.

Richard's letter referenced earlier also details a beating incident, where the victim was held down by one officer while the others struck him: "One of the officers who was at the serving table ran all the way back to the end of the dining hall and violently began to beat and kick the Negro inmate who was lying on the floor and being held and restrained by the said lieutenant. Upon his brutal, cruel, and unusual attack, the various inmates seated in the dining hall began to scream and showed signs of unrest, as they did question the fact that the state correctional officer would resort to this type of method."[68]

Grueling accounts such as this one combined with the rise of the Adjustment Center show how constructing Black militants as a social problem allowed for the reconfiguration of carceral apartheid as governance within the prison setting, through new official policies obscured under the terminology of rehabilitative treatment—further bolstered by clandestine intentions and extralegal violence.

Carceral apartheid intensified its grip on prison populations during this era, further permeating penal organizations to legitimize the extreme use of force against Black militants. Very similar dynamics were seen at this time, as free society was going through the height of the civil rights and Black Freedom movements.

The prominent Black militant leader George Jackson, both a member of the Black Panther Party and one of the founders of the Black Guerilla Family, wrote extensively about the violent, coercive tactics used to control Black militants in California prisons—from indeterminate sentences in Adjustment Centers to beatings and sadistic torture. George himself spent seven and a half out of ten years in prison in solitary confinement.[69] In 1961, he was sentenced to one year to life for stealing seventy dollars.[70]

In a December 1964 letter to his father, George described how he continued to remain in isolation in the Adjustment Center despite not committing any infractions:

> I am still confined to this cell. It is nine by four. I have left it only twice in the month I've been here for ten minutes each time, in which I was allowed to shower. Did I tell you?
>
> They have assured me that I have not been given a bad-conduct report. It is just that they felt I was about to do some wrong. It's always suspicions.
>
> What I was supposed to have done or was about to do, never, never what they caught me doing as it should be. The last time I was in a cell like this three months, from February to May (1964) for reasons that are not altogether clear yet! I have had no serious infraction in almost three years now.[71]

George's letter reveals how the protests by Black militants concerning the ambiguity of indeterminate sentencing to Adjustment Centers fell on deaf ears because they were considered "problem inmates." Their constructed threat to the penal organization alone was enough to warrant isolation, without evidence of any actual committed infractions.

Prison officials justified constructing the threat by citing incidents in other states where Black militants were blamed for riots and FBI investigations describing them as violent criminals, pro-Communist, and terrorists. They eventually came to reference the Watts riots at any chance possible in order to justify their unconstitutional treatment of Black militants.

For example, in one memo, prison officials wrote, "The Department is continually on the alert for any activity on their part. We have had a number of incidents were [sic] they have created disturbances, however, none have gotten out of control. In the last two or three years they have been rather quiet, but we do not feel that this can be attributed to a lack of interest on their part. An example might be the part they played in the Watts riot in Los Angeles in 1965."[72]

Prison officials also justified their practices by claiming the number of incarcerated people involved in Black militant groups would decline if the department could reduce the incentive to join. For instance, the same memo citing Watts further argued: "We have also found that their membership fluctuates with many members dropping out when they find themselves in difficulty with the prison administration."[73]

Despite many claims like the above, the department never conducted systematic studies to test whether or not Black militants were actually threatening to a prison's welfare and whether Department policies were effective at reducing violence and increasing public safety. From the official files available, it is evident that systematic analyses of inmate incidents in prisons did not begin until 1970, two decades after the rise of the Adjustment Center to control those labeled as problem inmates.

None of these reports used adequate analyses to determine whether there was in fact a correlation between Black militants and disturbances, or if solitary confinement and "treatment" was effective in reducing violence. Department records make it clear that rather than conducting such investigations, the department relied on the racist intention that Black militants were indeed a social problem requiring a solution, necessitating the implementation of policies and practices rooted in the logic of carceral apartheid.

In response, Black militants filed a number of lawsuits against the department, charging that official controls such as indeterminate isolation were unconstitutional and that other forms of violence such as beatings were extralegal, with most cases specifically citing the enforcement of Administrative Bulletin 58/16—although these cases were routinely dismissed. Still, California prison officials were very concerned about the lawsuits, so much so that they began sending internal strategy memos citing case law from other states as precedents for derailing lawsuits.[74]

Prison officials rejoiced when in 1961 the Supreme Court of California decided:

Muslim petitioners' were not protected by the guaranty of religious freedom set forth in the state constitution since persons convicted of felonies were expressly excluded from the coverage of that provision. . . .

Respondent admits that the above restrictions have been enforced only against the petitioners and other Muslim inmates, but claims that the discriminatory treatment is justified because: "In the petitioners' case, the Director determined that the principles petitioners allegedly espoused were in direct conflict with the health, safety, welfare and morals of the prison."

Petitioners, by their acts in rejecting the authority of members of the white race, displaying verbally and physically their hostility to the prison staff, interfering in the disciplinary proceedings of other inmates and the alleged doctrines advocated, present a problem in prison discipline and management.[75]

The court went on to say that Black Muslim claims consisted "merely of hatred of the white race and superiority of the black man," adding salt into the already-deep wounds of all Black militants. The court further complimented prison officials on successfully managing a difficult inmate population, as seen with the following statement: "The court must assume that the prison officials will treat the Muslim inmates as humanely as is possible, considering the difficult administrative problems presented by the Muslim actions and practices."[76]

In rendering their decision, the court also specifically cited two incidents, one in which a Black Muslim allegedly verbally assaulted a correctional officer, and another, in which a prison was found justified in preventing a Black Muslim from mailing a letter to his attorney.

The first incident occurred because, according to the Black Muslim petitioners, correctional officers routinely searched and harassed Black Muslims without just cause. In recounting the incident, the court wrote:

There appears to be considerable friction between the prison officials and the Muslim inmates as individuals and as a group. On August 16, 1960, two prison officials found it necessary to search two Muslim inmates for contraband.

The officials were soon surrounded by approximately 20 of the Muslim group, who manifested much hostility and a desire to protect their two "Brothers" from interference by the prison officials.

A number of the Muslims who had gathered were ordered to report to the Captain's office where they were questioned.

According to the report of a prison official, "All of those questioned looked down their noses at those present as if we were a very small piece of refuse."

At the close of the interview, petitioner Mitchell refused to leave and as an officer attempted to remove him, Mitchell told him "to get his 'stinking hands' off him as no white devil was allowed to put his hands on a Muslim."

Mitchell was forced to the floor so he could be handcuffed and removed from the office. Petitioner Johnson thereafter lunged at one of the officers, and he was also forcibly subdued and removed from the Captain's office.[77]

The second incident occurred after one of the Black Muslim petitioners tried to write a letter to his lawyer that detailed the first incident and a number of other abuses against Black Muslims, other Black militants, and in general, all imprisoned Black people. The court described this incident in the following manner:

> On August 21, 1960, petitioner Ferguson attempted to contact a Los Angeles attorney concerning alleged violations of the rights of the Muslim inmates while in Folsom prison, but it appears that the letter was not allowed to be transmitted to the attorney.
>
> Ferguson again sought help on August 28, 1960, by writing to his mother, with directions to take the letter to a specified address. The letter to his mother was also confiscated, and Ferguson was punished for abuse of the mail privilege. In the opinion of the prison officials the letter to his mother contained derogatory remarks about the prison officials.
>
> Ferguson stated in the letter to his mother that the prison officials had advised him that his letter to the attorney "Is being returned in your central file, and he is (not) an approved correspondent of yours and you will not be permitted to write to him. The charges you state in your letter are also untrue and we will not permit you to make such statements, criticizing officials of this institution."
>
> Ferguson continued: "Now mother what this man forgot, was that this letter I wrote to Mr. Berry. It was legal and he is a lawyer. And I have the right by law to write to a lawyer when it is about law."[78]

The Ferguson case reveals that, despite admitting discriminatory treatment against the Nation of Islam, the court felt that the department's actions were justified because Black Muslims and other Black militants did indeed constitute a recognizable problem population and presented a viable threat to the safety of correctional officers, prison staff, and other incarcerated people. This was allegedly evidenced by the petitioners' blatant refusal to submit to authority and their outspoken criticism of white supremacy in free society and within prisons.

Claiming civil rights violations by the Department of Corrections was difficult to show in court for several reasons. For example, any Black militant cases that contained solitary confinement and isolation allegations were particularly difficult to litigate because previous case law had found that "a cause of action will not arise under the Civil Rights Act because of solitary confinement by a State of a prisoner in its custody."[79]

Another case frequently cited as precedent had similarly found that prison officials could use solitary confinement because it constituted an administrative sanction. It was thus not judicial and therefore not a form of "double punishment" of an incarcerated person.[80] California case law was also cited to support the notion that prisoners were not citizens or thereby guaranteed civil rights.

The above kinds of cases often contained language and logic that argued in the following way: "The supporting affidavit states that he is a citizen. It appears that he is a prisoner confined in that prison. He has been convicted of a felony. As such he is not a citizen."[81]

In *Roberts v. Department of Corrections*, the petitioner challenged this finding, and though his disputes were validated by the Supreme Court of California, the court ultimately denied his motion while still requiring the original district court to correct their abuse of discretion when it came to his citizenship (i.e., writ of mandamus).

The Supreme Court concluded:

Petitioner, who is confined in a California state prison, sought to file a petition in forma pauperis for a writ of injunction in the District Court below. That court denied leave to proceed in forma pauperis, holding that petitioner was not entitled to the benefits of 28 U.S.C. 1915, 28 U.S.C.A. § 1915, because he was no longer a "citizen" as required by that section. The District Court reached that decision in reliance on California Penal Code, § 2600, which provides that one sentenced to imprisonment for a term of years is deprived of his civil rights for the period of imprisonment. The decision of the District Court is in error. Citizenship for the purpose of in forma pauperis proceedings in the federal courts is solely a matter of federal law. Congress has not specified criminal convictions, except for desertion and treason, as grounds for loss of citizenship. . . .

Finally, petitioner filed in this Court a motion for leave to file a petition for a writ of mandamus to the District Court. Mandamus is an extraordinary remedy, available only in rare cases. . . . Because of the ambiguous state of this record, and the fact that a denial of this motion will not prejudice petitioner in further attempts to proceed in forma pauperis, the motion must be denied.[82]

Despite the difficulty that Black militants faced in surmounting this kind of use of case law, and the ambivalence that judges displayed toward their complaints, prison officials were still anxious to find ways to derail complaints against the Department. One, because they did not want Black militants to win cases impeding their authority and two, they actually believed Black militants were a dire risk to security.

Prison officials and state actors, thus, often tried to prevent the success of cases by colluding with judges outside of the courtroom.

A 1966 letter reveals that a district judge went so far as to ask the California assistant attorney general how to "get rid of Muslim cases," in their words.

A follow-up letter from the assistant attorney general advised that Muslims or any Black militant could not file their claims under the Civil Rights Act, providing a list of legal ways to derail cases.

The assistant attorney general also advised prison officials to employ the following legal roadblocks: "Insufficiency of allegations, statute of limitations, immunity of judicial members and other public officials, executive immunity, and the state is not a 'person' meaning it is not a suitable defendant for suit under the Civil Rights Act."[83]

Despite the difficulty faced when making accusations against the Department of Corrections, imprisoned Nation of Islam members, in particular, continued to find supporters on the outside who would file lawsuits on their behalf.[84]

They were persistent and especially outspoken against confinement in Adjustment Centers, frequently arguing in court, "no other inmates are given solitary confinement for praying to God, or subject to punishment for the practice of their religious beliefs."[85] Subsequently, members of other Black militant organizations filed lawsuits against the department.

Eldridge Cleaver, who converted to Islam while serving time in San Quentin in the early 1960s and eventually joined the Black Panther Party upon his release from Folsom in 1966, wrote a letter to San Quentin's warden on behalf of Black Muslims and militants alike.

Eldridge accused the prison and the department more broadly of deliberately denying Black militants' access to due process:

Every effort to obtain Judicial Review in accordance with both the Constitution of the United States and of the State of California, has been thwarted and frustrated through one subterfuge after another, to-wit:

1. By guards on the yard confiscating our Writs and Affidavits while they are in a stage of preparation, and
2. By the Legal Department of the Counseling Center refusing to render us the same services that are rendered to other inmates of the institution who are involved in legal action of varying kind, and
3. When at last we are able to compose and execute a Petition for the Writ of Habeas Corpus and present it to the Supreme Court of the State of California, San Francisco, that Court, on the most frivolous of technical grounds, refused even to allow the Clerk to "file" our Petition—no [sic] on grounds of legality, but on procedural grounds merely—without, as far as we know, giving any consideration or weight to the fact that neither of us are trained in the Law and in fact are mere laymen seeking to place our cause before the Court for a just determination of it.

Whereas we are now of the unanimous opinion that it is futile to continue with our efforts to pursue our cause in propria persona, and whereas we find the present situation intolerable in that we are suffering spiritual desolation and ravishment. . . .

We unanimously agree that our cause should be entrusted to an Attorney who will be able to demand, on the basis of his knowledge of the Law, etc. that our Human and Legal Rights are no longer contemptuously, callously—and illegally—trampled underfoot. . . .

Until the moment when [our attorney] arrives here at San Quentin to confer with us, we declare that we will maintain a Hunger Strike—abstaining from all food and nourishment—even unto death.

L. Eldridge Cleaver, A-29498[86]

Black militants continued to fight the official, clandestine, and extralegal controls of carceral apartheid through legitimate legal means, consulting lawyers and community organizations that assisted by filing lawsuits against the department. However, as evident in Eldridge's 1961 letter, they became increasingly frustrated with the legal process and the courts' approach to complaints against the Department of Corrections.

To them, the Adjustment Center symbolized the department's intention to intimidate, control, and silence Black political opposition. This rising tension would eventually reach a breaking point for both the Department of Corrections and Black militants.

Over time, it became more evident to Black militants that working from within and using the "master's tools" would provide little immediate relief from the governance structure that held them captive and controlled their fate.[87]

This was a war.

After all, official policies such as solitary confinement were not the only means through which this structure operated. Black militants also had to contend with lies and secrecy, the routine use of extralegal policies, as well as the reality that in the carceral apartheid version of the world, it is "white above all."

3

WHITE ABOVE ALL

> I believe in white supremacy until the blacks are educated
> to the point of responsibility. I don't believe in giving authority and
> positions of leadership and judgment to irresponsible people.
> —JOHN WAYNE

Andrew was born in 1956, in a Chicago neighborhood that had traditionally been dominated by German and Swedish settlers since in the nineteenth century. The neighborhood experienced waves of Japanese and Puerto Rican migrants in the twentieth century, with a small population of African Americans nestled in between these communities. Andrew grew up in a working-class family, like most of his neighbors, and remembered playing with children from many different racial and ethnic backgrounds. But most importantly, he grew up as what wealthier Chicagoans pejoratively called "a poor white," a racialized status that would increase in its importance to him as he aged.

"I'm the fourth of five children," Andrew recalled as he sat across from me, both of us sitting on a porch in Southern California that was lined with tall palm trees. The old wooden boards creaked under our feet and the white paint chipped from the rays of the hot spring sun. He donned a bulky leather jacket full of worn creases, his eyes blue and wide, his hair blond and gray—with faded swastikas tattooed in black ink among the wrinkled freckles on his hands.[1] Andrew had spent the last four decades a sworn warrior for "white above all" and a self-professed enemy of every Black person on earth.

Over the next two days, Andrew and I met each morning to sit on that old wooden porch for hours so he could tell me what he felt was his life story. He wanted me to know who he was as a child, what he had survived, who he became as a man, and ultimately, how his life changed when he was incarcerated for just over forty years.

Ku Klux Klan parade in Washington, DC, September 13, 1926. National Photo Company Collection, Prints and Photographs Division, Library of Congress, Washington, DC.

I sat there with an open invitation to learn, and he showed up willing to share all of who he was and had become. At times during our conversations, he would look down at his hands and place them over each other, almost to hide his faded swastika tattoos, but I did my best not to look at them and instead looked into his eyes. Because, I really did want to understand his life history, how it was similar and different to the life histories of other men I had conversations with, men who also spent many decades and were sometimes sentenced to life, just like Andrew had been, within the California Department of Corrections during the second half of the twentieth century.

Men who similarly identified as white, but also Black, Chicano, Asian, and Native, described coming into prison with their early life stories and being fundamentally shaped and changed by their experiences during their incarceration.

These were men who ultimately founded or became sworn members or affiliates of various prisoner groups such as the Aryan Warriors, Aryan Brotherhood, Black Guerilla Family, Mexican Mafia, and Nuestra Familia. And for those who did not claim organizational ties, they still developed a strong allegiance in prison to their racial group and by default supported the organization that spoke for their racial group. I sought to understand what led to their feelings of [insert racial group] "above all"?

For Andrew: how does a young boy from Chicago, who moved to California with his parents, survived extreme childhood abuse, was eventually sentenced as an adult to life imprisonment, and almost died in an officer-orchestrated gladiator fight in Pelican Bay supermax come to believe and embody, "white above all"?

Andrew smiled. He came to life discussing his siblings, particularly his inspiring older brother Scott. Scott suffered from Perthes disease when he was young and walked using braces and crutches until he was an adult. Andrew spoke of him proudly, as someone he always looked up to, and the one person he could always rely on.

> From my earliest memories of my brother, he was the most positive driven person that I ever known in my life. Because he used to take me when I was five years old and I guess he was eleven, down to a movie theater somewhere in downtown Chicago and it was all lit up and all tiled along the walls and he would park with a shoe shine box and sit his crutches up against the wall and just sit on the ground and ask people if they wanted a shoe shine when they would come by and I think he charged like fifteen cents for a shoe shine . . . he would play baseball and wouldn't let anyone hit the ball for him and he would hit the ball and take off running with his crutches—very strong.[2]

When Andrew was seven, his parents separated, and his father Tim moved to California to be close to Andrew's uncle. His mother, Virginia, immediately packed up all of the kids in a Studebaker and followed his father out West, first stopping in Nebraska, before leaving Andrew and his siblings alone in various states for almost a month.

"All of us kids were separated and farmed out to a different house," away from their parents temporarily, Andrew remembered, rubbing his brows as he frowned while thinking about it. "My two brothers went, I don't know where . . . that was probably the first experience of abandonment that occurred in my life and because I never understood it and really my mom never explained it, not that I can recall or perhaps not that I even cared about."[3]

Andrew's mother eventually returned to pick him and his sister up, making stops to get the rest of his siblings, then driving onward to Southern California. They ended up back with his father, all together in a house in Los Angeles County.

By the time he was ten, his parents split again, but for good and both parents relocated separately to towns in Northern California. "I remember I was apparently a very sensitive child, and very upset by these things I didn't understand." His eyes hung low by now and he was shifting uncomfortably in his seat before settling into a held pose. Andrew explained how, as a child, he had felt very close to his father before his father left his mother. "My dad tried to talk me through it and help me understand that he was still going to be there." He hinted to me that his father did not keep this promise.

> There are a lot of things now as someone who is sixty-two years old and I've done a lot of work in recovery in self development, in understanding underlying cause and effect of why people make the decisions that they make, that I'm able to or have been able to with the work that I've done, been able to try to see things in a different light, a different perspective then I may have seen it previously in my life.
>
> And now I can look back at mom and see how a single woman with five children back [then] what choice did she have to find another man to help her afford to raise these children because she wasn't going to be able to do it on her own back then. Even women today struggle because they make so much less than a man does in the workplace.[4]

Virginia worked as a waitress and "now we had another person in the household [who] became our stepfather. And everything was fine while my brothers were there, until my older brother went to Vietnam in 1968 . . . and my brother Jason left home."

Right before Scott left for Vietnam, he worked odd jobs in their neighborhood to pay Andrew's boarding school tuition. Scott was persuaded by their mother and stepfather's assertion that Andrew required personalized care and instruction. "You'll hear time and again how much esteem I have for my older brother," Andrew told me from a place of knowing his brother was only trying to help, as he always had.

Because Andrew flunked the third grade, his mother felt he had developmental delays and sent him away to a boarding school for children with special needs in the mountains of Northern California. Andrew resented her for this and, as an adult, felt it was unjust. That she had maybe given up on him too easily. He struggled for a moment to find the words and then remarked angrily: "I actually flunked the third grade because I was so upset and traumatized with the family dysfunction and disintegration and my stepfather's abuse which was horrendous, that's why I was acting out and unable to concentrate and flunked the third grade . . . my mom put me in this boarding school in the mountains which facilitated my stepfather's sexual abuse of my sisters while I wasn't there."[5]

But eventually, Virginia could no longer afford the tuition, with her eldest son away at war, and so Andrew needed to return home, to what he described as a house of horrors—a fiefdom ruled by the narcissistic pedophile Harold, his new stepfather.

However, to keep Andrew away and his sisters close, Harold encouraged arrangements for Andrew to leave boarding school and instead go live with his father, his new wife, and stepsister in a nearby town, which he did for a year from ages eleven to twelve. "It was great," Andrew said, his voice noticeably elevated. A forlorn smile returned to his face and a light gleamed in his eyes as he talked about spending time with his father—but just for a moment.

The smile quickly dropped when he recounted how his father's new wife, his stepmother, did not like him living there, because eleven-year-old Andrew had a severe bedwetting issue that he said persisted until age sixteen. "I wet the bed every night and she's having to wash my pissy sheets and I know she didn't like it . . . rather than teach me how to wash my own sheets she had my dad put me in a diaper . . . with plastic and elastic legs . . . the elastic would cut into my thighs at night and it still didn't do any good because whatever the hell was happening I was still peeing into the sheets every night."[6]

By the time he was twelve, his father asked him which parent he wanted to live with, a question Andrew did not understand at the time. When he answered he did so from a place of wanting to protect his mom. Andrew felt terrified that if he gave the wrong answer, something bad could happen to her and his sisters.

So, he answered his father with "Mom," and the next day, he was sent back to his mother and stepfather's house.

It was just Andrew, his two sisters, his mother, and Harold.

"My first bedroom . . . which was the closet in my sister's room on a cot. That was kind of like the first prison cell I ever had. Once I was on that cot I wasn't allowed to come out until my stepfather was gone the next day. I would go into the closet, doors would be shut and if I came out of that closet

I would be beaten. I was beaten at least twice and I never came out that closet again."[7]

He paused speaking for a moment to drink water and collect his thoughts.

The wispy air began to feel thick, almost as if we were in a portal and had been transported back in time. I noticed the wind beginning to blow. The neighborhood stray cat, Chuey, walked onto the porch and sat near Andrew's leg. They were friends. It was almost as if the cat knew Andrew needed her support. He reached down to pat her head, saying hello and acknowledging her offering. It was clear this was a regular occurrence for them, these early-morning porch meetings.

The frown on Andrew's brow continuously grew deeper as he brought to memory what he survived in his childhood. His hand lingered on Chuey.

By the time Andrew was thirteen, his stepfather had moved them into a mobile home and once again "they got tired of me peeing in my sheets," Andrew recalled solemnly.

"It would be like having a dog that pees in the house all the time," was the metaphor he used to describe how his family saw him, and how he came to see himself.

He described how his stepfather bought a sixteen-foot travel trailer, with no bathroom and no power, that sat in the driveway. Harold kicked Andrew out of the main house and forced him to sleep there. Though freed from his closet prison, Andrew was no longer allowed to step foot in the house and was given a bucket to pee in. His meals were handed to him out of the main house backdoor. Andrew described it as fulfilling a dual purpose—keeping him and his bedwetting out of the main house and "facilitating him having his way with my sisters."[8]

Andrew agonized over how there was a lot he did not understand at the time and just felt hated, like a dog and a monster the family kept at bay in the trailer.

"My stepfather loved to hit people . . . I know he sexually abused my sisters . . . my younger sister struggles with drugs and alcohol because of it to this day."

If Andrew could have one wish come true, it would be to help his sister now that he was a former lifer and was released early after over forty years in prison. But the reality of our society continuously hit him in the chest each time he saw her, and her condition worsened without proper substance-use support and in-depth trauma therapy. "I just don't have the resources," he lamented, guilt filling his voice as it cracked. "That's something I struggle with."[9]

> My stepfather, one of the things he did to try to create a connection with me . . . every weekend on a Sunday he would go out to a rifle range, he was a part of a gun club and he had issued to him from the military as a veteran an M1 Duran rifle . . . he taught me how to use that weapon on the range . . . so we would go out on the weekends on Sunday and he would shoot in the competitions with these other guys and I would go to the side and plink these cans . . . well, my stepfather had guns and one of the things I like to do when he wasn't around is I would pull out his guns and I would look at them and they were big and they were heavy and they were cool. And I would aim them out the windows and I'd just look at them, play with them and put them back. He warned me about doing that a couple of times, just telling me . . . don't ever mess with your guns by myself . . . I kept defying that.[10]

When Harold found the guns slightly moved again, he immediately knew Andrew had been playing with them. Rather than call him out, Harold wanted to play a game. He smirked, his eyes flickering and sweat pooling on his brow as he lined all of the children up in the living room. They stood, shoulders hanging, looking up at Harold, hoping that maybe someone would come to save them. But no one was in the room except their mother and she sat on the couch, folding her legs and watching the display Harold had rendered.

"Who was playing with my guns?" Harold whispered, as if he knew that no one would speak to him.

When no one answered, Harold stood up and walked up to Andrew's older sister, the first in line, and asked her, "Were you playing with my guns, Cindy?"

When Cindy replied no, Harold asked her who was, his voice growing to a loud bellow. When she, in her small voice, shakily creaked "I don't know," he cocked his hand back and swung on her, hitting her face down to the ground as hard as he could.

Cindy crumbled to the floor screaming, clutching her small face.

Harold then proceeded to step in front of Andrew's younger sister and asked again, in a low voice, "Were you playing with my guns, Joyce?"

When she whispered, "No," he asked her who was, and when she similarly replied "I don't know," Harold raised his hand and slapped her as hard as physically possible, harder than he had Cindy, and knocked Joyce to the ground. The youngest of all, she lay there, barely moving.

Andrew took a moment and paused his story.

His fists were clenched, and he stood up from his seat. His voice began to crack, and he started pacing up and down the front porch. Chuey the cat watched closely, quickly standing up to see him. Andrew walked to the edge of the porch and stopped, shoulders sunken down, just before he looked back at me.

I saw large tears filling up his eyes, one rolling down got caught on his mustache. He froze there searching for words, opening his eyes to see Chuey at his feet, who went to meet her friend.

"They're down there crying defending their brother and he steps up to me and says 'You little piece of shit,' and he starts beating the hell out of me. He beat on me for nearly five minutes. My mom sat on the couch, legs curled up underneath her, didn't do a damn thing."[11]

He took a long deep breath and returned to his seat. We sat in silence for some time before resuming our conversation. It felt like the portal we were in was standing still. Chuey purred softly, walking back to her perch next to Andrew, and curling up into a ball. I took a deep breath and grounded myself, looking intently in his eyes. I slowly and calmly told him that he had survived more than any one person could ever imagine and that we could stop talking at any time—that he did not need to share anymore, and we could just sit there, and be. "I will just sit with you, Andrew."

After some silence, he asked if I would turn the recorder back on because there was so much more that he wanted me to know. He wanted me to understand that he had lived many lives before this point in time.

Before prison, during prison, and now the present.

I wanted to understand the human complexity of it all. I wanted to know Andrew. I wanted to know his role and that of the state. I wanted to know the whole picture.

"You can turn it back on," he assured me, turning to face me and placing his hands on his knees. "I have more to say."[12]

And so I did.

I ended up seeing the world as one governed through carceral apartheid—a way of doing business as usual in the United States that uses otherwise lower-status white people to do the bidding of the state, which is to control and dominate Black populations in particular by promoting "white above all" as a declaration of war.

Loyalty to Whiteness, Loyalty to the Badge

White supremacy is hegemonic. Whiteness is imbued with privilege and maintains this position through dominance, traditionally practiced as physical and epistemic violence. The state positions white men as the backbone of a strong society, placing a particular burden on white men to uphold this racial dictatorship, whereby the nation's political ascendancy rests on them "crushing out an effete civilization" and serving as "guardian of all peoples."[13]

Whiteness is historically contingent, yet since the first enslaved Africans arrived in North America, one tenet has remained true: white above all. Class analyses fail to articulate how people held together by an arbitrary clustering of alleged phenotypical categories maintain white solidarity, even when labor divisions should effectively prevent the bourgeoisie and proletariat from aligning.

Critical race theorists have long pointed to the significance of race for coalition building, collective identity, and allegiance. This occurs in part because of an emotional attachment to racial identity, status benefits, political claims, network and community ties, and state formation.[14] Less is known, in particular, about how race organizes people, who, based on status and class, "should not" see each other as allies (e.g., officers and inmates)—yet race and white solidarity reign supreme within a penal organization, such as prison.

Whiteness is worshiped so much that sociologist W. E. B. Du Bois once described it as a pseudoreligion in society.[15] As I argue in previous work, this piety also occurs behind bars because, similar to low-class white people in the outside world, incarcerated white people receive a social-psychological wage of whiteness or emotional boost by ascribing to whiteness, because it binds them to prison personnel, a higher-status group in relation to fellow Black incarcerated people. This wage facilitates the organizational creation of prisoner elites on the basis of white unity.[16]

Both correctional officers and incarcerated people enter prison with preexisting identities, political affiliations, and belief systems. These preexisting contingencies range from little interaction with non-whites in society to growing up in a Jim Crow–enforced region or experiencing severe childhood abuse. Officers and the incarcerated import with them the cultural schemas and social obligations that will significantly influence how they behave in prison.[17] Social groups based on preexisting, imported characteristics like race, age, criminal history, prior experiences with violence, and regional origin become significant for individual survival, prompting both correctional officers and incarcerated people to band together in groups for protection.[18]

This reality means that, as the population filters through the degradation of penal life, prior cultural schemas and social obligations reconfigure and harden into practices that intensify the tenets of carceral apartheid both for the incarcerated and penal actors. In sum, carceral apartheid as experienced in free society is heightened when occurring within a penal environment, where everyone is fighting for their own survival behind walls and will do anything to eliminate those perceived as threats to their supremacy.

In the mid-twentieth century, California segregated its prison population, keeping incarcerated Black people in worse housing conditions when compared to other racial and ethnic groups. Excerpts from a 1959 lawsuit brought against Richard McGee, director of corrections and the creator of Adjustment Centers, by an incarcerated Black man named Cornelius, outline systematic racial segregation and discrimination in housing conditions, which Cornelius claimed violated the equal protection clause of the Fourteenth Amendment.

Cornelius also pointed out that incarcerated white and Latinx people were allowed to integrate at their leisure, but that incarcerated Black people were forced by correctional officers to stay separate, and always in worse conditions:

> Plaintiff is presently an inmate of the California State Prison at Folsom, in which said prison he is confined under the California indeterminate sentence law for the crime of attempted robbery while armed.
>
> The complaint does not question the validity of plaintiff's commitment, but alleges that while lawfully confined he is subjected to systematic segregation, discrimination, and degradation solely on account of his race.
>
> Specifically, it is alleged that plaintiff is required to join an exclusively Negro line formation when proceeding to his assigned cellblock for daily lockup; that he is then lodged in an exclusively Negro cell within said cellblock; that he is required to join an exclusively Negro line formation for tally purposes; that he is required to join an exclusively Nero [sic] line when proceeding into the prison dining halls; and that he is required to eat in a walled-off and exclusively Negro compartment in said dining halls.
>
> In addition to its being segregated, plaintiff alleges that the Negro dining area would be dangerous in the event of fire or disorder, as it is located further from the available exits.
>
> Plaintiff admits that this segregation is neither required, nor authorized, by the codified laws or the statutes of California, but that it is maintained at Folsom Prison pursuant to the oral directions of respondents.
>
> It is argued, however, that such segregation is State action which, psychologically, causes a loss of self-respect, thereby making it difficult for plaintiff to effect the same degree of rehabilitation possible for

unsegregated prisoners of other races and, therefore, that this is not permissible in a public, tax supported penal institution of the State of California.[19]

The US Court for the Northern District of California disagreed with Cornelius, claiming that judges intervening in penal policy could disrupt the department's ability to secure and control those incarcerated. It is telling that department officials were so seemingly confident in their de facto immunity that they did not even show up to the hearing.

The white population across officer and inmate boundaries did not want an increase in incarcerated Black people and did not want integration. It is within this context that the increasing number of Black militants within California prisons in the late 1950s and early 1960s ignited passionate responses from white prison administrators, white correctional officers, and white incarcerated people alike, all in an effort to maintain both political and effectual dominance.

Racial and ethnic minorities simply being physically present in white majority-dominated environments constitutes political opposition and spurs reactions ranging from aversion to violence. For example, even if Black people were not overtly protesting anything, their physical presence was taken as a type of resistance, because it physically infringed upon white dominance.[20]

Between 1955 and 1965 alone, the incarcerated Black population increased by 7 percent to 26.9 percent while the racial composition in terms of the white population continued to decline.[21] With the Black population increasing in size and share of the imprisoned population, overt Black political opposition was considered the highest risk for institutional welfare, because it challenged hegemonic white supremacy. This phenomenon permeated both penal policy and everyday interactions within California prison walls. An even more pronounced commitment to carceral apartheid unfolded because the increasing minority population was perceived as politically radical and as a viable threat to white physical and ideological dominance.

White Unity

Correctional officers saw incarcerated white people as natural allies in the fight against incarcerated Black people, particularly those suspected or found to align with the Black Freedom Movement. Both groups came to feel their two stories of survival were intimately intertwined, with correctional officers planting and encouraging this worldview. But the original seeds came from the top.

Prison officials circulated internal memos warning that organizations constituting the Black Freedom Movement were seeking to disrupt the status quo and incite Black protest within California prisons. For example, in 1962, when the Observance Committee of the National Emancipation Proclamation Centennial began sending letters to Black people incarcerated in California, the assistant director of Corrections became very concerned that the organization was connected to the Nation of Islam.

The warden of Soledad State Prison sent the assistant director letters that the committee had recently mailed to his prison, agonizing over whether the content might incite protest among the incarcerated Black population. The warden wrote the following explanation to prison officials: "This letter contains a membership card, membership application form, and literature relative to making the US government pay for the slavery of their fathers. I do not know whether this has any connection with the 'Muslim' movement but I felt it should be referred to you for whatever action you may wish to take. No doubt colored inmates in other institutions will be receiving similar letters. A photostatic copy of this has been placed in the subject's file. He has not been informed of the receipt of this letter."[22]

Prison officials were particularly embroiled over a portion of the committee's letter, which encouraged incarcerated Black people to organize for racial justice. This snippet of the letter read as follows:

> We wish to assure you that every effort is being made to further your achieving reparations for the centuries of slavery and persecution endured by our forbearers. This is the last year according to international law that this claim can be made. We have presented to the President the required documents setting forth our claims for indemnity, and a budget of the proposed expense for proper and adequate observance of the Emancipation Proclamation Centennial. Your cooperation is urgently needed. We submit the following instructions for your participation in this struggle.
>
> Organize all those interested in staking their claim and who wish to work toward obtaining it, into a local committee in your community with five or more members who have paid their fee and accept our program. . . .
>
> We are in a life and death struggle for survival and need a militant mouthpiece. Let us join in spreading the knowledge of reparations to every descendant of slaves in this country. . . . Send to the Heralddispatch $6.60 for 100 copies. The profits from the sale of these papers will help provide funds for your local committee . . . contact all churches,

trade unions, fraternal and social clubs. Mobilize the people in the interest of this most urgent cause.[23]

Worried that Black political organizations on the outside were successfully radicalizing the incarcerated Black population, the assistant director of corrections sent the committee's letters to the Federal Bureau of Investigation, as a part of their information-sharing network with correctional systems. On the back of one of the letters, titled "Resolution on Reparations," a prison official wrote the racial slur "Spook" to demonstrate their hostility toward material and ideas that they felt challenged correctional and ultimately state sovereignty.

A parole hearing for an incarcerated Black man named Tigel, held some years later, exemplifies the rising tensions between prison officials and Black militants. This San Quentin parole hearing documents how, in this regard, Black militants represented a symbolic threat:

> One of the prisoners who appeared before them was a young black who had openly proclaimed that he was a member of the Black Panther Party. . . . When he sat down before the Adult Authority, the first question he was asked was: "Tell me, why are you a Panther? What do you see in them?" He replied: "All black people in America are really Panthers because all black people in America are oppressed."
>
> There followed a long discussion about the meaning of oppression and the legitimacy of the Panthers' response to that oppression. One of the Adult Authority members admitted that "there has been a certain amount of injustice against Negroes over the years, but things have gotten much better recently, and I just don't see how you can say that you are oppressed. This is a democracy, and if you have grievances, there are nonviolent ways that you can solve them." The prisoner replied, "It may be a democracy for you, but it isn't for blacks, and particularly it isn't for me." . . .
>
> The discussion continued, and one of the Adult Authority members asked the prisoner, "Well even if there are still some injustices against Negroes, do you think that it is justified to steal like you did?" The prisoner replied, "Everyone here steals. Everyone. This country is built on stealing. A shop owner steals when he raises his prices so that the people in the ghetto can't afford to buy enough to eat. That is stealing as much as burglary."
>
> After about twenty minutes of heated political discourse (nothing else was discussed), the hearing ended. The prisoner was denied a parole.[24]

In concluding the parole hearing, prison officials decided "a prisoner who expressed radical ideas [does] not respect authority and [is] likely to have difficulties adjusting on the outside."[25]

Similarly, Black politics and shifting racial and ethnic demographics among the incarcerated jointly angered and terrified correctional officers and prison staff. They received directives that reflected the prison officials' worries.

As a prison counselor at San Quentin put it: "You know, this is not like the outside. You can't allow prisoners to do things which might lead to a riot. If prisoners were allowed to read and discuss politics and to organize without restrictions it would only end up with people getting killed. We can't let prisoners do anything which might encourage a disturbance in the prison, and that is exactly what these revolutionary writings do. If you were the warden, what would you do? Would you risk letting prisoners become revolutionaries? What would you do? We don't have the choice."[26]

To cope and gain the upper hand, officers and staff achieved "white above all" by following official and clandestine control strategies which had been outlined as formal policy directives, such as secretly referring Black militants to the disciplinary committee so they could be locked up in the prison Adjustment Center.

In other instances, officers took things a step further and used extralegal control strategies, also in secret, such as extreme violence, to immobilize and torture Black militants. They often did this within those same Adjustment Center cells, which were far from the eyes of the general incarcerated population. Correctional officers also encouraged incarcerated white people to become more racist and used incendiary remarks, as demonstrated in statements from a white man incarcerated in San Quentin recounting this type of behavior:

> The guards here stir up prisoners. There hasn't been a serious race riot here now for over a year and things were going pretty smoothly, but the guards started spreading rumors that the cells were going to be integrated just to make things tense. No one wants that. The whites do not want to live with the blacks, and the blacks don't want to live with whites. The guards come up to a white prisoner in his cell and say, "How would you like a black cell partner?" That gets the white prisoner up tight and increases the tensions in the prison.[27]

His words are supported by similar claims from an incarcerated man who self-identified as Chicano: "There was a fight between a black and white inmate. The black guy won the fight, even though the white guy put up a good fight. The guards said to the white inmates afterward, 'Man that black dude really dusted the white dude. I thought you white dudes could fight better than that.' The guards said that because they hoped to start another fight."[28]

Some officers even took it a step further by spreading rumors of impending Black militant violence and proceeded to provide incarcerated white people with street weapons to use against the incarcerated Black population.[29] The consequences of these extralegal tactics are illustrated by a statement from a Black man incarcerated in San Quentin:

> Several months ago I overheard a white guard tell a white prisoner that the blacks in the East Block were arming themselves to stick some white dude and that the whites should stick together to protect themselves. Late that day the same guard came up to me and took me aside and told me that the whites in the East Block were going to stick a black dude and that we should be careful. The rumors spread, and by that evening everyone was scared. When we left our cells the next morning the black and the white prisoners were ready to jump on each other if anyone made a wrong move.[30]

A white man, also incarcerated in San Quentin, who self-identified as a Nazi—the sect that would later combine with biker cliques to become the original Aryan Brotherhood—felt officers were justified in supplying incarcerated white people with street knives. He adamantly believed that radical politics prompted Black militants to plot physical harm and so they needed to be dealt with expediently using a white officer–inmate alliance. The threat was seen as especially acute while Black militants' numbers continued to grow in the prison population:

> One of the n——s who stabbed a white was called Big Jim. We knew that he had done the stabbing. The day after he stabbed this white guy he went out to court on an appeal that he had filed before.
>
> A sergeant came up to one of the bike riders [Hell's Angels] and said to him:
>
> "We know that Big Jim did one of the stabbings. We would rather have him carried off to the hospital than to have to try to make a real case against him in court for the stabbings. I'll see that nothing happens to you for doing this. I'll make it worth your trouble."
>
> The bike riders will be waiting for Big Jim when he gets back from court. I know the guy the sergeant talked to well. Everyone knows that he has been involved in sticking the spooks. I know for a fact that he recently stabbed a n—— and killed him. If it weren't for guys like this, I think the blacks would cause even more trouble than they do.[31]

I argue this white officer-inmate alliance supported the formation and growth of white supremacist incarcerated groups with the sole intent of protecting white supremacy and violently annihilating Black militants.

What eventually emerged was the 1964 founding of the Aryan Brotherhood in San Quentin, and early members initially called their efforts the Blue Bird Gang.[32]

The Nazi sect that constituted the majority of the Aryan Brotherhood's founding membership had a reputation for successfully subduing Black militants through officer-sanctioned extralegal means. As one Nazi member put it: "If the spooks started anything, the Nazis went out and took care of things. They would stab a few spooks and get things under control so no real troubles would develop. If we had a strong party now, the blacks wouldn't start things so much."[33]

The Nazi sect, and the Irish-American biker cliques who joined them, proceeded to successfully strengthen their organizational reach by becoming useful in the fight for "white above all" and through expanding revenue streams in the illicit prison economy, with commodities such as drugs and forced prostitution.

They believed that incarcerated Black people had brought their own fate on themselves by seeking to challenge the sanctity of whiteness: "Most of the blacks at San Quentin are mentally defective, lazy, and vicious. I know that you disagree with me, but all you have to do is open your eyes and you will see. All that they want to do is play a game on whitey, live off our backs."[34]

The Aryan Brotherhood chose the clover and swastika as symbols because members originally had to be part Irish, and they aligned with Hitler and outlaw motorcycle clubs.

From the beginning, the gang was steeped in racial hatred and neo-Nazism. The founders adopted swastikas and Nazis SS lightning bolts as the Aryan Brotherhood's identifying symbols and tattoos. Recruits were ordered to read Mein Kampf and to "earn their badge" of membership by attacking—and often killing—black inmates.[35]

I argue the formation of the Aryan Brotherhood was the result of white incarcerated individuals—ranging from Nazis and bikers, to those without any prior organizational ties—joining forces to control what they felt was an impending Black militant threat. The Aryan Brotherhood provided the organizational base to carry out well-planned attacks against incarcerated Black people and counter any attacks that Black militants might plan in return.

Correctional officers already relied on a legitimate organizational base for protection and action, with significant resources and institutional backing to strive toward white dominance. The Aryan Brotherhood was the ultimate solution to achieve "white above all" for the white incarcerated population because in addition to providing a solid structural base, incarcerated white people now enjoyed the protection and support of corrupt correctional officers, who also aided in setting up the Aryan Brotherhood's initial drug trafficking routes by smuggling contraband into prison.[36]

In 1968, the Aryan Brotherhood aligned with the Mexican Mafia for further protection from Black militants, and to expand their lucrative drug trafficking and contraband networks. In return, the Aryan Brotherhood assisted them in their burgeoning war with the Nuestra Familia. The latter quickly replied by forming an alliance with Black militant cliques, who would soon organize into the Black Guerilla Family.[37]

White men incarcerated throughout the 1960s and 1970s had to pick a side, with many claiming that the prison environment fundamentally shaped their allegiances. Dean, a white formerly incarcerated man who grew up in Southern California, recounted in our interview how even though he was accustomed to racial segregation and white/Black tension, he was still shocked by the intensity of racial polarization that he experienced when he entered California prisons in the early 1970s:

> Prison, it's like going into a war zone.... California is a very racist state when it comes to prison. They don't put you in a cell with somebody of another race. If you're in a dorm, you don't get to bunk with somebody of another race. Very hateful. It was more of a shock to me. I mean I expected it because I grew up in the county jail. You're indoctrinated.... If you're here and another race, and I'm sitting here chatting with you. If you're Hispanic, it's all good. But say if I was white and you were black and we're chatting, my people, and I say my people [because] I'm using prison terminology. My people are ready to come over and say hey dude, what the fuck.... But that person sort of expect that to happen. If you been around you already know I'm not supposed to be over here chit chatting with you. We can talk, but we can't eat together.
>
> Like I said, whites and Hispanics are okay. Whites and southern Hispanics. This is the crazy thing. The Hispanics. The southern Hispanics and the white guys hanging out together, the northern Hispanics and the blacks hangout together. The Chinese or Asians hang out with the blacks. The American Indians usually hangout with the whites. I don't get it, I didn't write the rules. They were in effect long before I got there ... [break the rules] the whites are gonna come beat the shit out of you.... I've seen people beat up for borrowing somebody's shoes to go take a shower, you know flip flops.

Everybody is coming at everybody. So every race wants somebody who's gonna stand up for that race. And be a soldier. I hate to use that word too. [But] not crawl under the bench, while the guy who sleeps next to you is getting stabbed to death. You need to help, this is war.

If you don't get up and help, when it's all done, if you're still around, you're done.[38]

Dean went on to describe his experience with the Aryan Brotherhood trying to recruit him because he once won a fight against an incarcerated Black individual: "They've got these big swastikas on and everything else, the whites. [But] diplomatically, I'm not interested, you know what I mean. They would approach, especially if they seen you get in a fight or something, they'd be like 'oh you're down, you're down.'"

A white formerly incarcerated man named John who served decades in San Quentin, similarly explained to me in an interview, that at that time there was a primary need for "white above all," given the racial polarization he witnessed and lived: "San Quentin was absolutely terrifying. Not only are you a number, but also there's no real help available to you. It was a horrible place. Even the administration realized that was [for] protection. For instance, a single person of any ethnicity, alone, could be a target for one of the other groups. You needed to be in a group always, never alone."[39]

John went on to explain the emergence of leaders or "inmate shot callers" who had the power to declare war against another racial group if need be:

Let's say I bought, and I wasn't supposed to do this as a white guy, but let's say I bought a bunch of drugs from a Black man, a Black inmate. I would pay him of course, and I'd get more drugs. Then, suddenly, I'm in debt and I can't pay him. Well, I'll get a few threats. He can't do anything directly to me, because he's black and I'm white.

That would cause a war, a riot. He would then go to the black shotcaller, or the head man of the black race. He would get with the shotcaller or the head man of the white race, and they would figure out what to do with me.

It could be death, if it was enough debt. Some other circumstances they'd go from I got killed to any number of things. Just somehow so that nobody lost respect and the man that I owed the money to got repaid in some way.[40]

John's words help us understand how "white above all" and the historical crystallization of racial division through violence led to the emergence of internal governance among the incarcerated. The rules of engagement for incarcerated people were prescribed and determined by the governing structure of carceral apartheid. One consequence included strict self-policing, corroborated by a statement from a white man incarcerated during this period:

> On the streets I was never a racist. I was never down on the blacks. But here I have been forced to be a racist. I was told the first rule was that "you never talk with a black off the job."
>
> If you talked with a black you would be isolated by the rest of the whites and then attacked. . . . They made it perfectly clear to me that "if you associate with a n——, we'll kill you."[41]

There were also severe consequences for crossing officers who aided the Aryan Brotherhood. John described how the Aryan Brotherhood recruited him for a mission even though he wasn't an official member, because of his job assignment as a tier tender, which allowed him relatively unrestricted movement throughout the prison. They asked him to transport street knives, which, if lost, would place John at risk for retaliation from the Aryan Brotherhood and the officers who smuggled the weapons inside in the first place. As John outlined in our interview, he quickly accepted the mission, which if successfully completed, would secure John's place as a trusted associate (though not official member) of the Aryan Brotherhood. John agreed both for his own survival and to prove his allegiance to "white above all":

> I worked in the laundry at the time. One of my jobs was to push the carts of the clean, white clothing that all the inmates wore in the kitchens, like smocks and aprons. They all wore white and they'd be cleaned. I'd have to push it from the laundry all the way to the kitchen. The dining halls were one of the hotspots where riots would happen. I was told, really, asked slash told, that I was going to take this cache of metal knives, bone crushers they'd call them. They were smuggled from the maintenance building into the laundry building, and then from the laundry building to the kitchen.
>
> Since that was my job, I was the one that had to do it. Now, I didn't want to do it. I knew if I got caught, I'd get more time, I'd be in the hole for years. If the other groups found out it was me shuttling the knives, I'd have been a target. It was just horrible. There was no reason a sane person would do this, except under those conditions. How could I tell them no? If I told these guys, "No, I'm not taking your weapons to the kitchen," the first problem is, now I know there's knives in the laundry that need to go to the kitchen, so I could tell [snitch]. Then, who knows what else I could do? My choices were, pretty much, without it really

being stated, you die or you take these to the kitchen. If you take them to the kitchen, and you get there, and they're received, you're a hero. If not, you're a zero. There was that pressure as well.

Long story short, I took them. They got there. They were delivered to the right person. I went back to my job. That's the last I ever had to do with any of it. From that point on, I noticed that I had gained some, like a little more respect from the ones that I knew were really the gang members, even though I wasn't. I had gotten a little bit of respect. They allowed me to do some things, gave me cigarettes, like that. I seemed to be a little more accepted because I did what I needed to do and I kept my mouth shut. That was pretty much the two ways that you were initiated into service or the gang, per se.

You really didn't have a choice. You knew that and they knew that. For the most part, you thought about survival and status quo. Just went, and in this instance, it is for the white guys. The others are trying to kill me, so yeah, all right. I'll do it. You just did it. There was a little feeling of allegiance, even though I wasn't a gang member.[42]

As John's experience demonstrates, carceral apartheid created a social order where incarcerated white people had to abide by "white above all" for correctional officers and their fellow incarcerated peers, particularly those in position of great power, such as the Aryan Brotherhood. Those who did not abide by these rules faced certain consequences, such as death or maiming. John went on to explain this in our interview when describing white people who try to associate with Black people during their incarceration: "There are whites that are current Crips and Bloods from black neighborhoods. They jump into black and for all purposes they're black. But all the whites, all the wanna be tough guy whites are looking like they wanna kill that group. . . . It happens as soon as a riot jumps up. [When] it's like that, [that] white guy ain't staying on the yard."

Andrew described a similar story, one that shook him to his core. He recounted, like Dean and John had, how "back then" both officers and white supremacist groups violently policed any form of racial integration. Andrew stressed that this environment deterred him and other incarcerated white people from committing any actions that suggested they did not believe in white supremacy and support the mission of "white above all."

Andrew continued to pet Chuey. On this particular morning, it seemed she also felt uneasy. She kept fidgeting and purring loudly. I was convinced Chuey could feel the emotions of our conversation. Andrew hesitated again when speaking, but eventually led me through his thoughts. From his experience and people like him, "white above all" was not always a choice, but a coerced decision that one comes to trust and believe in overtime. Becoming who he became in this chapter of his life was the product of both terror and a desire to belong to something greater than him.

Andrew was incarcerated for the first time in the state of Nevada, where he'd spent some time as a young adult after escaping Harold and his childhood home in California. Years into his incarceration, something happened that left a mark so deep inside that he emphasized he would never forget it.

It was now the early 1980s, and Andrew had managed to survive the carceral apartheid regime so far. But Andrew knew that his time could come if he ever broke any rules—if he ever gave any inclination that his loyalties to whiteness were in question. Andrew learned this clearly when the Aryan Warriors set up a fellow incarcerated white man, named Ronald, for a brutal attack as punishment and a warning to all other white people. Ronald had decided to align with the Black population, and for that, the Aryan Warriors decided to make him pay. It was one of the worst lessons in "white above all" that Andrew had ever witnessed.

Remembering it all of these years later, Andrew abruptly stood up and shook, almost to kick the memory from his mind:

> The order of the day in Nevada was called "Hook up, Lock up, or Die." You had no choice. You had to align with whatever white prison gang was going on, or black, or Mexican, according to your race. Or you lock up in protective custody. Or you die.
>
> They'll kill you. And probably rape you before they kill you.
>
> I'd seen this one guy come into the prison system who was from Milwaukee, Wisconsin. And he was a white guy that was raised in a black neighborhood and so he affected all the mannerisms of a black guy in that he had a particular strut to him, he had a particular way that he spoke. Just differentiated himself from a white guy. And that was all right. His name was [Ronald].
>
> I remembered his name for so many years.
>
> He didn't align himself with the white guys because he felt more in-tune with the blacks. Because that was the community he was raised in. You know I intellectually understood it and took a neutral position, but also knew my place.
>
> And I saw him try to align himself with the blacks and I saw three probably 250 plus pound [white] guys, big because we had big weights and that was all there was to do. These dudes were huge.
>
> The doors that you had were electronically controlled outside by a cop in a bubble. Outside of the housing section, out in the rotunda, in his own little box, secure, safe, behind bars and bullet proof glass, he would

open and close the doors. Well, he wasn't opening or closing any doors, but it didn't matter. Because the doors opened in.

And these big guys kicked and kicked and kicked on that door until they busted that door open. And they went in there.

And there was a literal line of black guys down the stairwell that were one at a time going in there and raping [Ronald].

And uh, he was pretty messed up after that and I didn't want anything like that to ever happen to me.[43]

When Ronald was brutally raped, correctional officers were nowhere to be found and none came to his aide—their strategic absence during this setup was not lost on Andrew and signaled their willingness to look the other way. Given his experiences on the outside, Ronald had tried to align himself with the Black population during his incarceration. But if Ronald was allowed to stay, with the Aryan Warriors and white officers against it, the Black population risked an imminent race-war. This truth was something the Black population could not allow. Not for Ronald or any other white man. The officers involved and the shot callers from all racial groups jointly agreed that Ronald needed to become an example of what will never be tolerated to keep the peace. Word soon spread so everyone would know what happened.

Witnessing this vicious attack scarred Andrew, and regret filled his voice as he stopped talking and once again sat in silence across from me. It was as if Andrew couldn't escape Ronald's brutalized cries, which he claimed haunted his thoughts for years to come. He could even hear them when he dreamed, and sometimes Ronald's face came to him as he tried to sleep.

After that, Andrew made an even greater effort to never do anything that could be construed as being against white unity. He needed to survive, and rebelling against this social order would only bring about immense pain or death, a penalty he and others knew from proof should be adamantly avoided.

Andrew eventually became a member of the Aryan Warriors while incarcerated in Nevada, describing to me that he attacked and maimed members of the incarcerated Black population on behalf of the white population. He did not go into details with me as to whether or not he killed people, but like the Aryan Brotherhood, the Aryan Warriors have a "blood in, blood out" oath, meaning one must kill to enter the organization and be killed if they try to leave. Andrew attributed becoming a white supremacist in the 1980s to the need he felt to demonstrate racial solidarity. That he was socialized into an environment to act against his original moral code in order to protect his safety and life is evidence of carceral apartheid.

Andrew was very clear that, at some point during his life in prison, he did come to believe in what he was doing. He was not an innocent bystander. He did not play a role. He came to align himself ideologically, as well. He felt that it was all true, that it was "us versus them," and everything he and his white brotherhood did to survive their incarceration was justified. Andrew proved himself to be trustworthy, a feared fighter, and willing to commit extreme violence when necessary. He subsequently rose up the ranks in the Aryan Warriors organization, becoming a well-respected leader in the state of Nevada.

Andrew went on to describe the history of the Aryan Warriors in Nevada and detailed how the original Aryan Brotherhood—the one that began in San Quentin, California—tried to expand into Nevada by combining forces with the Aryan Warriors. This action ignited a longstanding war between the two white supremacist organizations:

> In 1972 while the Aryan Warriors had been established in the state of Nevada, the state of California sent a representative [Aryan Brotherhood], had him commit or admit to a crime that was in Nevada so that he would be extradited and sent to Nevada in order to bring the Aryan Warriors in line with the Aryan Brotherhood and say that, "You're no longer the Aryan Warriors, you're now going to be the Aryan Brotherhood. And I'm calling the shots. You'll fall in line or else."
>
> And they stabbed that dude and killed him.
>
> That created a permanent separation between the Aryan Brotherhood that's in numerous states in the United States and in the federal system and the State of Nevada. . . .
>
> But never have to my knowledge of the 1980s, I've lost track of the 1990s, has the Aryan Brotherhood has never taken or had a foothold in Nevada for one reason or another.[44]

After an unsolved murder in California was linked back to him, Andrew was eventually transferred from Nevada to California, back to his childhood home state. This transfer presented a dilemma: "I knew that if I ended up at Folsom or San Quentin I was going to have to align myself with the whites and if I aligned myself with the whites, you know as I had already done with what was called the Aryan Warriors in Nevada. Not the Aryan Brotherhood. Total different thing, same premise."[45]

As a result of this divide, Andrew knew that, once he arrived in California in the mid-1980s, his only choice would be to renounce the Aryan Warriors and join the Aryan Brotherhood, which he had no interest in doing—but he did not have a choice.

Andrew was immediately placed with the white population once he transferred to California, and at this time, the Aryan Brotherhood was at war with what remained of the Black Guerilla Family. Though Andrew had escaped the particular organizational histories that gave rise to the Black Guerilla Family in California, he was subjected to the remaining consequences once he arrived and had to pick a side.

Carceral apartheid spares no one, and all must adapt.

One must choose. Who must I be to survive?

And eventually, Andrew faced the most significant consequence: ending up at Pelican Bay supermax and being forced to fight "for the whites" in a prisoner gladiator match orchestrated by correctional officers—all while the officers placed bets on each of their lives.

REBEL

If there is to be any proving of our humanity,
it must be by revolutionary means.
—**WALTER RODNEY**

THE DRAGON

> If I could have convinced more slaves that they were
> slaves, I could have freed thousands more.
>
> —HARRIET TUBMAN

It was truly a beautiful day. The sky was a crisp blue, almost like a children's book, and the clouds wisped in the sky like cotton balls. Heat rose from the ground in waves, with dust particles visible to the naked eye. Much of the dirt looked as though it could use some moisture and crunched under my feet while I slowly walked on the side of the road.

And then I saw him, Anthony.

He waited for me outside of his home, and the closer I got, he began to pace a little, waving with a smile.

Anthony was a founder of the Black Guerilla Family and once a prominent leader of the organization during his incarceration.

His adult children were inside cooking and playing with Anthony's grandchild. When I finally stood only a few feet away, I could see his deep-set brown eyes and they appeared excited. It seemed he was happy to see me, and I felt the same. I had spoken to Anthony many times before on the phone and this would be our first in person conversation. I had taken a plane and drove many miles to meet him, and he had lived many lives—and gleaned insights from each.

Gratitude surrounded and filled me because no one ever *has* to tell their story. When someone chooses to, it requires the utmost transparency, gratitude, and care. Otherwise, there is a staleness to the energy that borders on offensiveness.

Anthony seemed comfortable in brown overalls and a white shirt, his hair mostly gray with some black remaining from all of his years on this earth. I immediately noticed his glasses and his hands, which looked as though he had been working outside. I later learned that Anthony took pride in cultivating the earth with those same hands, teaching his family many things from the books he was always reading and the secrets that the ground contains, if we only look more closely. Anthony held the esteemed role as an elder in his family.

Anthony welcomed me inside his home and introduced me to his family who warmly smiled and said that their father had been talking about my visit for quite some time. I sat at the dining room table while Anthony grabbed some notes from inside his bedroom, papers documenting California prisons that he kept for several decades. His family resumed cooking and bustling in and out of the dining room while Anthony and I caught up. He had read several books since we last talked. He was eager to see if I remembered to bring the book for him that I promised I would, which I excitedly had. We caught up about these books for about an hour before that conversation naturally faded.

Anthony then squared his shoulders toward me and said softly: "So, Brittany, what else do you want to know? I am so glad you came."

I was with Anthony, his children, and grandchild from the very early morning until the moon rose and night brought the day to an end. He and I talked, we ate dinner with his family, and talked some more until it was time to say "until next time."

I sat on the edge of my seat in silence as Anthony recounted his nearly fifty-year struggle against carceral apartheid within the California prison system. I asked him directly, "Why did you find it necessary to found the Black Guerilla Family, considering many Black militants were already members of [other] political organizations?"

He took a deep breath and answered plainly, using his hands as he spoke: "Everybody was against Black prisoners. So it was incumbent upon us to establish some kind of structure to defend ourselves against those attacks and defend ourselves against setups by the prison administration. And defend ourselves and eradicate predatory behavior amongst us in order to do and be that united front which for the most part we were able to do."[1]

The Black Guerilla Family consolidated earlier Black militant cliques and founded the organization as the prison arm of the Black Power Movement in 1970 in San Quentin.[2] In society, the Black Panther Party was the face of the movement, and the Black Liberation Army was the underground militia. First known as the Black Vanguard, the Black Guerilla Family organized in direct response to the governance system of carceral apartheid as perpetuated by the Department of Corrections. But the internal workings of the department weren't just a prison problem, hidden from view. The machinations

African American protesters outside the White House during the March on Washington demanding an end to white supremacist atrocities, voter suppression, and police brutality in Selma, Alabama. Photograph by Warren K. Leffler, March 12, 1965. US News and World Report Magazine Photograph Collection, Prints and Photographs Division, Library of Congress, Washington, DC.

of the prison hierarchy mirrored society in the outside world, a point that Anthony stressed continually.

This historical context is necessary to situate the rise of the Black Guerilla Family within broader movements to end carceral apartheid in the United States and its exportation abroad.

A Personal History of Carceral Apartheid and Its Racist Intent

Anthony and other founders of the Black Guerilla Family did not live their lives in a vacuum. As Black men, they came from generations of families who had survived the endless violence that carceral apartheid intentionally sows upon non-white populations. Their lives—and those of their ancestors—were a personal history of carceral apartheid, rather than some abstract theory of existence devoid of human embodiment and intergenerational transference. For this reason, they saw themselves as one ripple in a larger pool of watery pain and grievance that had plagued their people since the first

Europeans arrived, massacred the Indigenous population, and trafficked Black Africans across the Atlantic. Their rebellion was a revolution against all of it—a Pan-African Liberation that supported all revolutionary struggles against carceral apartheid worldwide—and not solely the manifestation occurring in California and US prisons.

Over the course of several generations, a set of institutional-level entities emerged within the United States with overlapping and mutually reinforcing customs, practices, and conventions such as chattel slavery, Jim Crow, and the entrenchment of segregated communities of concentrated disadvantage, known as "ghettos."[3]

The sinister depravity of racist intent to control and enact physical and symbolic violence undergirds each of these elements. Racist intent operates as a shadow system, one that becomes entrenched within the structural framework of institutions—the scaffolding, if you will. It has enforced and upheld America's institutions from the time of chattel slavery to mass incarceration, to the running of public schools and universities. I argue racist intent is the element that gives continuity to the succession of oppressive forms that have structured the Black historical and contemporary experience.

Chattel slavery created living property out of lives that were exploited for the socioeconomic gain of the white patriarchy. It and its legacy racialized the Black slave, creating the American Negro. Legitimized by religious, pseudoscientific, and liberal economic discourses, the institution of chattel slavery was maintained and supported by a system of psychological and physical violence against Black people. The enslaved were punished by shackles, mutilation, beatings, branding, imprisonment, and the rape of men, women, and children. These actions were positioned, as a response to perceived infractions or disobedience, with masters and overseers using an abundance of discretion to impose dominance.[4] Enslaved Black people were also pitted against each other, based on work role and on phenotype, for gladiatorial sport.[5]

In an effort to reduce rebellion, masters and overseers actively used social conditioning to produce the "ideal slave," an unrealistic persona who would maintain strict discipline and unconditional submission. This aimed to create a sense of personal inferiority, and instilled fear, teaching enslaved people to take an interest in the plantation's enterprise, depriving them of education and recreation, and enforcing a strict divisive colorline.[6]

Enslaved people were fiercely prohibited from congregating without a white person present, and banned from reading, especially after the large-scale uprising that became the Haitian Revolution (1791–1804), and notable preceding rebellions, such as the New York City Conspiracy (1741) and the

Stono Rebellion (1739).[7] Poor whites, often acting as overseers, were the masters' henchmen, working to enforce these systemic practices. These uprisings of enslaved populations provide evidence that the intended victims of racist intent, as a system of racial domination, have challenged even its earliest expressions in American history.

Even after the Emancipation Proclamation in 1863 and the Thirteenth Amendment in 1865, Jim Crow continued to uphold the coordination of racist intent through local and state laws that enforced legal discrimination and segregation. In 1896, with the *Plessy v. Ferguson* decision, the US Supreme Court upheld their constitutionality using the "separate but equal" doctrine.

Like chattel slavery, Jim Crow further established carceral apartheid as an intentionally racist process rather than a collateral consequence. In the aftermath of the Civil War, state actors such as police departments and local politicians often colluded with vigilantes like the Knights of the Ku Klux Klan in their efforts to suppress and intimidate African Americans.[8] Lynching and mob violence became the most emblematic control practices that accelerated in use during this era.

"Racial terror lynchings" were one of the most menacing, coercive practices used to enforce Jim Crow and stand as a blatant symbol of racial domination. These lynchings were carried out with impunity, often in broad daylight and in front of local courthouses. They were conducted by the white community as celebratory acts of vindictive punishment for those accused of not knowing their place.

Between 1877 and 1950, there were at least 4,084 racial terror lynchings in twelve Southern states, and more than 300 in other states. They differ from "hangings and mob violence that followed some criminal trial or that were committed against non-minorities without the threat of terror." Racial terror lynchings were "directed at racial minorities who were being threatened and menaced in multiple ways." Some states and counties were "particularly terrifying places for African Americans, [having] dramatically higher rates of lynching than other states and counties."[9] The 1955 lynching of fourteen-year-old Emmett Till and Bloody Sunday in 1965 are remembered as infamous examples of racist intent operating as the coordinated, systematic intimidation and punishment of African Americans who dared to challenge white supremacy.

Many Black families fled the South for the West, Midwest, and Northern states, seeking freedom and socioeconomic advancement. Instead, however, many fell victim to the very same consequences of racist intent, with Black migrants often finding their dreams of advancement through migration smashed. Before the Great Migration (1910–70), more than ninety percent of

African Americans lived in the South, with only one-fifth located in Southern urban centers.[10]

Roughly 6 million Black people left the South over the course of the Great Migration.[11] This rapid relocation of Black families was immediately met with the economic and social consequences of urban racial segregation and white supremacist violence, which created neighborhoods that became pejoratively known as Midwest, Northern, and West Coast ghettos. Furthermore, the Great Depression decimated job opportunities, particularly in the Northern industrial belt through 1940, when defense industries stimulated urban economies during the lead-up to and the onset of World War II.

As a coastal state and strategic military location, California developed a booming war economy based on blue-collar industrial and factory workers, which attracted Black migrants leaving the South. World War II countered the devastating effects of the Great Depression and reinvigorated collapsed economies, especially in the port cities of California. In the 1940s, 338,000 African Americans migrated to California from all over the United States to take advantage of new economic opportunities. The wartime boom increased in the 1950s, when the Soviet Union tested an atomic bomb and the Cold War began, prompting the United States to develop military technology in California. This gave rise to the modern military industrial complex that continues in the United States to this day.

To meet the demands of this growing economy, the US Congress passed the federal GI Bill, which enabled returning World War II veterans to pursue higher education. This newly educated workforce bolstered California's military industrial complex, but this population supplanted Black blue-collar workers, who were systematically denied access to education subsidies. Consequently, Black communities had a more difficult time acquiring the skills necessary to participate in the modern, technology-based defense economy.[12]

During this period, racist discriminatory housing practices fueled segregation, and white flight to suburban areas intensified, leading to high concentrations of Black Americans and Latinx communities in economically deprived neighborhoods such as Oakland, California.[13]

As a result, Black communities were left with high rates of poverty in addition to the violent consequences associated with isolation, unemployment, police brutality, and hypersegregation.[14] Black residents also reported roaming bands of white adolescents and adults, with the support of law enforcement, who would terrorize Black and Latinx communities to try and scare them from moving into other areas. The early political formation of Black organizations, such as the Crips and Bloods in Los Angeles, can be traced in part to communities' needs to protect themselves both from the violence of white civilians and law enforcement.[15]

As social inequality and violence rose in California, mirroring similar stratification processes in other US urban centers, we witnessed the rise of civil unrest, culminating in race riots across the country. Black families who had fled the South were left feeling disillusioned. Their hopes and dreams for a better life elsewhere were revealed to be simply unattainable due to the same racialized violence they had endured for generations.

Particularly for the younger cohort, joining Black revolutionary struggles in California became a way to fight back against new versions of the same carceral apartheid that their families fled in the Southern states. During the time that I first met Anthony, I also began to connect with several members of Black political organizations who joined in the 1960s.

Through this network I met Avery, a high-ranking leader in the original Black Panther Party who explained to me in an interview this sentiment in the context of Oakland, California:

> Oakland is probably very much the ideal place because Oakland had been an all White city up until the forties, 1940s, when, during the second Great Migration, Blacks came to Oakland, as they did to Chicago, whatever, from the south; mostly, in this case, Louisiana and Texas, to work on the docks and to answer the call of Henry Kaiser to come and build ships and what have you. So, Oakland went from being a white city to an almost half Black City, in like one generation. In the south, where you had the main part of the movement; where the majority of Black people had been living, the Whites were so violent and vicious. Wasn't nobody going to talk about, well, I'm just going to go here and do this and that. Nobody would have thought that.
>
> In the North, like Philadelphia, Baltimore, you know the older cities, people had settled in to the ghettos and they had made their peace, we could say, with a White World and a Black World, but they weren't under the gun because you could vote in Philadelphia, but you couldn't go to the beach. There were some theaters you couldn't go to; restaurants you couldn't go to, so there was segregation, but you could still live your life in Philadelphia or New York. You couldn't do that in the South.
>
> Now, why is that important?
>
> Because, who joins the Black Panther Party are the people who are living in the North because they are already disconnected from the Klan, so they don't have that fear; they don't have that fear of the Klan. But, now they have a consciousness; who is going to let somebody. . . . You talk to

somebody from the North; who is going to let somebody beat them up and you just sit down and take it.

So, you had the urban generation of northern and you had some Philadelphia, and so forth and so on, but on the other end here, this was Huey Newton and Bobby Seale's first generation that grew up in the North.

Their parents had still had southern attitudes and southern ideas, understanding the murders and all that.

But generally, the majority of blacks [had] lived in the South, and the great migrations came about because . . . What? We were looking for work, and we couldn't find it in the South. Right? So we walked, in some cases, to Detroit. We walked to Chicago, so forth and so on.

And those people that settled in the West Coast were actually different from the East Coast, who had been entrenched in life in New York, Philadelphia, Baltimore. Those are old cities. Blacks had been living in those cities for a long time.

This was a new group of blacks, on the West Coast.

Black communities on the West Coast, like others around the United States, soon realized that the Great Migration had not brought Black people freedom from white supremacist violence. This reality, in conjunction with key episodes of law enforcement brutality and publicized racist attacks against Black activists, sparked a nationwide Black rebellion and what poet and novelist James Baldwin described as "the fire next time."[16]

During the "long, hot summer of 1967," there were at least 159 race riots, with the biggest occurring in Newark, New Jersey, and Detroit, Michigan. Events like these and the preceding 1965 Watts riots in Los Angeles, California, reflected the struggle of Black Americans against carceral apartheid in society.

Avery recounted how this period further spurred the political consciousness of Black people. Avery knew George Jackson, also a Black Panther, who would eventually become a cofounder of the Black Guerilla Family:

The Black Panther Party was part of a continuing struggle that Black people waged from 1600s forward for freedom, but at the time, we had a convergence of a lot of things going on.

One of the biggest things you had during that time was the advent of the mass consumption of television. Prior to that, nobody knows what Harriet Tubman looked like, or being beaten down, nobody knows any of that. But we saw with our own eyes footage of people being beaten up trying to get the vote.

So something different entered into the picture and the government was unable to control the propaganda as it does now. Ordinary people saw the Civil Rights efforts and saw dogs being put upon innocent people and children being bombed. We saw that. That raised consciousness.

The reality was that if you are born black in America, you are not white. I don't care if you want to be white. I don't care if you think you are white. The realities of being black will overwhelm all that you think about yourself.[17]

Political consciousness grew in Black communities, creating perceived tangible threats to government institutions at the local, state, and federal levels.[18] At the local level, civil rights activists regularly faced violence, ranging from white civilians empowered by their adjacent status to law enforcement making threatening calls to their homes to physical attacks and unlawful arrests. According to the King Center, Dr. Martin Luther King Jr. alone was arrested thirty times and repeatedly fined for participating in boycotts, sit-ins, and marches.[19]

In 1956, over 100 church leaders were indicted alongside Dr. King for "illegally" boycotting Montgomery's segregated bus system.[20] Perhaps one of the most egregious examples of state-level white supremacist violence involved the Little Rock Integration Crisis of 1957.

Arkansas governor Orval Faubus defied the 1954 *Brown v. Board of Education* decision when he ordered the Arkansas National Guard to block Black students from attending Little Rock Central High School. Faubus closed all Little Rock schools the following year to block integration. The Little Rock Crisis revealed how—in addition to community-level violence including bomb threats and citizen-led beatings—African Americans who challenged the degrading conditions of Jim Crow also encountered resistance from local and state government institutions, including the wrath of the police, National Guardsmen, and cheering white civilians colluding to violently silence and stop rightful protest.

The federal government is arguably the most infamous perpetrator of white supremacist violence via its intentionally racist policies, notably through the implementation of COINTELPRO (the counterintelligence program). Beginning in August 1956, this clandestine program initially began as an operation to increase discord within the American Communist Party. However, in October 1956, FBI Director J. Edgar Hoover intensified the FBI's organized surveillance of Black leaders under COINTELPRO, targeting Black leaders with IRS audits, anonymous letters and phone calls, illegal wiretaps, undercover agents, and fake documents designed to increase factionalism.

COINTELPRO mirrored similar operations against Black leaders that disrupted political movements in the early twentieth century, most notably the

FBI's actions against Marcus Garvey and the Universal Negro Improvement Association. Early COINTELPRO targets included the Southern Christian Leadership Conference and its leaders, Bayard Rustin, Stanley Levison, and Dr. Martin Luther King Jr. Amidst increasing terrorism by white supremacists and civil unrest in urban centers, in 1967 Hoover created COINTELPRO-BLACK HATE and the Ghetto Informant Program (1967–73).

The former program focused on Black nationalist organizations such as the Nation of Islam, the Black Panther Party, and the Revolutionary Action Movement. The latter program used more than 7,000 people to infiltrate poor Black communities. The goals were to neutralize political threats, discredit Black movements, and disrupt protests.

The federal government went so far as to mobilize the army to prepare for martial law in urban centers while also establishing the National Advisory Commission on Civil Disorders, also known as the Kerner Commission. COINTELPRO reports described Black nationalists and civil rights leaders as having "backgrounds of immorality, subversive activity, and criminal records."[21] These depictions indicated how sections of the US government and American society more broadly viewed Black protest during this period.[22]

As Black resistance surged, the US Department of Justice laid the legal and political groundwork for the impending extension of carceral apartheid, which we now call mass incarceration. This period represented an organized attempt to reassert social control over racialized minorities, continue the war on Black communities, and extinguish the Black Freedom Movement.[23] The prison now reemerged as a racially concentrated American organization in which Blackness and criminality became synonymous.[24] Prisons were now functioning as a "surrogate ghetto."[25]

The self-described Black militants I interviewed had, for years, claimed that the social and economic degradation of Black communities and the War on Drugs were purposeful attacks. These laws and practices were designed to squash political opposition, sow racial and ethnic division, and produce racial exclusion and control. John Ehrlichman, the Watergate co-conspirator and Richard Nixon's domestic policy adviser, finally admitted to these purposes of the War on Drugs in a 1994 interview:

> The Nixon campaign in 1968, and the Nixon White House after that, had two enemies: the antiwar left and black people. You understand what I'm saying? We knew we couldn't make it illegal to be either against the war or black, but by getting the public to associate the hippies with marijuana and blacks with heroin, and then criminalizing both heavily, we could disrupt those communities. We could arrest their leaders, raid their homes, break

up their meetings, and vilify them night after night on the evening news. Did we know we were lying about the drugs? Of course we did.[26]

Republicans and Democrats gave bipartisan support for tough-on-crime policies, with anti-poverty schemes, the War on Drugs, and prison becoming the latest solution intended to control what the state had labeled as America's 300-year-old Black problem.[27]

During this era, prisons became disproportionately populated with Black Americans, many of whom were convicted of minor drug offenses or targeted by the police because of their Black militant affiliations.

As early as 1960, Black men were five times more likely to be in prison than white men.[28] Across the country, Black militants were viewed by correctional systems as "public enemy number one," with prison officials taking official, often clandestine steps to eradicate them. This echoed the FBI's COINTEL program, as prison leadership began sharing information with the FBI and local law enforcement. Prisons became routine organizations of carceral apartheid with internal structures to manage their growing Black prison populations, specifically targeting any signs of Black militant activity through official, clandestine, and extralegal means.

Life on the Inside

This was the world that Anthony had grown up in and when he entered prison as a young man in California during the early 1960s, he found Black political thought flourishing on the inside. Prior to co-founding the Black Guerilla Family in 1970, Anthony described this with pride. He wanted to make sure I understood that the Black Guerilla Family merely consolidated these efforts under a single banner but was not the first group to protest white supremacy within prison walls. He explained how "in every prison there always existed a group of brothers who are more conscious than the general population in terms of understanding the dynamics of racial attacks and so forth."[29]

Anthony was first incarcerated as a kid in 1963. He was quickly impressed by the Nation of Islam, finding their analysis of racial inequality and protest inspiring. As he remembers it, most of the Black people who actively engaged in political discourse in California prisons in the early 1960s were members of the Nation:

> When I first got to the Youth Authority, I used to see these brothers that would be standing tall, you know. Just standing tall. For lack of a better way of putting it, they would be shining, they would stand out. Most of them were Muslims because there was no Black Panther Party.

> They had a measure of confidence. They were more nationalist oriented. There was a level of cultural awareness. Then US Foundation came into existence and I was affiliated with that for a while when I was in prison.
> But I met these brothers like I said in the Youth Authority and most of them were conscious and aware of what was going on in the world and society.[30]

Before co-founding the Black Guerilla Family with Anthony, Hugo, George, and others in San Quentin, Benjamin also remembers encountering Black political activists as a kid in the Youth Authority. I met Benjamin and his wife Sherice through Anthony as they had kept in contact all these years later since being released from prison.

We sat in his kitchen while Sherice bustled around us, cooking and cleaning their home. I could hear her working most of the time in the other room for the four hours I spent with Benjamin, speaking over coffee. Benjamin explained to me how he spent one year in the Youth Authority before he was transferred in 1961 to the adult prison Deuel Vocational Institution (aka Tracy) at the mere age of seventeen, prior to his eventual transfer to San Quentin.

Entering Tracy as a teenager was an emotional and traumatic shock for Benjamin. Soon after arriving, he got into a fight with a counselor and was sent to the hole. On his way to solitary, a white correctional officer told him a few incarcerated white people were in the hole and would probably spit at him, and he must accept it or face consequences both from them and the officers:

> I went in when I was 16 and got out when I was 30. In the process of being in, I was transferred from my Youth Authority prison to Tracy. I was not even supposed to be there because Tracy is a place where they have gun towers and stuff. Man, I just turned 17 but they were sending people like me and other people there.
> The racism in California prisons was such that when I first went to Tracy in 1961, I got into a fight with a counselor. I was put in a hole. And I was told by the guard that while they [white prisoners] may spit in my face, for me not to do anything and just go along with it.[31]

Benjamin found himself having to battle carceral apartheid control strategies perpetrated by adult white men, and this angered him and created a deep-seated desire to retaliate and defend himself and his racial group. One night in the hole, he could not take it any longer, and began screaming at the top of his lungs until his voice went hoarse.

> I remember people yelling "n——, n——, n——" all night long. You can hear that, you know. And that was part of the racism then. You were 17 years old and you had motherfuckers calling you n—— all night. I mean one time later I was above segregation [Adjustment Center]. They got all kind of holes, right.
>
> So I was in the hole upstairs on the second floor, and I think there was one other brother up there besides me. The rest of them were white boys, and it might have been one or two Mexicans up there.
>
> I woke up one night screaming, saying, "suck my black dick," and I was responding to them in my sleep. Motherfuckers talking about black baseball players and just talking about my black people negatively.
>
> I just woke up screaming in my sleep, "Suck my black dick," and it got real quiet on the tier, right. Nobody said nothing. It was just the shit that people brought.[32]

The consequences of carceral apartheid clearly took a toll on Benjamin after only a few months of his incarceration at Tracy, much of which was spent in isolation. Soon after the spitting he endured, Benjamin got into a vicious fight with another incarcerated individual over more derogatory, racist behavior.

> I ended up picking up a case at Tracy. They were talking this racial talk and there is one dude saying that where he comes from (the Middle East), you could buy n——s for $50 a head. So he sided with the white boys in that stuff, right.
>
> A couple of months later, I'm downstairs in segregation and they put them down there. So as soon as he gets there, it's already "hey man, this motherfucker, he was talking that shit." So boom, he got moved on the next day. It might have took us two days to move, but we moved on him.
>
> I ended up getting an adult number. I was in an adult institution, but I had a white number. So that's how I picked up an adult number from stabbing. Most of the shit that went down was racially related. . . .
>
> And then there was other brothers that was coming down from Quentin and telling us about the wars that was going on at Quentin between the Nazis and the brothers.[33]

Benjamin's response demonstrates how Black militants internalized numerous mental assaults before retaliating against carceral apartheid with physical violence. Correctional officers did not intervene and either actively encouraged white supremacist attacks and retaliation, or punished Black militants for fighting back. Penal actors actively encouraged the violence, and this increased the level of cynicism among Black militants and convinced them of the need to meet organized violence in kind with organized violence of their own.

Their cynicism, in this context, arose from the perception that the law is illegitimate, unresponsive and ill-equipped to ensure safety.[34] People are less likely to comply with the orders of penal staff if they are cynical about the legitimacy of the penal organization giving those orders.[35] Incarcerated people battled inadequate legal pathways to rectify their grievances.[36] This, paired with the intensification of carceral apartheid during the Black Freedom Movement, created an opening for Black militants to organize to raise the odds of their imminent survival. They decided they would rather fight and potentially die than be tortured and possibly die anyway at the hands of officers aligned with incarcerated white supremacists. Benjamin described this alliance and the setups of Black militants as a key incentive to organize themselves behind one Black political banner:

> I mean the guards, yes, they favored the white boys. You know they did. You know, that's just the way it was. You know they'd rather see you get hurt than one of theirs. A lot of them is very racially bias like that. Wasn't about being a guard to serve on behalf of prisoners. They felt like whenever they can help a white boy, they will help him. They even bring knives to them and stuff.
>
> They're trying to break the back of anything that was going on. They would set something up if they know somebody, don't like somebody and put that person in a situation where he get taken off.[37]

Kendrick, a Black Muslim who became a lieutenant in the Nation of Islam in San Quentin and was a close associate of Anthony's, described a similar experience during our interview about prison life in the 1960s: "The guards were racist. At that time you had a lot of racist guards. You had a few good ones, but a lot of them was just downright racist. They allowed that. When one race would have knives that comes from the streets and another would just have homemade, there's something wrong. They was giving certain people certain things. Then the administration know if they could keep us divided among ourselves, then we could never use that against them. That was the main reason."[38]

He went on to emphasize that correctional officers aligned with the Aryan Brotherhood to plan attacks against the Black population. Their goal was to kill or maim Black militant leaders like himself and the others, who would go on to found the Black Guerilla Family: "They would have all that [street knives] because you'd have AB police. . . . It be the same type of people that work in the prisons that's in the prisons. Their mentality, a lot of them, is the same mentalities. At that time, they just take anybody. You could be a correctional officer as long as you had a 12th grade education . . . they disliked blacks. They blamed blacks for all they downfalls. They thought they was superior people."

Carceral apartheid fostered a deep-seated contempt for whiteness and its representations inside the correctional landscape within Black militants. The need to feel respected as a Black man and human being fueled their willingness to engage in violent combat with white officers and their incarcerated white allies. As Anthony explained:

> You get into prisons and jails and the racism is more. So automatically you are going to develop some animosity and hostility against the people who work in these institutions due to the way they treat you.
>
> You know, I used to tell them just because you got a uniform and a badge, it doesn't give you the right to disrespect me as a human being. I was somewhat outspoken and let them know how I felt about the treatment that was going on.
>
> There is a lot of disrespect that goes on in terms of the jailer and the prisoner. And then you put that with racist attitudes and you got a combination that at some point leads to outright warfare between you and them.[39]

Benjamin echoed this sentiment and described the violence as cyclical and retaliatory: "It was just a lot of instances where black people were actually fighting, actually engaging in combat, physical combat with white people in order to get some respect. Most of the time that people talked that shit to you, often they would not be where you all are face-to-face, where you could get at each other. It was a lot of racism. There were some people that got caught up in stuff like throwing shit back and forth on people."[40]

Black militants endured degrading conditions and became increasingly cynical about the legitimacy of the Department of Corrections. Many continued to face long stretches in the darkest corners of Adjustment Centers, designed to destroy their political will. George recounts solemnly, yet with conviction:

> The strongest hold out no more than a couple of weeks. It destroys the logical processes of the mind. A, a man's thoughts become completely disorganized.
>
> The noise, madness streaming from every throat, frustrated sounds from the bars, metallic sounds from the walls, the steel trays, the iron beds bolted to the wall, the hollow sounds from a cast-iron sink or toilet.
>
> The smells, the human waste thrown at us, unwashed bodies, the rotten food.

When a white con leaves here, he's ruined for life. No black leaves Max Row walking. Either he leaves on the meat wagon or he leaves crawling, licking at the pigs' feet.[41]

Revolution became their only way to survive, and it meant orchestrating a coordinated rebellion against carceral apartheid and the organized white supremacy that supported it. Black militants who co-founded the Black Guerilla Family saw the Department of Corrections as an insurmountable force, proven capable of dismantling their writs and lawsuits, and throwing people away to torture them within the belly of the Adjustment Center. Attempting to work within a carceral apartheid governance structure proved inefficient and antithetical for achieving justice, and as a consequence, the dragon would come.

"Long live the dragon" is a phrase that would affectionately refer to George Jackson for decades and to this day. Anthony had survived so much alongside his fellow cofounders that he needed to make sure this point was not lost. The world must know how carceral apartheid treated these individuals for years before they ever responded. He lamented, "It hardened us, you know and it got to the point where you know, if you fuck with us, you know we are going to fuck with you. If you don't want no problems, don't fuck with us. You know what I mean, you're going to lock us up 24 hours a day, just lock us up, don't fuck with us while we are there. You know, because if you do, you're going to have a problem."[42]

LIVE FREE OR DIE TRYING

*If you're not ready to die for it,
put the word "freedom" out of your vocabulary.*

—MALCOLM X

One incident in particular stood out in the minds of Hugo and George, and for Anthony and Benjamin, it remained even all of these years later. It was a precipitating event, convincing Black militants they must officially consolidate their efforts into the Black Guerilla Family, which happened a few months later in San Quentin. This event, known as the Soledad Incident, occurred January 13, 1970, in Soledad State Prison, where George and Hugo were incarcerated at the time.

While at Soledad, George and Hugo had become close to a fellow Black militant, W. L. Nolen, who was a well-respected leader within the Black population. W. L. became George's mentor and taught him what it meant to be a revolutionary, a person rigorous in their reading of intellectual and political texts, and one who also took care of their physical health and trained in martial arts.

Together, the two formed the Black Vanguard, the precursor to what became the Black Guerilla Family. George would go on to develop a reputation among Black militants for his martial arts capabilities.[1] The two had much in common, from their childhoods and contact with the criminal system, and, like George, W. L. had been sentenced to an unfair indeterminate incarceration in the California prison system for petty robbery.[2]

Because of his respected standing and outspoken disposition, W. L. was hated and feared by officers and incarcerated white supremacists alike. In 1969, W. L. filed a civil rights suit against the Superintendent of Soledad, Cletus FitzHarris, and the Department of Corrections for their carceral

Interior of Building E, room E-002 to E-002a, San Quentin State Prison (after 1933). Photograph by Robert A. Hicks. Historic American Buildings Survey Collection, Prints and Photographs Division, Library of Congress, Washington, DC.

apartheid regime. He circulated a petition among the Black population in Soledad, drumming up support.

The lawsuit named in court the following official and extralegal control strategies, including filing false disciplinary reports to send Black militants to the Adjustment Center, sowing racial conflict, leaving the cells of Black militants unlocked so the Aryan Brotherhood could attack them, "placing fecal matter or broken glass in the food served to New Afrikans," and overall "willfully creating and maintaining situations that creates and poses dangers [sic] to the plaintiff [himself]."[3]

Speaking these truths made W. L. a target, and he told those closest to him that he was afraid for his life. Officers at Soledad felt W. L. had to pay for speaking out, and they proceeded to make an example out of him. As vengeance, they would set up W. L. and two other leaders, both of whom had signed the petition against the officers four months prior, to die. The recreational yard served as their staging ground. It had been closed for two years after the Aryan Brotherhood had murdered two young Black men, but it was strategically reopened to orchestrate W. L.'s murder.[4]

Upon reopening the recreation yard, only one person at a time could use it to exercise according to official policy.[5]

However, white officers subverted this to their advantage. The officers' plan began with the tried and true clandestine, extralegal strategy of spreading lies among imprisoned white people that the Black militants were planning a massive assault against them. This rumor would give the Aryan Brotherhood a reason to intervene, like puppets on behalf of the officers' wishes.

After months of sowing dissent, officers intentionally integrated the exercise yard by putting a small group of Black militants with a large group of white and Chicano prisoners, who were members of the aligned Aryan Brotherhood and Mexican Mafia. The officers included men responsible for stabbing a Black prisoner a year earlier in this group.[6] The founders of the Black Guerilla Family believed that W. L. Nolen was the true target that day in January, and alleged that the officers put the other Black militants on the yard merely to mask their preconceived corrupt intentions.[7] The men had been checked before entering the yard, and no weapons were officially found.

However, not long after the yard opened, violence ensued as planned.

Witnesses claimed it began when members of the Aryan Brotherhood cornered W. L. Nolen, who was forced to turn and punch a man nicknamed Chuko in the face. The yard erupted into a mass fight.[8]

As W. L. and Chuko brawled, Chuko went for Nolen's legs, exposing W. L.'s chest.

Their most valuable target was now visible.

Officer Opie Miller chose not to fire the standard warning shot that officers are supposed to use in order to break up a fight. He was a twenty-year army veteran and began working at Soledad in 1962. He quickly racked up a list of violent attacks against the incarcerated Black population and was known to incite and commit racial abuse.

When W. L.'s chest was exposed, Officer Miller aimed his rifle and carefully took his chance. A direct shot.

As W. L. lay bleeding to death, both halves of the yard continued to clash in hand-to-hand combat. Black survivors claim that, as Cleveland Edwards went to go check on W. L., Officer Miller turned his rifle on him and shot him in the stomach. A second Black militant down counted as success, it seemed, for the officers.

Alvin Miller tried to run toward the commotion and saw his brothers fallen, dying.

Officer Miller aimed his gun and cut Alvin down as he tried to help his friends. A third Black militant cut down.

Harris, a member of the Aryan Brotherhood, was accidentally wounded when a bullet ricocheted off the ground and hit him in the groin.

Tellingly, Officer Miller had not aimed the gun at Harris, as he had with the Black militant victims he murdered.

Witnesses claimed that all three wounded Black men were still alive for at least fifteen to twenty minutes after the shootings, but that officials let them lie there until they were either dead or close to it. They were purposefully allowed to fill the cement with blood, their bullet-riddled bodies splayed across the O-Wing yard, gasping for air and looking to the sky for what seemed like an eternity to shocked onlookers.[9]

This public, graphic display was strategically prolonged to remind the Black population, with their Black militant leaders, of who held absolute authority over their destinies. This was a clear message about the fate that would befall anyone who dared to challenge carceral apartheid.

Black witnesses screamed from afar in horror, quivering, angry and grief-ridden as they watched their own bleeding to death on the yard, unable to do anything. Pointing, shaking, and gasping, they clenched their fists, knuckles turning white, willing the fences to break so they could be free.[10]

Officer Miller stood in the tower above, silently watching, calmly clutching the .30 caliber rifle. He hated Black militants especially and had a fondness for his fellow whites—officers and the incarcerated—as a staunch proponent of "white above all." Black militants described him as ruthless, with a keen eye for terror:

> A short, stocky man with an oval face and slightly receding cropped hair, Miller was a product of Woden, Texas. A small agricultural town that is excluded from most atlases. As a guard, Miller had a reputation among prisoners and staff of being sullen and severe. That was probably the reason he was often assigned to standing watches in gun towers, where he would have little, if any, direct contact with inmates. Two days before the opening of the yard, Miller was checked out the use of the .30 caliber rifle. As in the past, he performed well.[11]

Hugo was devastated by the murders and knew that Black militants' demands for justice would never be realized in a legal manner. After all, W. L. had been, essentially, killed for filing a lawsuit and circulating a petition. As far as Hugo was concerned, the department was blatantly aligned with incarcerated white supremacists as a collective effort to destroy Black militants.

Hugo wrote a haunting account of how he'd experienced the shootings at Soledad:

> I swear on my life and on those who have perished unmercifully under the cruel hands of these racist anti-Black officials, that what you are about to read is the pure, honest truth and nothing but:
> To All (Blacks) Concerned:
> (1969) On October the 27th, Eugene Grady, Eddie Whiteside and myself, were transferred to Soledad Correctional Institution Facility, from Folsom Prison. We were placed in the Max Row section of O-Wing [Adjustment Center].
> Immediately entering the sally port area of the section, I could hear inmates shouting and making remarks such as; "N—— is a scum, low down dog, etc."
> I couldn't believe my ears at first because I know if I could hear these things, the officers beside me could too and I started wondering, what was going on?
> Then, I fixed my eyes on the Wing Sergeant and I began to see the clear picture of why those inmates didn't care if the officials heard them instigating racial conflict. The Sergeant was and still is Mr. M., a known prejudice character towards Blacks because of previous unforgettable experiences with Blacks.
> I was placed in cell #139 and since that moment up until now I have had no peace of mind. The white inmates made it a 24 hour job of cursing Black Inmates just for kicks and the officials harassed us with consistency also. On October the 28th, my personal property was handed to me and I only received one third of what I had in Folsom, plus it was torn along with half of the photographs they allowed me to have. But I still kept collectively at ease.
> Soon, on November the 12th, they had the first shake down since I was there. The officials went straight to Whiteside's cell and I didn't believe my eyes at how they operated. They only went in the cell for seconds while Whiteside was hand-cuffed in another cell. They came out and without a cause, took Whiteside to the other side of O-Wing which is considered Isolation. I asked the officers where they were taking Whiteside and one of them told me to shut-up. About two minutes they came back and shook my cell down and I figured they would take me to the other side also, but they didn't!! They only accused me of having a torn sheet in my cell and they charged me $1.26 for it. Their records show that the

set of sheets on my bed were untouched, so I asked them how they came about with a torn sheet and again I was told to shut-up and was given ten (10) days cell exercise which means I don't come out of my cell for ten days! I still didn't say anything.

The next day, I got a visit in a visiting room and when I came back, inmate Meneweather (a Black) told me that the police had attacked W. L. Nolen (a Black) while being hand-cuffed and he had been taken to Isolation! Now, this was a little too much to accept, so Edwards (a Black), Meneweather and myself protested accordingly to their ways; we threw some liquid on Officer D. since he was the cause of W. L. Nolen getting attacked.

We didn't have any means of defense. No one knew how we were doing down here, so, we could only respond in protection of each other! They came back and threw gas in our cells until we almost died. Seriously, I had to wave a towel since I was choking from the gas.

They told me that they wouldn't open the door until I undressed, backed up to the door and stuck my arms out. I did just that, they hand-cuffed me and dragged me to the other side, naked. Meneweather and Edwards received the same treatment. We were placed in the so called strip-cells in the back of the tier.

The next day the doctor came by, not specially to see us, but mainly making his once a week routine. He asked me if I was okay and I told him, "yeah, I'm alright." I wanted to say "No sir, my eyes and skin are burning from the gas," but I couldn't do it because I didn't have any hopes of getting help from anyone except my own people.

Then, we were given 29 days isolation, including 15 days R.D. (Restricted Diet). This R.D. is served twice a day and believe me, even a dog wouldn't eat it, perhaps not even a pig!

In that dark cell I did a lot of thinking on what all this harassment would lead to because surely, the officials could see how well together we were and we didn't let the White inmates' fat-mouthing affect us in the least.

Then, my visits were restricted to the Captain's Office and I kept cool because all my brothers were being mistreated, some worse than me. For instance, W. L. Nolen was disliked by all the officials and what angers me is that, these officials don't hide it, they just come out in the open and let you know, you are not appreciated in O-Wing if you are Black.

After our 29 days were over, we returned to Max Row but before that they had brought inmate Grady to Isolation trying to frame him also.

I asked him why they (officials) did so many petty things and he said he couldn't understand it either, but in our eyes we could see the answer.

We were Black and we weren't fooling ourselves. We merely try to give each other encouragement.

When we came back to Max Row (Edwards, Meneweather, and myself) Whiteside and Nolen were already back. Again we laid back and accepted the insults from White inmates.

These officials didn't allow no one to exercise except inmates of their own race in group of three at one time, so that no Mexican, white or black inmate came in contact with one another at any time. They violated this rule by letting whites and Mexicans exercise together and get haircuts on the same day, so that this way it made it obvious what they meant to plant in people's mind by segregating Blacks from everybody else.

So, it was no secret that racial tension existed on Max Row and Blacks were housed as follows: Nolen (#134), Satcher (#144), Whiteside (#140), Pinell (#139), Randolph (#137), Meneweather (#134), Edwards (#132), Miller (#130), and Anderson (#126). Anderson was harassed the next day (around the 16th of Dec.) and taken to Isolation.

On the 18th day, Nance (a Black) was brought in from Isolation and placed in cell #128. That same day, I was informed by officials that I was to go to Sacramento County Jail, the next day. I couldn't figure out what would be the reason for me going to Sacramento. So, on the 19th, before I left, Grady was returned to Max Row and house in #127.

Now, we were all wondering why all of a sudden so many Blacks were being moved on our side, because, really, when I first came on this tier, there were only four (4) Blacks (Nolen, Meneweather, Edwards and Anderson) and they have been there for quite a while putting up with officials', as well as inmates' insults.

The only thing we had going for us, was ourselves, and we behaved so civilized that it enraged everyone to try more mischievous plots against us hoping we would react savagely as they did, but without triumph!

Anyway, on the 19th I left for Sacramento, it was a Friday and I didn't return until Tuesday the 23rd. I was put in the same cell #139. It was the same environment. The air stayed stuffed with "N—— here," and "N—— there."

On the 28th of Dec., a list was passed out announcing the opening of the Max Row yard on the 29th. But it didn't open because there was still some work yet to be done.

But I did notice that white inmates and officials were awfully cheerful for some reason or another, and they continuously didn't forget to remind us of the yard opening soon.

Nolen kept telling me that these officials were up to no good and the white inmates would pass my cell asking me, "Are you coming out when the yard opens?" Most of the time I would laugh at them, and sometimes I would just sigh and roll on my other side, trying to sleep.

Days went by, and on Monday the 12th, I left for Sacramento County Jail again. It was raining like hell up that way, so I figured the weather was the same at Soledad. Tuesday morning I was taken to Court, but someone said it was a mistake, that I was supposed to appear that afternoon, so I was taken back to County Jail, where I met other friends of mine.

Well, me and my friends (not from Soledad) went to court that afternoon, when we returned, we happened to hear the news on the radio where it announced the killing of three inmates at Soledad Institution while scuffling in the yard.

Damn, for some reason I knew what yard that man on the radio was referring to, because I fell to my knees against my will, and tears rolled out of my eyes.

Believe me. I'm a man in every respect, but if you felt the tension we live under, you could easily understand a grown man crying. I was sad, glad, angry, and hateful; Gordon (a Black) also cried and he wasn't even at Soledad and yet we know how it is for Blacks in prison.

Everybody stopped and stared at me not understanding. I cursed people out for no reason because, after all, it wasn't their fault. I returned here the next day, and I could smell death in the air.

The tier was like a tomb. I was put in my, what used to be, personal friend's cell:

W. L. Nolen.

I asked what happened, and they told me (Blacks) that W. L. Nolen, Cleveland Edwards and Alvin Miller were shot down like ducks in a pond.

Pay full attention to what I have said, because even today we live under the same conditions, and that murder out in the yard could have easily been me or the rest of the Blacks down here. Or maybe we get it next time? All I do is ask myself, "Is this the price a man has to pay for wanting to be Black and respected as such, as he respects others?" I tell you, it is cold blooded!

I speak on behalf of all Blacks who know and understand the meaning of being Black and in Prison. If it wasn't for those killings of W. L. Nolen,

Edwards, and Miller, I would have never sat down to write this, but if my people keep on getting killed in this fashion, what is the sense in me living when their heart is also my beat?!?[12]

The killings did not have their intended effect, however. Instead, they convinced Black militants in Soledad that they would rather die in battle against carceral apartheid than die on their knees.

The Black population protested these deaths with a hunger strike at Soledad, demanding a formal investigation into Officer Miller and anyone else involved.[13] The Monterey County grand jury did not allow any Black witnesses to testify at the hearings. Three days later, on January 16, 1970, the jury acquitted Officer Miller and ruled the Black militants' deaths "justifiable homicide."

The Black population anxiously tuned in, immediately hearing the ruling on the radio. Thirty minutes later, a white officer was brutally murdered in Soledad, a killing that many attributed to Black militants avenging the Soledad Incident.[14] A rookie officer, John V. Mills, died after being viciously beaten and thrown from a third-floor tier.

Witnesses described the three days between the Soledad Incident and the killing of Officer Mills as explosive and seething with hatred so palpable, one could feel it on their skin:

> Word of the triple killings flashed quickly throughout the Soledad main line. Within hours various groups of black inmates were demanding the arrest of the gun guard and a grand jury investigation. Investigators and attorneys from the Monterey County district attorney's office poked and probed, but after a passage of three days, there was no word on the progress of the investigation.
>
> The prison continued tense, "like a fire-cracker fixing to explode," as one white inmate described it.
>
> During the evening of the third day, the Monterey County district attorney told reporters in an interview that Opie G. Miller's killing of the three black prisoners was, in his personal opinion, "probable justifiable homicide by a public officer in the performance of his duty."
>
> When the black inmates heard this report on television, they were incensed. Within an hour a white guard named John V. Mills lay dying on the concrete pavement of Y-wing. He died in the prison hospital without regaining consciousness.
>
> Mills probably never knew any of the truth about the killings on January 13. His death was revenge, cold detached revenge.

Opie Miller—the man who shot Nolen, Edwards, Miller and Harris—took an extended vacation in Germany.[15]

Three Black militant leaders were charged with Officer John Mills's murder on February 14, 1970, including George.[16] These three became known as the Soledad Brothers. Their legal and advisory team consolidated into the Soledad Brothers Defense Committee.

The case garnered national media attention, with many well-known Black activists and white celebrities rallying for the cause, including George's partner, Angela Davis, Marlon Brando, and Jane Fonda. Fay Stender, a white lawyer working on prisoners' rights and an ally of the Black Freedom Movement, formed the committee and worked endlessly alongside lawyers and activists, dedicated to both exonerating the three and publicizing the rampant abuse of Black militants within California prisons.[17]

Fay introduced George to Gregory Armstrong, the editor who published his first book later that year, *Soledad Brother: The Prison Letters of George Jackson*.[18]

Eliza, a white anti–Vietnam War activist who worked closely with Fay Stender on the Soledad Brothers Defense Committee, recounted her experience of this period to me in an interview. She became close with George and described the events leading up to the Soledad Incident, their significance, and the role of the Black Panther Party in connecting the Soledad Brothers to valuable resources for their defense:

> Huey was the one who made George known. That is, Huey asked Charles Garry and Fay Stender, asked their law office to take on the case for George. Most people didn't know about it because of that.
>
> But most of what I knew of that period, starting from 1970, when George was accused, came primarily from George and secondarily from other people that George had told, especially lawyers and investigators that George had said things.
>
> I'm seeing that period the way I remember, that George told me, and the way George saw that period.
>
> One thing is that he became politicized, primarily he said, because of Nolan. Nolan was already a prison teacher. He was the one who got young people like George reading all of the great revolutionary intellectuals from around the world, who George lists in his book. . . .
>
> They had both been in isolation. But they were kept segregated by race, and the guards would regularly bait them, and tell the blacks the whites are gonna get you . . . they'd be saying things all the time and dropping these hints to them, getting them.

As well as the other kinds of torture that they described. [Officers] putting glass or feces or things in their food and then claiming that it was from one of the other [racial] groups.[19]

Word about the Soledad Incident would soon spread to San Quentin.

To combat these carceral apartheid strategies, the approximately nine to ten Black militants who founded the Black Guerilla Family felt their only recourse was to form their own paramilitary organization.[20] They accomplished this only a couple months after the January 1970 Soledad Incident, when a critical mass of Black militant leaders ended up together that year in San Quentin.

Anthony, for instance, was transferred from Soledad to San Quentin just before W. L.'s murder and remembers clearly the effect the incident had on him and his cofounders:

Before I got shifted out of Soledad, I was in a cell in O Wing (Adjustment Center) and I was in the cell next to W. L. Nolen. . . . I knew all of them personally. . . .

When they opened the yard on January 13, 1970, that was the first time that yard had been used. The first time they opened that yard is the same time they killed our street brothers. They killed W. L. Nolen outright. . . . I got to understanding in talking to other brothers who were in Soledad who later got transferred to Quentin. . . . And then the court is going to rule it justifiable homicide. That didn't sit well with black prisoners. As a matter of fact, it didn't sit well with the prisoners at all.

And when it got ruled justifiable homicide, like I said, they declared war on black prisoners.

And in return, black prisoners declared war on guards. . . .

When you have stuff like that taking place, particularly within the context of the prison system, a lot of us felt it necessary to defend ourselves. One of the actions that was taken was guards got killed.

You say, "Hey, you can't keep killing us. You can't just kill us and not expect some type of response." Or retaliation. It's like what choice do you have when the court says, "It's all right for them to kill you." That may not be the direction that you want to go but it's the direction that you're forced in.[21]

George was also soon transferred to San Quentin, where he awaited trial for the killing of Officer Mills. There, George, along with those who had been closest to W. L., recruited trusted militants to form the first cadre of the Black Guerilla Family in 1970. Anthony describes the motivation behind their decision to found the organization: "In every prison there was always a group of progressive brothers, who were concerned about defending the black population against the racist attacks, against brutality by the police. That always has been. When the BGF came into existence, one of the goals was to unite all these different autonomous elements under one banner."[22]

With their alliance in its infant stages, George's case continued to gain worldwide attention from the efforts of the Soledad Brothers Defense Committee.[23]

During this period, George was concerned for the safety of his partner. George advised that he only trusted his teenage brother, Jonathan, to act as Angela's bodyguard. Angela had been facing credible threats to her life because of her public assertion of her right to teach as a Black communist and activist. Unbeknownst to Angela, Jonathan was plotting to free the Soledad Brothers from prison and save his brother from being killed by corrupt officers. George was in constant danger of being set up to die, especially as he became more visible. According to the pair's father, Lester Jackson, George told Jonathan in July that officers were planning to kill him in August.[24]

On August 7, 1970, Jonathan stormed the Marin County Courthouse with Angela's guns in tow and attempted to save his brother by taking hostages to negotiate for the Soledad Brothers' release. He kidnapped Superior Court Judge Harold Haley, along with the deputy district attorney, and three women from the jury. As Jonathan attempted to leave the courthouse, he, along with Judge Haley and two incarcerated individuals, was killed. Judge Haley was a casualty of the sawed-off shotgun that had been taped to his neck.[25]

Jonathan's escape plot ignited the now infamous nationwide manhunt for Angela Davis, landing her on the FBI's Most Wanted list. The federal government accused her of buying the firearms used in the plot, and she served eighteen months in jail before she was acquitted in 1972 due to a staunch lack of credible evidence. Critics of the proceedings called Angela's trial a "witch hunt."[26]

To commemorate his brother, George dedicated the publication of *Soledad Brother* to Jonathan:

> Tall, evil, graceful, bright eyed, black man-child—Jonathan Peter Jackson—who died on August 7, 1970, courage in one hand, assault rifle in the other; my brother, comrade, friend,—the true revolutionary, the black communist guerrilla in the highest state of development, he died on the trigger, scourge of the unrighteous, soldier of the people; to this terrible man-child and his wonderful mother Georgia Bea, to Angela Y. Davis, my tender experience, I dedicate this collection of letters; to the destruction of their enemies, I dedicate my life.[27]

Those closest to George Jackson described this incident and its aftermath as motivating George to take charge of the movement and lead, despite his upcoming trial.[28] Two days after his younger brother died trying to free him, George wrote Jonathan a final message, revealing his intentions: "Cold and calm though. All right, gentlemen, I'm taking over now. Revolution, George."[29] George would go on to write what would eventually become his famous "insurrectionary text," *Blood in My Eye*.[30]

Plotting Insurrection

Following the Soledad Incident and the Marin County Courthouse escape attempt that ended in Jonathan's death, Black militants felt empowered to advance their new organization and believed it could effectively challenge carceral apartheid from within prison. Their preexisting ties to Black political movements gave them the knowledge and political savvy to request resourced support from other movement organizations, structure the BGF in a paramilitary fashion, adopt a clear ideological standpoint, recruit and educate members, and design coordinated plans to enact revolution.

As Anthony put it, the goal was to unite Black militants under one banner, and they recruited members from the Black Panther Party, Nation of Islam, Republic of New Afrika, US Foundation, and Black Liberation Army, all of whom wanted to fight for revolution behind bars.[31] They felt the momentum brewing and framed the structure of the Black Guerilla Family around linking societal conditions to struggles within prison:

> At that time there was several incidents where the police had attacked the Muslims. Like how they attacked the Muslims in Los Angeles. That was a big thing with us when we talked about police brutality. Before the attacks on the Panthers by the police, police were attacking the Muslims.
>
> You had the civil rights movement going on . . . of course the general social conditions that existed at that time. Lack of jobs, being harassed by the police. Substandard living conditions. . . .
>
> Like I said, the continued racist attacks and racist murderers, the brutality of the guards, the guards' involvement in killing people. It's just like when they killed the brothers on the yard. Those brothers didn't have any weapons. It was a fist fight [the Soledad Incident].
>
> Just like when these police kill our unarmed Black people on the streets. Most of the time, the court rulings, you see a lot of acquittals even though the evidence might be blatant that the police use extreme force. The courts, they're going to be found not guilty. They're going to

say, "They were justified in killing them." But in reality, it may not have been justified. . . . But they used extreme violence or extreme force to do whatever they did. . . .

The Black Panther Party was forced, whether or not they wanted, to take that position. Police driving by, doing drive-by shootings of the Panther offices. Or like what happened in Chicago, arranged in the middle of the night and he [Fred Hampton] was assassinated.

Or using dirty tricks to have different political organizations clash with each other and enemies, conflicts, taking place [referencing disputes between US Foundation and Black Panther Party and internal Nation of Islam struggles].

Look what happened to Martin Luther King Jr. Look what happened to Malcolm X. Violence always plays a part in suppressing any kind of movement that goes against the status quo.[32]

Anthony and his fellow cofounders recognized carceral apartheid as an all-consuming force that fully dictated the day-to-day survival of Black militants in society and prison. For him, one thing was certain: the only way to attack this force would be through a coordinated, direct assault.[33] As a founder, he had learned lessons from his experience with carceral apartheid and engagement with radical Black political movements. He decided that revolution rather than reform was the only solution that would bring about significant, permanent change:

It counters the system and what it was doing. It was forcing opposition to the practices that were taking place within the context of that institution. The brutality, the indefinite lockup, the censorship of mail, the indefinite sentence. All those things played a part.

It's no different than what took place in the Civil Rights Movement in the South. Whites only, you can't vote, being kept in a certain place, being brutalized. You can't just do that to people and not expect some kind of response.

In the context of the Civil Rights Movement, they took a more passionate approach to it. But I'm a part of a generation that said, "Oh no." They weren't just going to accept this. We're not just going to sit by and let you do this.

So we became more of a threat than the Civil Rights Movement.[34]

Sean, a member of the Black Panther Party, described to me in an interview that he became an early member of the Black Guerilla Family because, as he saw it, revolution was the only way to survive the state's regime behind bars:

I got involved with the Black Panthers because it was a heck of a racial time back then. A lot of good people died on both sides, white folk, black folk, Mexicans. A lot of people died. . . . A lot of good people died for nothing.

George, he tried to put everybody together, all races, because it wasn't just us that was being exploited. They was being exploited too.

The prison guards was giving them guys knives, bringing knives, some of them Buck knives and stuff like that from the streets. Bringing it in prison, and we had no way of getting Buck knives. They was giving them to the white boys. They was giving them to the Mexicans. They wasn't giving them to us, though. George said, "Oh well. I guess we got to protect ourselves."

We started with you can't go nowhere by yourself. If you went to take a shower somebody had to be standing outside the shower for protection, for security. That's how we survived. Our prison experience back then was a mess.

I look on here on my phone sometimes. I read up on all this. I read some of the stuff that they put in, ain't none of that happened. Ain't none of that happened. Saying that we was a prison gang back in the day.

We weren't a prison gang. We were revolutionaries.

You can't tell the black experience if you ain't lived the black experience.[35]

Like the Black Panther Party, the Black Guerilla Family continued to engage with other revolutionary organizations in society, such as the anti-Vietnam War movement. Black militants believed they were fighting for a common revolution to upend what could be described as a carceral apartheid system dependent upon racialized, gendered capitalistic oppression, and the anti-war protestors had similar ideologies.

Black Guerilla Family members routinely sent letters to leftist organizations, mainly in California, explaining their experiences within the prison system and urging them to publicize the abuse and expose the department: "In realizing the reality of our situation, we know that we are not merely dealing with other racist prisoners, but also dealing with the administration, the pigs and neo-Nazi right wingers on the outside. We are seeking as much support as possible from the progressive and revolutionary elements on the outside to assist us in combatting the escalating racism, fascism, that confronts us all."[36]

Activists on the outside quickly responded by putting up flyers in their communities and contacting their congressional representatives. The founders relied on these outside connections to publicize their struggles to wider audiences. Without these cross racial alliances in society, they felt their movement would not be able to gain nationwide traction.

Ideology and Structure

Founders used their preexisting movement experiences as reference guides for designing a social movement organization. One of their first objectives was to solidify a clear ideological foundation, which they then bolstered with an efficient, paramilitary structure, as described by Anthony:

> Its initial purpose and intent was to unify all black prisoners, so they wouldn't be just a group and we could come together under one banner. With a common goal or objective as black guerrillas. To have a political foundation, be conscious and move on a political level, not engage in criminal activities, not trying to control the drugs in the prison. But a political goal and objective to defend ourselves against these attacks and inflict as many casualties on the prison guards as possible in retaliation for the brutality and deaths they had caused.[37]

Based on what they had already survived, this was war, and in war times, one must create a militia. The founders put together a guerrilla force based on Marxism-Leninism, according to the model provided by the Black Panther Party and the Black Liberation Army.

This excerpt from the BGF Constitution also illustrates their belief in Maoism, with some lines coming directly from writing by Chairman Mao Zedong, the founder of the People's Republic of China:

> We use Marxism, which is positive in spirit, to overcome liberalism, which is negative. A communist should have largeness of mind, and he/she should be staunch and active, looking upon the interest of the revolution as his/her very life and subordinating his/her personal interests to those of the revolution. Always and everywhere he/she should adhere to principles and wage a tireless struggle against all incorrect ideas and actions, as to consolidate the collective life of the Party, and strengthen the ties between the Party and the masses. He/she should be more concerned about others than about himself/herself. Only thus can we be considered a Communist.[38]

Members followed the "Blood Oath of the Guerilla," modeled after the Mau Mau Oaths of Black freedom fighters, who opposed British colonial forces in Kenya. The founders viewed all fellow revolutionaries as eternal brothers engaged in a global communist struggle led by the Lumpenproletariat.[39] The oath states:

> If ever I should break my stride, or falter at my comrade's side,
> This oath will kill me!
> If ever my word should prove untrue, should I betray the many or you few,
> This oath will kill me!
> Should I be slow to make a stand, or show fear before the hangman,
> This oath will kill me!
> Should I misuse the people's trust, should I submit ever to greed or lust,
> This oath will kill me!
> Should I grow lax in discipline, in times of strife, refuse my hand,
> This oath will surely kill me![40]

Founders provided political education opportunities to indoctrinate new recruits and cultivate this new worldview. Prior to these education classes, incarcerated Black people had long exchanged political books, fostering a culture of racial solidarity. However, the Black Guerilla Family formalized their practices by modeling their classes according to the structured frameworks used by the Republic of New Afrika and the Black Panther Party.

Recruits followed a curriculum and were required to read a specific reading list and participate in discussions. They were also required to learn martial arts, something George had long been known for, and the basic tenets of hand-to-hand combat. Founders described political education as their main tool to remodel "criminals into revolutionaries." They read texts ranging from the work of Emile Durkheim and Karl Marx to Mao Zedong and Frantz Fanon.[41] Jerome, an early member of the Black Guerilla Family, remembered his political education fondly and described it as a transformative experience:

> I can tell you that they taught me how to read, they directed me of what to read that could be useful for me. It saved my life. . . .
> My political consciousness started with political education classes. I couldn't wait to be the one that got to stand up in front of all these black men and read a chapter of a book for lunch. For those of us who couldn't really read, there were other people that read to us.
> When there was no TV in prison, we had full access to our imagination. We read everything we could. Books were of a value, all books were of a value, some a little bit more than others. Good political books sold and were traded. If you had good reading material it was a part of an economy.

People were motivated to join the BGF movement because of all the questions that arise when walking into such an unjust environment. The discourse was vibrant, but you didn't have to be affiliated to attend the classes.

I thank Anthony and all of them because when I went into society, I would think to myself, "What would George think about what I'm doing."[42]

Carl, an early recruit of the Black Guerilla Family, also remembers personally teaching new recruits about security and self-respect as Black men:

For security reasons you had to school certain brothers who didn't know because there was nothing going on at the moment. They would be really lax. Like guys would get up in the morning, then it's time to go to chow and they act like they are at home coming downstairs from their bedroom going to the kitchen. They would be unaware of the dangers around them. So we spent a lot of time schooling them.

The other thing was that back then, it's changed since then, but back then the N-word was taboo. People would check before referring to themselves or anyone else by the N-word, so there was an educational process that took place.[43]

Sean remembered how new recruits often had to prove themselves in order to be fully accepted, in addition to keeping up with their political education:

We had set times at night. In the evening we had to go to the cell and do our reading and stuff and get tested. Some of the guys would come and slide the oath under somebody's door and if you picked it up and read it you was a member. Sometimes you get tested.

They give you a knife and tell you what. It's supposed to be blood in, blood out. A lot of people didn't have to do that, but some people did. If you show them weakness you had to do that. I guess I got lucky because I didn't have to do that. I was in Youth Authority with a lot of them.[44]

Founders even disagreed at times about whether to prioritize political education or combat training when indoctrinating new recruits. For example, Benjamin described these differing views and the constant need to compromise: "Some of the people in the BGF were warriors. There were some people that were warriors that would throw the book away. Some brothers felt like the only thing you've got to do was be a warrior and stand up. Be willing to move on somebody that deserved to be moved on. Others felt you need to always read, keep yourself updated, strive to become richer in your knowledge. And some of them just felt like being a warrior was good enough."[45]

Benjamin, along with others, felt that these differences weren't weaknesses, however. Each founder had their own strengths and used these skills to better the organization and attract new, quality recruits. At its inception, the Black Guerilla Family inspired many in the Black population to organize for change. However, the founders were very selective with their membership offers and designed the organization's eligibility tests to root out undercover agents, or those who were not absolutely committed to revolution by any means necessary.

Prisoners Above All

While defending the Black population and enacting revenge against the department were the organization's foremost priorities, the founders also believed that uniting the incarcerated under a prisoner class of all races would successfully destroy the system of carceral apartheid for good. "White above all" could not survive in the face of such coalitions, although this arguably was the most dangerous proposition the Black Guerilla Family put forth.

"Prisoners above all" threatened to destroy the entire foundation of the carceral apartheid regime.

One of the first actions the organization initiated was a statewide prison strike to protest carceral apartheid within California prisons in November 1970. As members of the California Prisoners Union, the founders contributed to a manifesto, listing their demands in such a manner that imprisoned people from all racial groups signed on and agreed to participate in the strike. This document became known as the Folsom Manifesto and was released November 3, 1970. The incarcerated in Folsom kicked off the strike by refusing to show up to their work assignments.

For nineteen days, approximately 2,400 people refused to leave their cells, enduring hunger and physical and psychological intimidation—carceral apartheid at its ugliest. Excerpts of the first two pages of the Folsom Manifesto show its ability and that of the founders to unify the incarcerated against the department:

THE FOLSOM PRISONERS MANIFESTO OF DEMANDS
AND ANTI-DEPRESSION PLATFORM

WE THE IMPRISONED MEN OF FOLSOM PRISON SEEK AN END TO THE INJUSTICE SUFFERED BY ALL PRISONERS, REGARDLESS OF RACE, CREED, OR COLOR.

The preparation and content of this document has been constructed under the unified efforts of all races and social segments of this prison.

We the inmates of Folsom Prison totally and unlimitedly support the California state wide prison strike on November 3rd 1970, under the united effort for designated change in administrative prison practice and legislative policy.

It is a matter of documented record and human recognition that the administrators of the California prison system have restructured the institutions which were designed to socially correct men into the FACIST [sic] CONCENTRATION CAMPS OF MODERN AMERICA.

DUE TO THE CONDITIONAL FACT THA [SIC] FOLSOM PRISON IS ONE OF THE MOST CLASSIC INSTITUTIONS OF AUTHORITATIVE INHUMANITY UPON MEN, THE FOLLOWING MANIFESTO OF DEMANDS ARE BEING SUBMITTED:

"MAN'S RIGHT TO KNOWLEDGE AND THE FREE USE THEREOF"

We the inmates of Folsom Prison have grown to recognize beyond the shadow of a doubt that because of our posture as prisoners and branded characters as alleged criminals, the administrators and prison employees no longer consider or respect us as human beings, but rather as domesticated animals selected to do their bidding in slave labor and furnished as a personal whipping dog for their sadistic psychopathic hate.

We the inmates of Folsom Prison, say to you, the sincere people of society, the prison system of which your courts have rendered unto, is without question the authoritative fangs of a coward in power.

Respectfully submitted to the people as a protest to the vile and vicious slavemasters:

THE CALIFORNIA DEPARTMENT OF CORRECTIONS
THE CALIFORNIA ADULT AUTHORITY
THE CALIFORNIA STATE LEGISLATURE
THE CALIFORNIA STATE COURTS
THE UNITED STATES COURTS
AND THOSE WHO SUPPORT THIS SYSTEM OF INJUSTICE.
CALIFORNIA PRISONERS UNION[46]

This show of interracial unity terrified the department, placing an even larger target on the Black Guerilla Family for their ability to move past what the founders called "racial tribalism" and unite the incarcerated as one prisoner class against the department and its status quo.

The Black Guerilla Family was very proud of the strike and believed that it represented a real possibility that one day prisoners could permanently unite and move beyond racial boundaries, conflict, and division. Yet as the founders and early members recalled in their interviews with me, the Department of Corrections made sure this success was short lived. Their recollections are, understandably, tinged with contempt:

Repression breeds resistance.[47]

A guard said, word for word, "When they're fighting each other, we don't have to do anything. It's just when they band together it creates problems." That's what he said. He said, "As long as they're fighting each other, we just keep pushing them to fight."[48]

The environment in which we all lived, of people who controlled the environment, stirred the mix because if we actually became friends and we never actually decided to organize collectively, what they were afraid would happen was that it would introduce other George Jacksons. To their advantage, they made sure that they were forming always a dissatisfaction among the races and they treated some people better than others.[49]

August 21, 1971

The Black Guerilla Family's next move—and its most famous—was to plan and execute a statewide prisoner rebellion against the Department of Corrections. Once the main organization conquered San Quentin, their newly formed cadres at Folsom, Tracy, and Soledad would receive word and follow suit. The founders of the organization were optimistic, hoping that just maybe, incarcerated people in other parts of the country would see their efforts and be inspired to bring rebellion beyond California.[50] They were also realistic, knowing full well that they could die in the process and never see the future they so ferociously envisioned. Members assured me in interviews that they accepted death as a very real possibility, exemplified by Benjamin's harrowing words: "I mean it is so enraging. Man you would be so angry, it didn't make us scared. It made us want to get their ass even at the risk of losing our own. You know that's what that kind of shit did to us, you know. . . . George was committed to the point where he was willing to give up his life."[51]

Members described themselves as warriors, willing to die in the pursuit of freedom and Black liberation. In order to plan this rebellion, the Black Guerilla Family knew they must first break George out of San Quentin. Shortly before George's trial for the murder of Officer John Mills, the organization received word that correctional officers at San Quentin were planning to murder George. They planned to kill him using a setup similar to Soledad Officer Opie Miller's shooting and killing of W. L. Nolen.

George was incredibly valuable to the Black Guerilla Family. A skilled tactician and political theorist, he inspired the incarcerated—and those beyond the walls—to commit to collective action as a counter-death grip.[52] George embodied the private and public face of the Black Power Movement's prison faction.[53] The Department of Corrections believed his public demise would cripple the movement, inside and out.[54]

The Black Guerilla Family orchestrated an elaborate escape attempt to free George from San Quentin and prevent his extermination. They yearned to subvert the correctional pleasures that the department and its proxies seemed to derive from indefinitely suspending Black militants between life and death. The organization spent months planning, training a secret prisoner army to protect George during the escape, which Hugo was a part of. They secured connections to the Black Liberation Army, entrusting them with transporting George to a safe house in New York City. The Black Guerilla Family relied heavily on the Black Liberation Army and their expertise with guerilla warfare and tactical operations. Prior to August 21st, the Black Guerilla Family practiced the escape scenario numerous times.[55]

Corrupt white correctional officers pretended to be sympathetic to the Black Guerilla Family's plight, manipulating their desperation, which was being relayed to the department by carefully planted snitches. Indeed, eager and desperate to save George, the organization paid the officers to smuggle C4 into San Quentin and hide the explosives along a carefully plotted escape route. The original plan was for Jackson and a few founders to make it to the end of a side corridor and use C4 to blow the wall. Contrary to popular sources, they did not use nitroglycerin.[56]

What the Black Guerilla Family did not realize was that the seemingly sympathetic officers were actually working with the Department of Corrections and Federal Bureau of Investigation, feeding fellow law enforcement as many details as possible about the upcoming escape attempt. The officers provided the Black Guerilla Family with faulty C4 rigged to stall when ignited, and enlisted the help of incarcerated white supremacists to suppress the escape itself.[57] It's important to note that the official state narrative deliberately erases this connection from the story.[58]

End Times

On August 21, 1971, the Black Guerilla Family initiated their escape plot, several months earlier than planned, because they received what they believed to be reliable intelligence that correctional officers were plotting to kill George within days—either by setting him up to be killed by the Aryan Brotherhood or by staging self-inflicted demise.[59]

As soon as the plan unfolded, weeks of practice did not prepare them for the way it all fell apart.

Dark paths thought to be open were closed.

Impossible doors meant to be unlocked were sealed.

Unbearable spaces meant to be clear of opposition were guarded by the department's trusted Aryan Brotherhood. Furtive solidarity with white officers had been exposed as impossible.

Didn't you know? The founders realized. "White above all" trumps all other social obligations.

Their sweat curdled, dripping forcefully down each triggered brow. Movement ceased to provide meaning. The panic settled nicely in their spirits.

George knew it was over, but he could not bring the words to light. Brothers in captivity or in death, the meaning was the same. Oaths were made, revolutionary suicide likely, though at the time not certain.

Certainty was engulfing. Filling and wrenching like gray clouds, swirling and falling on heavy shoulders.

The weight of a people, battling generations of racist intent, calling.

Continuously reaching for something, the end of the hall came closer with each step.

Was it hope they were feeling when the brown corridor walls became clear?

Even still, their C4 refused to free them. Instead, choosing to deal a dose of soul binding despair.

George and his fellow comrade instinctually turned to the nearest exit, a mere few paces away. Their quivering hands buckled when a last attempt confirmed freedom was bolted shut.

Everything had been a lie. For now at least, it was over. "White above all" had won.

Staring at each other, no words needed, a decision was made in silence. The only way out was to run for their lives across the courtyard. To live free or die trying never before felt so true.

Would they run fast or would they run slow? The choice was theirs.

Both men paused silently, studying the courtyard gates.

After a few moments, they gently exchanged glances—accepting the end.

Together, they crossed to the other side.

George calmly emerged first and ran for his life, appearing to move as though he were suspended underwater, projecting forward with an effortless grace. George's eyes looked up at the bright sky, fixated on the blue disparate clouds. He was determined to die with his head held high.

Riddled with bullets, George's eyes fell dark.

As his lifeless body slumped to the ground, Johnny Spain surrendered. Unable to break his gaze upon George, his brother in spirit, he put his hands up to the same azure above.[60]

The department had purposefully rerouted George's escape using a sophisticated plot involving correctional officers, colluding Aryan Brotherhood members, and C4 that would not fire. George and Johnny were forced into the courtyard, running straight into a well-placed firing squad that quietly waited for them to open the corridor gates.[61]

If the escape had gone according to plan, Jackson would have assumed leadership of the underground Black liberation movement. Once the C4 blew the corridor wall, the founders would have jumped into a getaway truck and used Black Liberation Army networks to make it to a safe house in New York City. New York City was chosen because it was the main Black Liberation Army stronghold. When the opportunity arose, the organization would smuggle Jackson to Cuba where he would continue to lead the underground movement. If escape to Cuba seemed too risky, Jackson would have continued to hide in plain sight in New York City, running the movement from a safe house.

But according to those involved in the plot, the escape was doomed from the start, poisoned by planted "snitches" and undercover correctional officers who divulged to the Department of Corrections and Federal Bureau of Investigation every move the Black Guerilla Family made.[62]

Ninety-nine books were found in George's cell after his murder.[63]

However, the officers involved were not able to anticipate everything. George's death planted seeds, and they blossomed in Attica, all the way across the country. The November 3, 1970, Folsom Manifesto drafted by founders of the Black Guerilla Family, and the legacy of the August 21, 1971, rebellion and escape attempt in San Quentin, would eventually inspire the September 9, 1971, Attica Uprising.[64] So much so that the Attica Liberation Faction reproduced the Folsom Manifesto almost verbatim when listing their demands.[65]

Two weeks after August 21, on September 9, 1971, the incarcerated at Attica State Prison in New York were inspired by George's murder, and initiated a revolt against a similar system of longstanding carceral apartheid—a protest against the state's ordained right to inflict social, civil, and physical death against incarcerated people.

On that fateful day, New York state troopers were determined to erase the memory of George Jackson and the Black Guerilla Family as they carried out a brutal public display. They deliberately executed the incarcerated and their hostages, with witnesses reporting them smiling, laughing, and joking as they did so. Their main goal was not to take back the prison, but instead to teach the incarcerated a lesson—never question your place in this world, for each breath you take is only possible because we allow it. The audacity of the incarcerated to claim manhood and humanity and then frame these claims in tandem with Black Power struggles earned them the barrel. And, the state troopers enjoyed every minute of it.[66]

PART IV

AFTERMATH

One day you'll wake up.
    The chains,
    Evaporated.
    Your breath,
    Liberated.

—BRITTANY FRIEDMAN

ADAPT TO SURVIVE

*I believe I'm going to die doing
the things I was born to do.*

—FRED HAMPTON

Black Guerilla Family founders were immediately put back into the most secure wing of San Quentin's Adjustment Center following the August 21, 1971, failed attempt to escape and save George. The next phase of their lives included some of the most brutal carceral apartheid practices ever recorded in California history. Anthony and Benjamin remembered being beaten with clubs while being called "n——" and described how much of the abuse at the hands of white officers happened during court transport procedures or within the Adjustment Center.

Six Black militants were charged with murder and felony charges related to the escape attempt, with Johnny Spain and Hugo Pinell among the men found guilty. Three were eventually acquitted, and together, they became known as the San Quentin Six.[1]

Like the Soledad Brothers, the San Quentin Six captivated the American public and were considered martyrs to some and violent Black terrorists to others. The six men adamantly fought their cases and faced an extreme intensification of the carceral apartheid regime—in the form of backlash—in the months leading up to and during their trials.

Benjamin described his experiences to me in intimate detail, with his wife walking in and out of their kitchen, listening and gently checking in on him. Sometimes, as she passed, she would place her hand on his shoulder, resting it for a few seconds to lightly lend a sign of reassurance, and then continue on with her household routines.

At one point, Benjamin began to cry. He placed his head between his hands while he whispered:

Interior of Building B, with light well to vent at road level, San Quentin State Prison (after 1933). Photograph by Robert A. Hicks. Historic American Buildings Survey Collection, Prints and Photographs Division, Library of Congress, Washington, DC.

Anthony and I got locked up in the court, in the holdup cell at the courthouse. We were both getting ready to go back to Quentin and they forgot to open the door . . . he comes grabbing me and banging me like that. He stepped in front of me, he opened up the damned door, snatched it up, bam! And knocked him (Anthony) out with a club. That's what kind of conditions happened. This happened at the courthouse in the holdup cell that we were in. So of course we felt there was no division between the court system and the prison system.

We felt they was part of the same thing. There was no justice in the prison, there was no justice in the courthouse. That's how we felt. . . .

After August 21st they had us kind of subdued somewhat. I remember being forced to crawl on my elbows and my knees. I'm on my elbows, my knees, the motherfuckers calling me n——. We are lying out there stripped on the yard and motherfuckers making racial tones. . . .

They go to take us upstairs. As they're taking you they're beating you and then when you get on the second floor, they are making you crawl on your knees and your elbows. And they're calling you n——s while they're on it. . . .

A lot of them guards they can't even whoop you in a one on one fight if it came down to that. But it's not about that, it's about control. They use as much force as they deem necessary to control the situation. They do it through intimidation of inmates. Because if a person is intimidated, then you don't have to worry about them as much, they're scared to react. They're scared. They will accept almost anything.[2]

Some founders described wishing for death after being repeatedly beaten, starved, shackled, and sexually assaulted by correctional officers in retaliation for founding the Black Guerilla Family and attempting to escape. Everyone interviewed emphasized the struggle of clinging to their political beliefs while enduring the torture alongside their brothers. But they claimed that this faith and solidarity were the reasons they were able to mentally survive such extreme extralegal control strategies.

As I sat with Benjamin, I hesitated to continue our conversation about the weeks following August 21, 1971, because I knew that he still carried the emotional scars of that day and its aftermath, even though his physical wounds had long healed. I paused and sat silently, looking down at his hands, doing my best to hold the space as one of compassion and learning.

He took a deep breath, as if he knew the next question I was going to ask. He squeezed his eyes shut, willing himself to speak.

More tears fell. Keeping his eyes closed, Benjamin hugged himself as he recounted Hugo's experiences. He recalled Hugo as a fellow founder that he was close to, and whose friends had affectionately nicknamed him "Yogi."

As Benjamin told it, Hugo was a key leader who was repeatedly raped by officers during his time in isolation and when he travelled to and from court in the San Quentin Six case, which was an act of vengeance for the August 21 escape attempt. This allegation was later substantiated by all of the other Black Guerilla Family founders, early recruits, and political activists from aligned movement organizations, both in prison and society.

Benjamin shook as he spoke, as though he was reliving Hugo's experience vicariously:

There was a lot of rage inside of us because of no respect, no justice. Some of the people that were involved in stuff were never indicted. . . . One I had the most empathy for was Yogi because Yogi used to get beat ruthlessly all the time. He had clubs stuck up his rectum and stuff and they got away with that shit.

Yogi had to go to court, so after August 21st they would take him and torture him. Lieutenant Nelson was involved in that torture. And Yogi would come back and sometimes we see him, he would have tears in his eyes, but he held on. They was able to do stuff in the back to him, the cops with trucks anyway. . . . I would imagine it's two hours maybe. However long it is, they would use it to their advantage.

This sergeant named Shane stuck a club up his rectum.

He told me that and that it was embarrassing for him as a man to tell me, another man, that they did that to him.

I didn't know what to do.[3]

White officers used extralegal control strategies such as rape to humiliate Black Guerilla Family founders and early members, including Hugo. Sexual assault was one of the officers' preferred torture methods, and it was routinely used against Black militants for at least a decade, as explained by the founders. Those perceived as having committed the most blasphemous affronts to white supremacy were at high risk for this particular racialized and gendered degradation. This type of violence escalated in the wake of Black militant efforts to formally organize themselves (e.g., W. L. Nolen's lawsuit and petition originating in Soledad, and the August 21st incident in San Quentin). Since Hugo was accused of murdering officers and members of the Aryan Brotherhood during the August 21 escape attempt, he fit this description and was brutally victimized by officers in an effort to destroy him psychically and physically.

Jerome personally experienced similar treatment. He was an early member of the Black Guerilla Family who recounted to me in an interview the sexual assault he endured and survived at the hands of officers, who targeted him as a result of his Black militant status. When I first met Jerome, we spent the majority of the time discussing his experience on the outside as a community advocate and the leader of a major prisoners' rights organization. I met his colleagues and toured their offices before he took me to a seminar room to finish our conversation in private. There were details Jerome wanted to discuss with me about his past that he did not feel comfortable describing with onlookers present.

As he turned on the light in the seminar room, he beckoned for me to sit and take off my jacket, asking if I had brought my recorder. I pulled out the recorder and he instructed me to turn it on while pulling up a chair adjacent to me, at the head of the long wooden table. He took several deep breaths before speaking, which resembled the types of breaths I do in daily meditations. It became apparent to me that Jerome was setting the space for himself to open up and do so from a grounded place. I soon understood why because almost immediately the topic of sexual assault emerged as a weapon of extra-legal control against Black militants.

Jerome continued to take deep breaths and lean his elbows heavily into the tabletop, crossing his fingers and rubbing his palms together. He slowly explained how he had survived his brutal sexual assault by clinging to his political training, viewing the experience through the lens of the carceral apartheid he encountered. This perspective helped him fight off the sinking feeling of worthlessness and self-blame that overtook him after his assault—feelings which he realized the officers had intentionally inflicted upon him.

Jerome was raped by white officers because a white woman visited him—a Black man + militant—in prison. Officers were particularly enraged by this visit. They used it as a justification, among many, to target him and make an example out of him for any other Black militants who would dare to even speak to a white woman—especially in front of the officers. For Jerome, this experience only solidified why Black militants needed the Black Guerilla Family as organized protection for Black self-defense and a platform for justifiable revenge against a department that not only overlooked this violence, but encouraged it.

I listened intently as Jerome struggled through his sobs to tell me how he survived the sexual assault:

> One day I'm on my way to visiting this person and it was the first time I ever got a visiting pass. To see a one on it, the first visitor. It was the first visitor who came to see me and that's a prideful thing when you're in prison. That somebody love you so much that they would come up and stand in that line, probably in the dark, to come visit you inside of a cage.
>
> And on my way to visit this person, being that she was white and I was black, they assumed or was vicious enough to lie and say they seen something in the middle of a skin search on the way to the visit.
>
> They drug me, on the way to the visit, to the hospital. Strapped me down on the bed and stuffed their hands up my ass looking for drugs.
>
> At that point in my life, I, as a result of my involvement with her, wrote a letter to Women Against Rape because it had been defined to me as an act of power as opposed to an act of sex. And everything that I was defining came out to be the same thing. It was the only organization that I knew that was concerned about rape.
>
> Because I figured that's what had occurred, no matter what they said.

And they said [Department of Corrections], they were calling it using euphemism and sophisticated terms to hide the brutal assault. "So we did a digital rectal search, we did this search, that search."

No, you did rape dog, because what you wanted to do was assert power. It wasn't about dope, it wasn't about environment, it's not about those things when they have every black man in the universe that comes to a system that makes you stand on one foot, touch your toes, squat, cough, bend.

It's not about that, it's about how you break the spirit. So that's what that shit was about. It's about how you break the spirit.

My activism picked up in a different way after that incident. And I became much more defined and focused in terms of my activism.[4]

As Jerome realized firsthand, his sexual assault was about power and racial domination because of his political beliefs. Furthermore, his association with a white woman violated white supremacy. The thought of a white woman even speaking with a Black militant, let alone their assumption it was possibly in a romantic manner, enraged the perpetrating officers.

Surviving this experience convinced Jerome that he belonged in the Black Guerilla Family.

A legal aid nonprofit sued the Department of Corrections in court on Jerome's behalf—the same organization that led the Soledad Brothers Defense Committee. Even with this attempt at justice through official legal channels, Jerome's dedication to the Black Guerilla Family intensified. He remained absolutely certain that an extralegal, militant opposition to carceral apartheid was the true vital savior for the survival of all Black incarcerated people.

Regarding the lawsuit, Jerome acknowledged: "I felt like I owed them [the nonprofit] in part for helping me because if they hadn't stepped forward and sued, I was looking for the guards to kill them."[5]

Jerome decided against attacking his assailants in retaliation, but maintained if anything like the assault ever happened again, he would die fighting back after killing the perpetrating white officers.

Prison officials battled a new wave of lawsuits following the intensification of carceral apartheid as backlash against Black militants for the August 21 escape attempt. In particular, members of the San Quentin Six experienced an unprecedented spike in violence, including: "Continuous segregation [for] 24 hours a day, the denial of fresh air and exercise, the use of tear gas to remove inmates from their cells . . . and neck chains for all inmates' out-of-prison movements."[6]

In 1973, the San Quentin Six sued the Department of Corrections for placing them in the San Quentin Adjustment Center for an indeterminate amount of time, shackling them with twenty-five-pound neck and waist chains during all out-of-cell movements, denying them outdoor exercise, beating them, and preventing them having contact with outside visitors.

The evidentiary hearing validates their accusations in vivid detail:

> Testifying in support of their entitlement to relief, plaintiffs described how they go to the AC, how they have been treated there, and the effect which such treatment has had on them. Physicians, including the Medical Director of the San Francisco County Jail and the Director of the Security Ward at San Francisco General Hospital, testified in support of plaintiffs' allegations that their health had been adversely affected by the conditions of their confinement.
>
> Two ex-guards who used to work in the AC testified in support of plaintiffs' allegations that guards have beaten, threatened, and harassed plaintiffs and other first tier AC prisoners, that prison reports are at times altered, and that the AC guards have a stereotyped view of plaintiffs and treat them in a dehumanizing fashion.
>
> A professor of pharmacology at Stanford University who is a tear gas expert described the nature and effects of tear gas. A prisoner who had been incarcerated in every portion of San Quentin testified that incarceration in the AC was the most debilitating. Mothers of two of the plaintiffs and two of plaintiffs' lawyers described the visiting difficulties and the effects visiting problems had on plaintiffs, their visitors, and their access to the courts.
>
> Psychiatric and psychological experts testified that AC conditions threaten the sanity of and dehumanize plaintiffs and have already damaged plaintiffs in a way that will only be fully known after they are released.[7]

While the department's first line of defense in the period following August 21 was prescribing isolation in the Adjustment Center, this time, Black militants were also shackled at the waist, neck, and ankles whenever they left their cells. For example, during Johnny Spain's trial, prison officials forced him to wear "leg irons, a waist chain to which each of his hands was bound by individual chains about eight inches long, and chains that apparently held him to his chair."[8]

Johnny described the great pain this dehumanizing treatment caused him in his suit against the department: "I could feel the pain before the chains were ever applied, and that is an hour or two hours before these chains were put on. I could feel those chains and the pain of it, two and three hours after they were removed when we returned to the prison. And in terms of pain, we are talking about 14 and 15 hours a day of having to deal with this. That consumed every aspect of my life at that point."[9]

However, Judges Cynthia Hall, Alex Kozinski, and John T. Noonan Jr. of the US Court of Appeals for the Ninth Circuit upheld the Northern District's original court ruling, arguing that Spain did, in fact, present a risk to the courtroom's physical safety, and that the chains were not unconstitutional.

These court cases reveal how prison officials combined indeterminate solitary confinement with various torture methods into carceral apartheid strategies that attempted to destroy the minds and bodies of Black Guerilla Family founders. These weapons were deployed to upend their original social movement foundation by any means necessary.

"I'm With George" and the State Criminalization of Politics

Prison officials were successful at rounding up the Black Guerilla Family's original founders and early members and segregating them in Adjustment Centers to decimate the founders' ability to control the direction of the organization. Those in solitary mainly used prison kites, or small notes held together with string that can fit through crevices, to pass messages to the general population and relied on trusted recruits to carry out the founders' original goals.

The founders did not anticipate the exponential spike in membership after George Jackson was killed on August 21, 1971. From 1970 to 1974, the organization's numbers exploded to nearly 1,000 people across the California prison system.[10] As a result, new cadres formed in other prisons, reaching beyond the original small interest groups that had been previously building in Folsom, Soledad, and Tracy.

The founders described the exponential growth as "deeply troubling," on the one hand, but a source of "inspiring potential," on the other. They lamented their inability to control the movement that they had spearheaded. It was inspiring that their escape attempt, and George Jackson's death, made them martyrs and prompted hundreds of Black incarcerated people across California to claim "I'm with George" and stand in solidarity. The drawback, they felt, was that the majority of these aspiring members would have to be vetted or put through the original membership program they had carefully cultivated. But that program had experienced a significant shock. Prison officials banned all of the ninety-nine books found in George's cell when he was murdered, and enforced the ban with the Adjustment Center for anyone caught reading or requesting those books.

Further, the original leadership was locked in twenty-four-hour isolation, unable to control how the organization moved forward and how new recruits were trained. This was problematic considering the massive influx in people claiming to be a part of the movement. Founders pointed to the significant fact that the department also relied heavily on planted snitches who claimed to be a part of the Black Guerilla Family, but reported to the administration instead. They targeted anyone who read or taught political ideology to other prisoners. Founders alleged, however, that a large portion of people who joined the new Black Guerilla Family—those who mainly wanted to participate in the prison contraband economy—were overlooked by the department-planted snitches. While there were new recruits who believed in the organization's original foundation, which placed them at significant risk for keeping the dragon alive, the department was, in fact, successful. Their early efforts kept the organization at odds using COINTELPRO-era extralegal strategies, sowing more confusion during this all-important growth stage.

Importantly, the Aryan Brotherhood and Mexican Mafia enjoyed relative political immunity from prison officials, even as the department systematically targeted all of the original Black Guerilla Family membership and locked them up, only a few managed to escape gang validation and stay in the general population. In the eyes of the department, the Black Guerilla Family was the most threatening "prison gang" and eventual "security threat group" in the state because of their proven aggression toward law enforcement. A 1974 FBI investigation echoes their concern: "From a review of the inmates in control and the leadership of the BGF, it readily becomes apparent that leaders have attained their rank due to their bloody backgrounds and history of violence . . . members of the BGF are hostile toward staff and tend to act out through aggressive behavior. Several staff members have been informed that they are in the way of the BGF."[11]

The FBI assisted prison officials in identifying the original membership so they could be placed in indeterminate solitary confinement.

Newly formed BGF cadres tended to operate autonomously and did not completely abide by regulations issued by the leadership, members of which were still locked up at San Quentin. Founders described in interviews how this inability to control the direction of the organization angered them and their loyal associates on the outside. They claim that by 1973, Black Guerilla Family cadres began entering the illicit contraband market, focusing a notable amount of energy on securing a stake in the prison economy, rather than planning the next Black militant revolution.

As Anthony put it, prison officials only allowed Black Guerilla Family cadres to function if they (1) did not publicly identify as BGF, and (2) if they focused on the illicit contraband market rather than putting significant time and resources behind plotting revolutions. He acknowledged that their political ideology remained unchanged, but he questioned the practical direction that the movement would take once he was forcibly removed from his leadership position by the department.[12]

Because the Mexican Mafia and Aryan Brotherhood operated without much department intervention at this time, both organizations continued to grow in size, expanding their control over various prison rackets. Seeing the Black Guerilla Family in distress, the Mexican Mafia and Aryan Brotherhood declared war on the organization in 1974, prompting the Nuestra Familia to come to their allies' defense:

> After George's assassination, the black progressive leaders in the BGF got locked up by the administration. Those with political consciousness, who kept the ship righted were taken out of the general population. So you have a lot of less aware people in control who were susceptible to falling victim to the gangs that the institution were orchestrating.
>
> After that, then a war broke out between the Mexican Mafia and Aryan Brotherhood against the Black Guerilla Family.
>
> For a period of time, the BGF comprised of the best people. Just anybody couldn't be a part of it. You had to be tried and tested and had to be political first and foremost. You had to embrace the principles that had been established. That is what George was talking about, the transformation of the mentality to a more revolutionary one. You had to have that kind of understanding to be a part of it.
>
> After a while it just changed, so that's why I stopped relating to it when they removed the main body of the political leadership. They left those that were less conscious who had not rejected the criminality that brought them into the institution.
>
> Now they are involved in predatory activities.[13]

As Anthony described the organization's turmoil and inner conflict, his biggest regret was being unable to fulfill the revolution he, George, and the other founders so passionately dreamed of. To this day, Anthony and Benjamin do not claim the Black Guerilla Family and only refer to themselves as "former members"; however, when it comes to contemporary Black Guerilla Family efforts that are aligned with the original political mission, both founders do claim those and point to them with hope for their original dream.

Both founders remember a turning point in 1974, when the original leadership proposed a summit between leaders of other cadres and the mid-level leadership in San Quentin. At the meeting, members circulated information to all leaders that the founders wanted the Black Guerilla Family to split into two organizations. The founders would form a new organization with a social movement focus and align its goals with the original Black Guerilla Family's purpose. This organization would be called the United Guerilla Front and would be aligned with the Black Guerilla Family, yet distinct. Original members loyal to the founders felt that the United Guerilla Front was necessary because the organization had dramatically evolved:

> The BGF was deteriorating and degenerating. We wanted the best people from the BGF to be in the UGF ... to try and reestablish the political principles since the leadership on the mainline was concerned with criminality. The new leadership wasn't interested in politics. They were more interested in trying to create a criminal organization. Their concerns and interests were into promoting criminal activities as opposed to political consciousness or advancement.
>
> For a period of time it was a clandestine organization and was meant to stay that way. But after it deteriorated, people started getting tattoos and identifying themselves with the organization. Now those tattoos validate locking them up.
>
> Like George said, you are not supposed to be marking yourself and telling everyone what you are about. You don't tell the enemy who you are. Now the system uses those symbols to validate locking people up as gang members. People are mad but they gave them justification to be locked up by telling them and showing themselves as a member of an organization.
>
> We used to see these younger members come in with all these tattoos and I used to ask, "Why are you doing that? If you want to embrace the principles of the organization, you are going against it by identifying yourself." Most didn't have a legitimate response because they didn't have the insight or the foresight to see how this was and could be eventually used to justify the continued segregation....
>
> Before there had been a set of principles and guidelines that governed the direction in which the organization was going and objectives. Progressive, positive, and geared toward being about a more just and equitable society free from racism, free of suppression, to promote the unity, harmony and development of a new society. Moving your people from being predators, dope dealers, pimps, and robbers to people who are interested in building up the society.[14]

The new leadership, which greatly outnumbered the original Black Guerilla Family, voted against the proposed split in the organization. Their biggest concern was that the fracture would hurt their recruitment efforts and weaken their political position within California prisons. Many people associated George Jackson with the Black Guerilla Family, and the organization could not afford to lose any members to a United Guerilla Front, considering their constant battles with the Mexican Mafia and the Aryan Brotherhood.

White officers were still using the Aryan Brotherhood as hitmen against Black militants, and the Black Guerilla Family in particular. Black political activists in society circulated flyers, such as this one found in Oakland, California, trying to publicize this alliance and garner support to save the Black Guerilla Family and what it stood for: "End California Dept. of Corrections support and collaboration with white supremacist prisoner organizations in their attack on black prisoners! Expose and defeat the Aryan Brotherhood, Ku Klux Klan, and Nazis! Fire Warden Sumner! End the lockdown! Stop the torture of black prisoners! We demand an investigation of institutionalized white supremacy at San Quentin! To be conducted by community organizations and ex-prisoners. End legal lynching . . . support the revolutionary prisoners' movement!"[15]

Even with an ongoing battle raging against many aligned enemies, the original leadership remained steadfast in the idea that the organization needed to split to save its political origins. Enraged by the decision to block the United Guerilla Front offshoot, some founders renounced the Black Guerilla Family, claiming, "That is when I withdrew from dealing with it, that ship couldn't be righted."[16]

Others refused to give up and tried to reroute the Black Guerilla Family's direction by force.

Carl was an early member and loyal to the founders. Carl acted as a hitman, executing Black Guerilla Family members and potential recruits that a subset of founders had deemed traitors to the original political causes. We talked many times in Southern California over meals and coffee, and on one such occasion, after knowing one another for a year, Carl opened up about his role:

> At that point there was a drug element that was associated with dominating for a period of time. They wanted to function with the mafia leaders in terms of those that are in control, so there was a lot of conflict as a result. Internal conflict as well as conflict outside the structure related to drugs.
>
> It took some time to weed all that out. Weed out what's referred to as "old guard" and allow the original intent of the structure under the leadership of George Jackson and others, what their original intent was, and

that was to build a political, revolutionary style organization. To align themselves with the politics that existed in the community related to the liberation movement....

I would say that the late '70s, early '80s, was where most of the turmoil existed internally. Trying to weed out those that were intent on seeing this being a structure that controlled drugs....

There was both elements that I came to be made aware of. Those that were intent on using this for monetary reasons through the use of drugs and those that were interested in seeing a political foundation develop and have an impact on the liberation struggle in prison and outside the walls.[17]

Carl also claimed that much of the drug trafficking occurred in Northern California cadres, with the exception of San Quentin. He, along with others, claimed that the Southern California cadres were able to maintain the original political structure for longer, though they still eventually folded into drug trafficking, much to the delight of the Department of Corrections:

If you were living in Northern California and you came to prison, then you would gravitate towards one faction. If you lived in Southern California, then that was the more politically correct structure. There wasn't a solid dichotomy between the two. It's just generally, that's what it was because a lot of the brothers that I had relationships with were brothers from Northern California....

Brothers came down from San Quentin where the responsibility could be shown that the political structure was developing correctly. One of them, who was part of the leadership, had got to know me pretty well. Those leadership responsibilities transferred to me. I continued to push that line along until I was locked up ... stayed in the SHU for approximately four years before I was released from prison.[18]

Prison officials directed wardens and their officers to purposefully police Black militants, as they had done for decades. This progressed into successfully infiltrating the Black Guerilla Family with double agents, criminalizing Black political activity to incentivize participation in the illicit prison economy, and ignoring long-standing white officer collusion with the Aryan Brotherhood against Black militants.

While the landscape of the prison system and the shape of the Black Guerilla Family organization transformed after the murder of George Jackson, official, clandestine, and extralegal carceral apartheid strategies of control and warfare against the imprisoned Black population continued to be documented in the 1980s and beyond.[19]

GUERILLA

> In every human Breast, God has implanted a Principle,
> which we call Love of Freedom; it is impatient of
> Oppression, and pants for Deliverance.
>
> —PHILLIS WHEATLEY

The durability and intensification of carceral apartheid forced the Black Guerilla Family to adapt and transform, well before the height of mass incarceration. Even though it was battling upheaval, the Black Guerilla Family would remain a revolutionary political voice for the Black imprisoned population in California for decades to come—the frontline defense against the ongoing war on the Black population, particularly the targeting of Black militants. It still serves this function today, in California and beyond, even though there are questions about its current form and trajectory in other states. By designating the organization as "security threat group public enemy number one," deliberately sowing dissent among the members, and continuing to privilege the Aryan Brotherhood, the California Department of Corrections succeeded in effectively decimating its original foundation, at least for a number of years.

In forcing the Black Guerilla Family to adapt to survive, the department purposefully incentivized what remained of the social movement to reorganize into an organization reliant in part on illicit prison economy revenue in California and, eventually, nationwide. This adaptation did not mean that the Black Guerilla Family was no longer a social movement, but rather that the state criminalization of politics pushed a subset of the organization into practices contrary to its original purpose. These new practices were used by that faction to attain both monetary and political goals. And most importantly, the Black Guerilla Family's internal battles and the war it faced with the Department of Corrections made it much easier for the Mexican Mafia and Aryan Brotherhood to nearly destroy what remained of the organization by the late 1970s and early 1980s.

Even still, another battle loomed on the outside. This was the fact that the Black Guerilla Family was also reeling from a very public brutal attack on Fay Stender, one of George Jackson's biggest supporters and the lead lawyer on the Soledad Brothers Defense Committee. In 1979, a recently paroled man—claiming to be a member of the Black Guerilla Family—broke into Fay's home and shot her several times. Before he shot her, the gunman forced her to write, "I, Fay Stender, admit I betrayed George Jackson and the prison movement when they needed me most!" She was paralyzed from the waist down due to her debilitating wounds. It was a devastating loss to the Bay Area prisoners' rights community when Fay eventually committed suicide a year later.[1]

The original Black Guerilla Family leadership was outraged over what happened to Fay Stender. Founders alleged that a faction within the transformed Black Guerilla Family was complicit because those members felt Fay did not do enough to help George Jackson and prevent his murder. There were claims that, after he was gunned down in 1971, the organization felt she had effectively washed her hands of the prison movement. She left the movement in 1973, which is true. However, it's noteworthy that the new leadership did not claim responsibility for the attack and did not speak out publicly against her, leaving a mysterious trail of allegations and disagreements as to who was truly behind her brutal targeting.

Anthony, as an original founder, described this event as "unfortunate, senseless violence," and noted how it caused an even bigger split within the Black Guerilla Family.[2] Others expressed similar feelings, and felt Fay had never betrayed the prison movement. Founders remember retaliating against the new leadership by killing a few of their trusted associates.[3] That was meant to show them that not just anybody could claim to act in the name of the Black Guerilla Family.

Behind bars, the Department of Corrections used Fay's 1979 attack as evidence that every Black Guerilla Family member should be discovered and placed in indeterminate isolation.[4] And by the 1980s, the racist and politically orchestrated War on Drugs was raging in full swing, causing the incarcerated population in California, especially Black people, to skyrocket.

Aaron, a former leader of the Crips in San Quentin, described to me in an interview that the Crips and Bloods were the new Black organizations on the scene. They quickly assumed majority control of the drug trade inside prisons, giving them a formidable leadership role within the Black population.

Their numbers would eventually surpass those of the Black Guerilla Family, though they still maintained their identity as a street organization, first and foremost, and not as a prison-based organization. Aaron suggested the Black Guerilla Family was a symbolic figurehead from the Black Power era to these new flows of incarcerated individuals, and he clocked their lack of interest in being part of the past.

Aaron, who entered prison in the early 1980s, put it bluntly:

> The original BGF, and I had to preface that because right now, although there still are BGF members on the mainline, most of the BGF are isolated in the SHU (Secure Housing Unit). You get locked up just for being a BGF. They have a bunch that makes it into the general population that the administration lets hang out because their values have deteriorated to such an extent that they're no different than street gang members.
>
> My relationship with the BGF has always been respect and also I step cautiously with them guys.
>
> They didn't like the fact we were Crips. We saw our enemies as Bloods. Fellow Africans.
>
> They were cautious with how they dealt with us. We had an agreement. They did their thing, we did our thing. We didn't do anything to arouse or to provoke them because they're the BGF, the biggest prison gang in the state of California. Most blacks pay homage, including the Crips, to the BGF, the original ones. Mainly because that's our leaders. . . .
>
> When it comes to racial issues, that's really when the BGF will step up. Tensions between another race, you know it's going to be them that's going to make the call. Is this going to be a race riot? Is this not? They make the call.
>
> Inner conflicts among African Americans, they usually are the ones that act as buffers between the Crips and Bloods. Not wanting to see any black blood being shed.
>
> Before anything happens, they're usually given the opportunity to either speak up or let it go.[5]

Though the Black Guerilla Family had a say in racial disputes, Aaron stressed that, ultimately, the Crips and Bloods maintained a high level of autonomy and gained considerable traction within the Black population. He described to me how both organizations would attack the Black Guerilla Family if they attempted to meddle too much in their affairs. Aaron's point was to highlight the Black Guerilla Family's waning political ability to exert complete sovereignty over the Black population in the 1980s, like they had in the years prior since their founding.

This fact was considered a win for the Department of Corrections and their imprisoned white supremacist allies.

Aaron remembered needing to order attacks against the Black Guerilla Family in order to prevent them from "overstepping" on Crips' affairs in San Quentin. This was especially the case if the Black Guerilla Family refused to accept the feuding between the Crips and Bloods, and tried to forcefully maintain an incarcerated Black alliance:

> Most times though, they don't interfere with our stuff.... They don't like it. They try to get us to stop. What has happened in history is they've tried to act as inter-mediators between the two and conflict was with them.
>
> Caused conflict and we actually had armed resistance against the BGFs. We had to stab some of them while they stabbed some of us. Matter of fact, I had a couple of buddies killed by the BGF's because of that. So they pretty much ended up avoiding getting involved with our conflicts....
>
> By the time we came on board, they [BGF] were the ones setting down the law.
>
> We just decided we weren't going to listen to the law.[6]

Importantly, during this era, the Crips and Bloods were fighting over territory on the streets of Los Angeles, specifically, and Southern California, more broadly. This made a secure Black alliance in prison difficult to maintain when members were incarcerated. Aaron did provide some nuance, noting that, when other racial groups attacked the Black population in San Quentin, all Black people would stand together and fight. However, the ongoing feuding between Crips and Bloods, coupled with internal struggles that the Black Guerilla Family was dealing with as it grew and changed, made it very difficult to develop and foster trust within the Black population. This same sense of community seemed like a relic from the version of the Black Guerilla Family that existed prior to and shortly after George Jackson's murder in 1971.

Aaron adds to claims from founders, early members, and activists that, by the mid-1980s, the Black Guerilla Family was coerced by the Department of Corrections to adapt into a new organization that struggled to maintain political control over a fragmented Black population. In addition, the organization was still constantly at war with the Aryan Brotherhood and Mexican Mafia—much to the delight of officers. To the Department of Corrections, it must have seemed that the organization would fail from the inside out. All they had to do was sit and wait and stoke the fires of dissent like a Machiavellian war tactic.

Bill, a retired Department of Corrections sergeant with over thirty years of experience validating and investigating "security threat groups," described to me in an interview that law enforcement considered the Black Guerilla Family the most hostile organization. This put them above the Aryan Brotherhood, Mexican Mafia, and Nuestra Familia in terms of priority for infiltration and decimation. And as a result, Black militants needed surveillance and segregation in Adjustment Centers, and they were eventually shipped to the Secure Housing Unit (SHU) at Pelican Bay State Prison from 1989 onward.[7] Bill's sentiment was echoed in a memo that the warden of San Quentin sent to department heads back in 1971, which read: "I am witnessing the deterioration of our ethnic organizations, which were once dedicated to the education improvement of our men inside San Quentin, to paramilitary organizations with revolutionary overtones."[8]

Bill was well-versed in the Department of Corrections' official narrative of the Black Guerilla Family and had spent decades developing "security threat group" protocols and educating officers about the dangers of Black militants and how to identify them in the general population. When I told him I was researching the Black Guerilla Family, he laughed and asked, "Why would you do that?" He implied that law enforcement agencies and think tanks had already produced a wealth of information on the organization, describing it as nothing more than a "political prison gang" so additional research was not warranted.[9]

Bill explained how, in the department's point of view, Black militant groups required the development of a more rigorous validation system, one in which the department was simply reacting to a viable threat:

Back in the 1970s, inmates were being identified just by associating with another inmate.

In the late 1980s the CDC (department) devised a gang management policy where it required three sources on one inmate to identify him as being in a gang: self-admitted, a tattoo, or corresponding with another validated person. We could use those three sources and validate that guy.

Prior to that, we would just identify by association.

When you lock someone up you are taking away his liberties, his freedom in terms of being incarcerated.

When you lock a person up and identify him, you are removing him from the general population and placing him in ADSEG (administrative segregation/secure housing unit) where he only gets out of his home one hour a day.

But if a guy is identified as a threat he will be restrained every time he gets out of his cell.[10]

Bill was adamant that the Black Guerilla Family would kill officers if the department did not have policies in place to identify, surveil, and restrain them and, ideally, disrupt their ability to organize. As I was very curious about his experience with other prisoner organizations, I asked him to contrast the department's treatment of the Black Guerilla Family to other groups. After all, Bill had eventually labeled multiple organizations as "security threat groups" using the validation system that he helped build over the course of his career.

I questioned, "Why wasn't the Aryan Brotherhood significantly targeted [by the department] until the 1980s?"

Bill chuckled again at this question and responded by narrating an incident that occurred in the federal system in 1983, when a member of the Aryan Brotherhood killed a correctional officer. He replied to me boldly, "Well, have you ever heard of Marion? They got too big for their britches."[11]

Bill explained how, after the Marion incident in the federal system, the Aryan Brotherhood was put on the radar of state correctional systems, including the Department of Corrections in California.

This turn of events suggests that the officers were reevaluating their once secret ally, which they depended on to handle their Black militant problem as prison officials continued to overlook it. Now, the Aryan Brotherhood seemed like a potential threat to the sovereignty of the entire carceral apartheid structure, as it had been given too much privilege.

"White above all" is, in fact, structurally contingent, and alliances can shift if elite incarcerated groups, which have been given an intermediary status, are seen as falling out of line or trying to subvert those at the top of the political hierarchy. The Department of Corrections was helmed by the bosses and correctional officers, and sometimes all of the incarcerated population needed to be reminded of the colloquialism of, "Don't bite the hand that feeds you."

Still, Black people who had been validated as members of "security threat groups" continued to receive harsher sentences and are more likely to face prison discipline, including isolation in secure housing units or SHUs, which Chapter Two documents were contemporary versions of the Adjustment Centers first conceptualized by the department in 1953.[12]

Fareed Nassor Hayat, a legal scholar, documents how people who are validated by law enforcement using security threat group and street gang databases are prosecuted more harshly because they face both criminal and gang statutes. This results in being tried multiple times for the same offense, which he argues is in violation of double jeopardy protections. Hayat also points out the dearth of prosecutions against white supremacist organizations using the same tactics.[13] Hayat's work, along with the research of other scholars such as sociologist Patrick Lopez-Aguado, and the research in *Carceral Apartheid*, supports the need to abolish security threat group and street gang databases, and gang statutes altogether.[14] This unequal persecution supports the state's history of warfare against Black communities in particular, and non-white communities more broadly.

"It's All Sport to Them"

By 1989, the department opened Pelican Bay and promptly transferred each validated leader of the Black Guerilla Family to supermax confinement. The August 21, 1971, escape attempt was brought up time and time again by prison officials and state legislators as they lobbied to finally solve California's alleged Black militant problem. The supermax facility that had been newly constructed—in part, for this purpose—was their latest attempt at controlling the Black Guerilla Family and other organizations like it.[15] Extralegal and official control strategies—all of which privileged racial violence, conflict, and oppression—effectively set the stage for California to justify prisoner racial segregation and extreme isolation units. It is the only supermax or administrative maximum (ADX) institution in California, and the main objective is to secure incarcerated individuals in long-term housing units (C and D units), confining them to solitary confinement twenty-three hours per day, seven days a week in the SHU. It also has two maximum security units and a small minimum security unit for the incarcerated orderlies who maintain the prison.

Hugo Pinell was quickly transferred to Pelican Bay and became one of its most famous "residents," along with other notable Black militants the department claimed to validate as Black Guerilla Family members. The few original leaders who had diligently worked for years to maintain their anonymity managed to avoid Pelican Bay.

The Black militants transferred to Pelican Bay shared a common history of decades battling the official, extralegal, and often clandestine control strategies of carceral apartheid. It's impossible to overstate the centrality of the Adjustment Center to this experience. As this book has shown, Adjustment Centers were the precursors to Pelican Bay and the original site of indeterminate housing in isolation for Black militants in California.

A 2017 letter by Abdul Olugbala Shakur illuminates this arc and connects the dots:

Over 30 years ago I was placed in the dungeon cell in the infamous Adjustment Center.

Over 90 days of complete darkness, no running water, butt naked, no mattress/blankets and sheets, with cold air blowing from the vent, not to mention the constant company of the roaches and rats. This was both my introduction and initiation into the sarcophagus vortex of solitary confinement and isolation.

Thirty-two years fighting the demons conjured up by a tormented mind, contorting within the confines of a man-made hell, a concrete hell that is designed to suffocate the spirit and paralyze the mind.

Twenty-five of those 32 years were spent in the notorious Pelican Bay State Prison [supermax], where it is easy to forget what the sun looks and feels like, even the moon and stars become distant memories. One even forgets what it feels like to walk on dirt and grass, let alone touch it with our hands.

After so many years of sensory deprivation, it becomes easy to make friends with the critters that stalk our concrete coffins in search of their own humanity in an artificial world not of their making....

I was the most censored prisoner in the CDCR.... Both my placement and retention in solitary was political.[16]

Importantly, once Pelican Bay opened in California in 1989, it wasn't just Black militants—like Hugo—who were quickly shipped there. It also became a breeding ground for correctional officers who set up the incarcerated for gladiator fights, labeled incarcerated people as snitches to get them killed, and placed bets on their lives. These were familiar tactics they had used on imprisoned Black militants for decades. At Pelican Bay, the supermax culture of extreme isolation empowered officers to feel freer to escalate their engagement with these extralegal strategies.

The department soon started shipping leaders of the Aryan Brotherhood and other white supremacist organizations there, too, in addition to leaders of the Mexican Mafia and Nuestra Familia.

As a validated member of a white supremacist organization, Andrew remembers his experience with the SHU at Pelican Bay in the 1990s with rage toward the Department of Corrections. By that time, the official and extralegal control tactics of carceral apartheid that were institutionalized and perfected on Black militants for decades had become routine practices against those in the SHU, even white supremacists like Andrew. Twenty-three hours a day of isolation was the norm, and setups like gladiator fights were an unfortunate weekly occurrence—sometimes nightly—used to entertain and amuse the officers and promote division among the incarcerated. For the officers, it seemed like a win-win.

Andrew spent almost two years in the Pelican Bay SHU. He grimaced, shuddered, and broke into tears while describing his time there. He survived being set up in a gladiator fight against members of the Nuestra Familia:

> They had me transferred to Pelican Bay Security Housing Unit. . . . They put me in the D unit, in D1. When they brought me off the bus this big ole' giant Mexican guy, a lieutenant pulled me aside, slammed me up against the wall, almost broke my nose. And told me, "You think you're an escape risk, you think you can escape from here, go ahead and try, motherfucker you're never gonna get out of this SHU alive. This is your last stop. You're gonna die in here. You've got a life sentence. You're never gonna see the outside again. . . ."
>
> Over the period of time approximately a year, year and a half that I was locked up in there from 1991 to late 1992–1993, every night the cops would set up gladiator fights amongst the inmates. They would bring an inmate to the opening of the eight-cell pod. They had several pods in the building, in each wing, 1–7, D1–D7. And they would bring an inmate there in his leg, arms, and belly chains. You do not leave your cell unless you're in leg, arm, and belly chains unless you are going to the pod door.
>
> They'd open the food slot on that door and take off your belly chains and crack the door a little bit and take off his leg iron or maybe the leg irons first and the belly chains second.
>
> And then there would be a door opened and the inmate knew that they were bringing them here for a gladiator fight. And he knew that whatever cell door opened is where he's going. He would walk up to that cell door and you would hear fist pumping and tennis shoes squeaking and then all the inmates in the pod would start flushing their toilets trying to cover up the fight between the inmates so that the guard in the tower doesn't hear, because they [tower guards] can't see that the [other guards] just set up a gladiator fight.
>
> Because I'm the one in the closest cell and I can see it. And I'm standing with my back against the wall peeking so they can't see me peeking. Because if they see me peeking, I'm done for. I'm a witness.
>
> But I'm hearing them laughing and joking and patting each other on the back and betting and all kinds of crap all while this is going on.
>
> It's like this. You're either going to go up to that cell and fight, and potentially fight to the death because you don't know what weapon that guy might've just made up there or has standing by.

You don't know if in the fight, surrounded by nothing but concrete and a steel toilet and steel walls that's got three thousand six hundred and thirty blocks in it that you can have your head bashed up against. Or the steel posts holding it together. Or the concrete bunks.

You don't know if this guy's gonna knock you out, do something vicious like open up your mouth and pop it on the edge of that concrete and just smash his foot in the back of your head breaking your jaws and your teeth out of your mouth. Something that's been known to be done.

It's just the extraordinarily excess violence and potential death was something you lived with every minute of every day in that place. And I saw potentially being set up every night.

What would happen is these guys would get in a fight. They would beat each other up, the cops would then come in with all their riot gear, what we called "booted and suited." Because they've got armor plated shin guards, thigh guards, torso guards, got helmets on, front shields, face shields. They've got steel batons, they've got fire extinguisher sized canisters of mace and they'll come up and they'll hose everybody down through the holes.

And then they'll go in there and beat the crap out of these two guys, hog tie and gas 'em, and bring them out and then routinely, face down, picking them up by the belly chain and leg chains and the chain that's now running between the belly chain and the leg chain. Three guys on either side.

There's stairs going up to the second floor that had teeth on them, so you wouldn't lose your footing as the correctional officers would go up and down. More for them than for us.

But for them, it was a nice little platform for to try to ram the inmate down onto as they're taking them down the stairs. And if you didn't hold your head up right, your head may hit it, your teeth, whatever. So not only are you getting the shit beat out of you by this guy, but now the cops are beating the shit out of ya.

It's all sport to them.[17]

Andrew's detailed account of ritualistic abuse, corruption, and gladiator fights reveals the long-term consequences of carceral apartheid on correctional accountability and the sheer collective enjoyment that comes from state violence. Because officers were allowed—and even encouraged—to routinely commit torturous offenses against Black militants, over time, those same officers, and the control strategies they espoused, became invincible.

Prison culture had already reduced incarcerated people from human beings to mere disposable numbers. But carceral apartheid made it clear to officers that their charges weren't just numbers, but their animals, and at the mercy of correctional will.

Legacy

But the Black Guerilla Family's founding mission wasn't extinguished in the Pelican Bay SHU. They continued to resist. In 2012, something notable happened, something that members of the Black Guerilla Family had hoped for since they founded the organization: cross-racial mobilization around a prisoner class. It superseded the department's fifty-year-long effort to keep them fighting each other in a race war, deliberately placing Black militants at the bottom of the political hierarchy.

The leaders of the four major prisoner organizations banded together to initiate a series of hunger strikes across prisons in the state. Their attorneys released statements about how these leaders sat in isolation units in Pelican Bay and, after years, eventually became conscious of the fact that all of their enemies had ended up right beside them in the SHU, many eventually subjected to the same fates. These men followed with a joint lawsuit against the department.

When one of the lead plaintiffs was asked about how the Department of Corrections had routinely dehumanized people in isolation, he responded: "From the deprivation, keeping us from our families and our loved ones, harassing our mail, everything—the severe isolation, lack of stimulation, lack of education opportunities, rehabilitative opportunities, lack of decent food, proper medical treatment. Lack of just human dignity."[18]

Another stated amidst tears that: "I be wanting to write the judge and say 'just give me the death penalty, just give me the death penalty.' Everything around you becomes numb. . . . I would like to hope that the SHU will shut down. I don't think that no human being should have to live in that SHU as long as we have had to live in that SHU."[19] While a third lead plaintiff rightly called the Pelican Bay SHU "psychological low-intensity warfare against the mind of a human being," a fourth described solemnly the deliberate removal of sunlight and access to the outdoors for decades.[20]

Filed May 31, 2012, *Ashker v. Governor of California* was a federal class action lawsuit on behalf of prisoners held in Pelican Bay's Security Housing Unit (SHU) who had spent a decade or longer in solitary confinement. They claimed that prolonged solitary confinement constituted cruel and unusual punishment and violated the Eighth Amendment of the Constitution, and they accused the CDCR of using an arbitrary protocol to sentence prisoners to the SHU, which further violated their rights to due process. On August 12,

2012, these leaders also released a historic statement called the Agreement to End Hostilities. An excerpt reads: "We can no longer allow CDCR to use us against each other for their benefit!! Because the reality is that collectively, we are an empowered, mighty force that can positively change this entire corrupt system into a system that actually benefits prisoners, and thereby, the public as a whole."[21]

Several of the lawsuit's plaintiffs were leaders in their respective organizations, and many of them participated in hunger strikes that had been initiated by people incarcerated in the SHU in 2011 and 2013. This historic lawsuit signaled widespread unity among historically adversarial, enemy prisoner organizations, such as the Black Guerilla Family, Aryan Brotherhood, Mexican Mafia, and Nuestra Familia, all of whom had rallied around the question of prisoners' rights. The long-term vision of the Black Guerilla Family's 1970 founding was realized once again despite the decades-long war the Department of Corrections had waged to prevent it.

The department fought the historic lawsuit, arguing that the SHU and supermax confinement in general were an essential component of penal policy, which had been designed to reduce disturbances and increase public safety.

In fact, carceral apartheid intensified as retaliation for cross-racial mobilization against the department.

Roughly four years after the 2011 and 2013 hunger strikes, and the 2012 Agreement to End Hostilities, on August 12, 2015, Hugo was murdered in a fashion similar to his Black militant brothers who were slain before him. Hugo was stabbed to death by members of the Aryan Brotherhood, two weeks after his release from isolation in the SHU to the general population.[22] In the wake of Hugo's slaying, much of the work of prisoner-led efforts to foster cross-racial mobilization against the department broke down. Despite incarcerated witnesses and a wrongful death lawsuit filed by Hugo's family against the department for employing the tried-and-true official and extralegal tactics, the Department of Corrections has yet to comment on the allegations. Hugo's murder strategically enlivened racial animus and distrust among the incarcerated population, spurring waves of chaos that threatened to upend the years of organizing that went into the Ashker lawsuit.

Very quickly after Hugo's murder, the Ashker lawsuit was settled September 1, 2015. Plaintiffs, their attorneys, and activists held onto the hope that it would end indeterminate solitary confinement in California SHUs and dramatically reduce the number of people kept in isolation given this ruling: "Pursuant to the Settlement Agreement, the CDCR shall not place inmates into a SHU, Administrative Segregation, or Step Down Program solely on the basis of their validation status."[23]

However, indeterminate isolation has continued in California to the present in 2024, and it continues to be used against those who signed the Agreement to End Hostilities, with the department using their resistance to carceral apartheid to justify continual confinement in the SHU. Prisoners' rights activists have touted the aftermath of the settlement as a major failure and continue to document the ongoing degradation and violations within the prison system, including the department's continued stubborn use of the SHU.[24]

The illusion of American progress has led to the continued torture, genocide, and caging of humans in the darkest corners imaginable at home and around the world—human beings our government wishes we would all simply forget.

CONCLUSION: INVITATION TO AWAKEN

For the dreamers who see beyond the veils
For the lovers who move with integrity
For the liberators who catalyze
For freedom.

—BRITTANY FRIEDMAN

Carceral apartheid never sleeps, but just like with any golem, we can create the means to dismantle it and the pathways to build the structures needed to thrive. Conflict energy is a natural response to change whether the light is incremental or revolutionary. And often, conflict energy is a distraction designed to blind us and glamor us away from the very real opportunities for a new world that currently exist. The old world, which is based on the illusion of freedom and the desire to control fate, is fading away yet still fighting to maintain an imperious stronghold under the guise of both democratic capitalism and communism.

If we look closely, however, there is a new world being built. One that prioritizes love, human and nature connection, joy, and ultimately healing on a collective level. A world that rejects the old paradigm of extraction, division, commodification, and ultimately the strategic promotion of psychic, social and physical death of the masses for the benefit of an elite few. It is free of the "isms" that have promised a brighter future, but instead decayed into totalitarianism, violence, and greed.

Abolitionist dreams are not fantasies but concrete realities that both exist and are in the making. As Historian Robin D. G. Kelley reminds us, "freedom dreams" have taken many forms and philosophies, but all are ultimately visions of future worlds for the here and now.[1]

At the root of carceral apartheid is the desire to maintain control of the past, present, and future at all costs—it is a quest for total power. This desire thrives with false promises of inclusion and prosperity for those who will keep the faith. But we can reject this introduction to fate. Where we focus our intention, our creative energy, herein lies the key to the new world and whether the introduction to fate will hold or crumble in the wake of a world that now prioritizes the heart over fear. But the counterfeit dreams, ideologies, and patriotic saviors that have come before, that spin lies through the media, propaganda history books, national anthems, and pledges of allegiance, are at the edge of their reign.

"It is only after slavery and prison that the sweetest appreciation of freedom can come," in the words of Black intellectual leader Malcolm X.[2] After many rounds of this dance with death, we are at a precipice, an invitation to awaken. If we only look, we will see the fruits of many visions in the form of community-led justice, cross-racial coalitions, and what abolitionist geographer Ruth Wilson Gilmore terms "life-giving institutions."[3] She further teaches us that "where life is precious, life is precious."[4]

Our invitation to awaken demands an end to the heteropatriarchy, criminalization, racism, and surveillance that creates the conditions upon which carceral apartheid thrives domestically and globally. We will no longer be introduced to a fate bought and paid for with lies, white supremacy, and ultimately social control. Instead, we rewrite the past, create a new present, and envision a future where true joy is based in radical love and compassion, not profit and chasing fleeting highs.

This is a reality where the sanctity of connection and life in the natural world—the divine grace of the earth and creation—is the currency of our hearts.

APPENDIX

TRUTH-TELLING AS METHOD

People have risked their lives, survived torture, been imprisoned, and died to save information the state has sought to destroy. Truth-telling as method is a practice of discovery, of rebuilding that which has been attacked, and of digging in the dark corners of our society to reveal the hidden. Black feminists have been doing this work for centuries, weaving together histories and creating methods for revolution. Truth-telling as method has taught me that without access to key records and oral histories, the state can prevent us from fully theorizing the reality of racist intention that is rooted in the operation and structure of entire systems and institutions, rather than solely the individual racism of a few bad actors. If we could hear the backroom conversations, see the secret letters, texts, and covert emails, then we would not be debating the theoretical necessity of centering racist intent, even in a contemporary world that, at times, feels colorblind.

For example, when whistleblowers exposed emails that proved the mid-2010s coordinated effort by government officials to poison the water of Black communities in Flint, Michigan; or when whistleblowers leaked hidden correspondence and directives proving the 1932–72 orchestration—in part by the Centers for Disease Control—of the Tuskegee Syphilis Study, once again the deliberate destruction of and declaration of war by the state on the Black community was revealed in the light of truth. Cover-ups, clandestine activities, whistleblowers, and intentionality should be central to our sociological understanding of racism in the United States as foundational to the continual facilitation of imperial rule over the descendants of chattel slavery. As scholars, truth-telling as method is a process of catharsis, of raising lies up from the dead, and of dreaming a new reality in their wake.

The work of sociologists is to aid in the "reckoning" that occurs as a result of truth-telling. As a mentee of sociologist John Hagan, I was always encouraged to keep pushing and to not back down, as Hagan demonstrated himself in his coauthored book on the police torture cover-ups in Chicago orchestrated by Chief John Burge and Mayor Richard M. Daley or in his coauthored book on genocide in Darfur.[1] Through the mentorship of sociologist Aldon Morris, I learned to reject others' fear-based projections onto my work and stand true in my convictions, as Morris does in his book centering W. E. B. Du Bois as a founder of the discipline of sociology.[2] From the encouragement of sociologist Nicole Gonzalez Van Cleve, also a mentee of Hagan and Morris, I felt motivated to tell the truth about what I discovered despite knowing that those in positions of power would not like what I had to say—just as Gonzalez Van Cleve does in her book exposing the real crooks (i.e., legal actors and police) of Chicago's Cook County.[3] Through the mentorship of sociologist Mary Pattillo, I learned to ground myself and to be fearless in my research. At Northwestern University's Department of Sociology, there is a legacy of faculty and former students dedicated to truth-telling as method. And from my dear friendship and writing exchange with sociologist Michael Sierra-Arévalo, I was encouraged to stay in my power and to never lose my authentic voice, as he maintains in his work on policing and its culture of violence.[4] Supporting the collective reckonings happening within our society is a key part of our methodological work as sociologists, and building conscious communities who support this vision is essential to maintaining "staying power" and subverting white supremacist conventions in our discipline.

In her chapter "The Black Feminist Roots of Scholar Activism," sociologist Shaonta' E. Allen beautifully details how sociological research within this vein "could and should facilitate social action."[5] *Carceral Apartheid* takes up this call as a historical ethnography, meaning I use life history interviews to invigorate and triangulate archival sources with the goal of producing both social facts (patterns and themes) and historical facts (dates, places, events, and people). I identify deceased persons by name, but in line with sociological methods and ethics, I use pseudonyms for living persons. It is important for historical sociologists to "think like an ethnographer," in the words of sociologists Armando Lara-Millán, Brian Sargent, and Sunmin Kim.[6] This is particularly true for studies of Black life that are often muddled with white notions of history and patriotism, as noted by sociologist Marcus Hunter in "Black Logics, Black Methods."[7] Notably, Hunter, Lara-Millán, and Sargent also trace their intellectual legacies to Northwestern's Department of Sociology, along with other fearless truth-tellers like sociologists Carla Shedd, Robert Vargas, and Jean Beaman.

Carceral Apartheid continues this tradition to deliver a timely social critique. In its pages, I ask readers to journey through a land of control outside the purview of everyday life and take the lessons learned to understand how these patterns govern free society, first and foremost, even before they ever permeate prison walls. I implore readers to use all their senses to understand this regime, as reflected in my method and writing style, in the spirit of what I and sociologist Michael L. Walker term "intuitive social science": "An ontological, epistemological, and methodological stance that takes seriously sentiment and mood through sensing transparencies (touch, taste, sight, sound, and smell) married to imagination and intuition as heuristics. . . . Indeed, sentiment and mood are elemental contributions to knowledge, not novelties to be trotted out for more poetic writing. . . . Philosophies of race and racism . . . are woven throughout the preference for mechanical writing and against intuitive social science."[8]

To build what historian Kelly Lytle Hernández describes as a "rebel archive" was an incredible undertaking that took a decade to complete and write up.[9] At the start of my archival and interview research, I corresponded with three scholars studying California prisons, two of whom made introductions to separate individuals; these contacts eventually snowballed into the same group of founders and early members of the Black Guerilla Family I interviewed for this book, which then further expanded the network of self-described Black militants I was able to connect with and interview. The second scholar also suggested I begin at the Freedom Archives, which also led me to connections with people who had access to private archives run by political activists who had kept and preserved original documents for several decades. The third scholar suggested I begin my research at the California State Archives in Sacramento, California.

In addition to the California State Archives, the most significant archives include the Bancroft Library at the University of California–Berkeley, the Freedom Archives

Table A.1. Primary documents from public and private archives

Archive	Collections
Bancroft Library, University of California–Berkeley	Eldridge Cleaver papers George Jackson letters Black Panther Party internal correspondence and publications
California Department of Corrections	Historical trends reports, 1956–2007 Inmate incidents in institutions reports, 1981–2006 California prisoner demographics, 1961–2015 Prisoner and parolee reports, 1851–2010
California State Archives, Sacramento	San Quentin inmate racial distribution statistics, 1947–48 San Quentin incidence reports, 1945–50 California Department of Corrections interdepartment communications/memos, inmate racial segregation, prison conditions, inmate treatment, incidents, 1945–70 San Quentin incidence reports, 1951–95 Asst. Director of Corrections investigation files—internal memos, private correspondence, and policy reports, 1961–68 Prison Adjustment Center files—minutes, internal memos and correspondence, policy reports, and surveys, 1953–75
Digital Commons—Golden State University Law School	California State Assembly meetings on correctional institutions
Federal and State Court Case Depository—Lexis Nexis	Black Guerilla Family and other black militant cases Briefs, pleadings, and motions Jury verdicts and settlements Statutes and legislation Expert witness testimonies and interviews with law enforcement members and organization members Depositions about organizational structure, activities, and names of members

Table A.1 (continued)

Archive	Collections
Federal Bureau of Investigation—The Vault	Black Extremist, Parts 1–23, COINTELPRO Black Guerilla Family, Parts 1–3 George Jackson, Parts 1–5 Black Panther Party, Parts 1–34, COINTELPRO Nation of Islam, Parts 1–3, COINTELPRO Aryan Brotherhood, Part 1 of 1
Freedom Archives	Arm the Struggle correspondence and publications New Afrikan Prisoners Organization letters and publications COINTELPRO internal correspondence Black militant prison movement letters, publications, and internal correspondence Black militant organization newsletters
Gerald M. Kline Digital and Multimedia Center, Michigan State University	Black Panther newspapers Huey Newton essays Black Panther media clips
Green Library, Stanford University	Huey Newton letters San Quentin Six letters Black Panther Party letters and publications
It's About Time, Black Panther Archive	Black Panther newspapers Court case transcripts involving black militants Black Guerilla Family essays and prison letters

of San Francisco, the Golden State University Law School Digital Commons, the Federal Bureau of Investigation Vault, the Stanford University Green Library, and the It's About Time, Black Panther Archive of Sacramento. I also draw from memoirs and autobiographies written by people during their incarceration in the California prison system, and from the firsthand accounts of prison staff and officials documenting their life and work as penal actors.

I also reached out to activists and prisoner reentry organizations suggested by people I interviewed and connected with, in addition to doing my own research to find organizations across California. I passed out fliers to organizations providing contact information for the study and posted public fliers.

In total, from 2014 to 2018 I conducted forty-one life history interviews. Each interview lasted between two and four hours; some took several days; others were ongoing, with sessions held over the course of years. These interviews were with formerly incarcerated founders and early members of the Black Guerilla Family; with formerly

Table A.2. Memoirs

Memoir	Social Group
Leo L. Stanley, *Men at Their Worst*, 1940	Retired prison surgeon
Clinton Duffy and Dean Jennings, *The San Quentin Story*, 1950	Retired warden
Kenneth Lamott, *Chronicles of San Quentin: The Biography of a Prison*, 1961	Former prisoner
Eldridge Cleaver, *Soul on Ice*, 1968	Minister of Information, Black Panther Party
George Jackson, *Soledad Brother: The Prison Letters of George Jackson*, 1970 George Jackson, *Blood in My Eye*, 1972	Cofounder of the Black Guerilla Family, Black Panther Party
Gregory Armstrong, *The Dragon Has Come*, 1974	Friend of George Jackson
Huey P. Newton, *Revolutionary Suicide*, 1973	Cofounder and chairman of the Black Panther Party
Malcolm Braly, *False Starts: A Memoire of San Quentin and Other Prisons*, 1976	Former prisoner
William Richard Wilkinson, *Prison Work: A Tale of Thirty Years in the California Department of Corrections*, 2005	Retired correctional officer
John Lee Brook, *Blood In, Blood Out: The Violent Empire of the Aryan Brotherhood*, 2011	Former prisoner
John Clayton and Richard McNamara, *Pelican Bay: Guard McNamara's Story*, 2013	Retired correctional officer

incarcerated men self-identified across racial and ethnic groups, both with and without a racialized organizational affiliation or membership; with social and political activists connected to the civil rights and Black Freedom movements; and with a former correctional sergeant and a former public correctional officer turned prison official of a private prison. These interviews yielded hundreds of pages of transcripts and notes. I also conducted and recorded life history interviews with living founders of the Black Guerilla Family who were no longer incarcerated. Our interviews ranged from four to five hours in one setting to many conversations over the course of multiple days; and for some founders, I interviewed them multiple times over the course of years of sustained contact and conversations.

This unprecedented amount of original and high-quality data on the Black Guerilla Family, prisoner organizations, and the California Department of Corrections from 1950 to 2018 is used to substantiate the novel empirical and theoretical claims made throughout the book. The vast majority of my data covers this period; however, I do include memoirs and archival sources from the early twentieth century to describe institutional policies and penal life prior to the rise of Adjustment Centers in the 1950s.

During the writing process, on the advice of my editorial team at UNC Press and my developmental editor Mary Kole, I hired Alex Colston, a professional fact-checker. Highly acclaimed also as an editor, Colston has worked for years with historians and journalists publishing with academic and trade presses. Fact-checking is a paramount aspect of truth-telling as method and to that end, this book underwent two full rounds of fact-checking, in addition to traditional peer review, to produce the final version.

NOTES

Prologue

1. To read more about this protest and the role of the Southern Tenant Farmers' Union, see Jarod Roll, "'Out Yonder on the Road': Working Class Self-Representation and the 1939 Roadside Demonstration in Southeast Missouri," *Southern Spaces*, March 16, 2019, https://southernspaces.org/2010/out-yonder-road-working-class-self-representation-and-1939-roadside-demonstration-southeast-missouri/#:~:text=This%20essay%20revisits%20the%201939,of%20New%20Deal%20agricultural%20policy; and "Oh Freedom After While: The Missouri Sharecropper Protest of 1939," *Zinn Education Project*, accessed January 18, 2024, www.zinnedproject.org/materials/oh-freedom-after-while/.

Introduction

1. Gary Bingham, "My First Two Weeks at San Quentin Prison," *Gary Bingham's Blog*, February 7, 2008, http://westwood2.blogspot.com. Bingham is a retired associate warden who worked within the California Department of Corrections for twenty-seven years. He began his career as a correctional officer in 1973. He currently runs a personal blog on which he reflects about his time in law enforcement and the military.
2. Hugo Pinell's emotions about arriving at San Quentin are taken from my interview with Rose (a member of his family), which I conducted in person.
3. Interview with John. The respondent also noted, "San Quentin was a terrible place," and along with all others in my interview sample who served time there, described it as a "gladiator school."
4. *Allegra Casimir-Taylor v. State of California, California Department of Rehabilitation, Scott Kernan and Ron Rackey* is a wrongful death suit filed by Hugo Pinell's daughter with the US District Court for the Eastern District of California on September 23, 2016. The suit alleges that even after department officials became aware of a hit on Pinell authorized by the Aryan Brotherhood, he was still transferred into the general population in California State Prison–Sacramento (also known as New Folsom State Prison, it is a high-security facility with about 2,000 prisoners). One of the most damaging allegations is that correctional officers placed bets on how long it would take for Hugo to die at the hands of the Aryan Brotherhood while in the general population. The suit was dismissed with prejudice on July 25, 2017.
5. Gary Bingham, "Hugo Pinell Killing Serves Justice," letter to the editor, *Daily Republic*, September 12, 2015, www.dailyrepublic.com/all-dr-news/opinion/letters-editor/hugo-pinell-killing-serves-justice/. See note 1 of this chapter for more information on Bingham.

6. Karen Wald, "The Web of Death & Struggle: The Genesis of California's Political Trials," *Alternative Features Service*, April 28, 1972, San Quentin Six Collection, Freedom Archives, www.freedomarchives.org/Documents/Finder/DOC510_scans/SQ_Six/510.webofdeathandstruggle_sq6.1972.pdf. Full quote: "If you put men in cages and treat them like animals, how do you expect them to behave? A prisoner once asked. In the California prison system it seems clear that most of the prisoners have retained the essential characteristics of their humanity far better than have their jailers."
7. Wald, "Web of Death and Struggle." Full quote: "In the California prison system it seems clear that most of the prisoners have retained the essential characteristics of their humanity far better than have their jailers, but injustice heaped upon injustice inevitably produces rage, and then retaliation by the prisoners."
8. From interview with Rose. In addition to a direct quote from Hugo Pinell, "Mother of Love," June 25, 1972, in *Letters to Mother from Prison*, pamphlet, 1975, San Quentin Six Collection, Freedom Archives, www.freedomarchives.org/Documents/Finder/DOC511_scans/511.SQ6.LetterstoMother.pdf.
9. Direct quote from Hugo Pinell, "Quotes from Hugo Yogi Pinell," Fair Chance Project, January 29, 2013, http://fairchanceproject.com/campaigns/yogi-quotes. In May 2018, I met with the coordinator of the nonprofit Fair Chance Project and confirmed the quotes are valid. See also interview with Rose; and Pinell, "Mother of Love."
10. Interview with Rose. I use the term *moreno*, given that according to a member of Hugo's family, whom I interviewed, Hugo identified as *moreno*, which for him meant he saw himself as both an Afro-Latino man and a Black man.
11. Brittany Friedman, "Carceral Immobility and Financial Capture: A Framework for the Consequences of Racial Capitalism Penology and Monetary Sanctions," *UCLA Criminal Justice Law Review* 4, no. 1 (2020): 177–84. The article puts forth the theoretical devices "carceral immobility and financial capture" while analyzing the intergenerational human toll of racial capitalism through the lens of financial penalties in the criminal and civil legal systems. Racial capitalism is a theory that was first proposed by Cedric J. Robinson to understand extractive processes on the basis of race; this can be seen in Robinson's body of work, but most notably in his book *Black Marxism: The Making of the Black Radical Tradition* (Chapel Hill: University of North Carolina Press, 2020).
12. Emile Durkheim in *Suicide* (1897) and W. E. B. Du Bois in *The Philadelphia Negro* (1899) are the earliest proponents of strain theory, though Du Bois specifically outlined the theory in relation to race and justice. Strain theory maintains that societal structures constrain what goals are culturally acceptable while simultaneously dictating legitimate means for how people should attain those goals. This structural dilemma causes strain because many do not have access to culturally defined "noncriminal" or legitimate pathways to achieve such goals. For Du Bois, such strain was reflected in the migration of Black people during and following Reconstruction and the specific barriers to full social, political, and economic incorporation they faced as a result of institutional racism: debt peonage, the convict-lease system, racism in the courts, the lawlessness and barbarity of white mobs (e.g., lynching), and racial segregation. Such structural barriers are applicable to the continuous migrations of Black people across the United States and, in the above case, to Hugo's early introduction to the

criminal justice system. For DuBois, race and criminal (in)justice were inextricably linked and justified by pathologizing blackness rather than acknowledging that society was built upon systemic, institutionalized racism and violence. Robert Merton, in "Social Structure and Anomie," attempted to produce a nuanced version of strain theory, drawing heavily from Durkheim's notion of anomic suicide to argue strain leads to individual anomie. The significant issue with Merton's rendition of strain and anomie is that he neglects to account for racism as a determinant of strain and of state-definitions of criminality; this neglect causes him to overlook how deviance is socially constructed from the top-down and built upon power asymmetries between white people and Black people. In doing so, Merton focuses exclusively on class and does not fully question the process of labeling deviance as fundamentally connected to power. See Robert K. Merton, "Social Structure and Anomie," *American Sociological Review* 3, no. 5 (October 1938): 672–82. For additional context, see Robert Wortham, *W. E. B. Du Bois and the Sociological Imagination* (Waco, TX: Baylor University Press, 2009).

13. Mumia Abu-Jamal, "Yogi's Time," July 30, 2006, Political Prisoner News, Freedom Archives, http://freedomarchives.org/pipermail/ppnews_freedomarchives.org/2009-January/002061.html. In addition to interview with Rose.
14. Description from Hugo's emotions about his experience while in custody taken from my interview with Rose. Emphasis added in italics to show areas where metaphors are used to articulate his relative's recounting of his emotional state.
15. Interview with Rose.
16. Interview with Rose.
17. Abu-Jamal, "Yogi's Time"; interview with Rose. The full statement from Hugo is as follows:

> In 1964, a white woman accused me of rape, assault and kidnap. I was 19 years old. I turned myself into the authorities to clarify the charges against me which I knew to be falsified. The deputies beat me several times because the alleged victim was white, and the Public Defender and the Judge influenced my mother into believing that I would be sentenced to death unless I pled guilty. At their insistence and despite my innocence, I pled guilty to the charge of rape, with the understanding that I would be eligible for parole after 6 months. When I arrived at the California Department of Corrections, I was informed that I had been sentenced to three years to life.

There are multiple sources arguing that Hugo's sentencing was trumped up or bogus, and there is also the testimony from the alleged victim as transcribed by the courts. The evidence presented by the prosecution in the case does not add up beyond a reasonable doubt. See "Hugo 'Yogi Bear' Pinell," Prisoner Solidarity, accessed September 10, 2022, https://prisonersolidarity.com/prisoner/hugo-yogi-bear-pinell; "The Black Panther Party and Hugo Pinell," It's About Time, Black Panther Archive, Sacramento, accessed May 10, 2016, www.itsabouttimebpp.com/Political_Prisoners/pdf/Hugo_Pinell.pdf; Abayomi Azikiwe, "Former Black Panther Killed in California Prison," *Workers World*, August 19, 2015, www.workers.org/2015/08/21455/. For a detailed account of the state's case, see *Pinell v. Superior Court*, 232 Cal.App.2d 284 (Cal. Ct. App. 1965).

18. Interview with Rose.
19. Eventually, following an incident in Soledad in 1971, Hugo Pinell acquired a reputation in the media as "a Nicaraguan life-termer who prison officials say attacked three other guards in three different prisons since 1968." See "Soledad Guard Stabbed to Death," *Daytona Beach Morning Journal*, March 5, 1971, https://news.google.com/newspapers?id=M04fAAAAIBAJ&sjid=jtEEAAAAIBAJ&pg=970%2C1162725.
20. I use self-identified white supremacists and self-identified Black militants to distinguish between people who reported allegiance to a movement and who participated in a corresponding movement organization versus people who showed allegiance to their racial group but who may not have been a member of a movement organization.
21. "Death on the Yard: Behind the Killings at Soledad and San Quentin," *Ramparts*, April 1973, It's About Time, Black Panther Archive, Sacramento, accessed July 22, 2016, www.itsabouttimebpp.com/underground_news/pdf/Ramparts_April_1973_1.pdf. For additional support, see Dan Berger, *Captive Nation: Black Prison Organizing in the Civil Rights Era* (Chapel Hill: University of North Carolina Press, 2014).
22. Interviews I conducted with founders and early members of the Black Guerilla Family led me to conclude there were about nine or ten founding members of the organization. This approximation is based on slight disagreements among the interviewees as to whether an individual was indeed a founding member or recruited shortly after the organization's formation. The consensus among founders and early members is that the organization was officially founded in 1970. See Jonah Walters, "Black Radical Prisoner Organizing Didn't Die with George Jackson: An Interview with Brittany Friedman," *Jacobin Magazine*, August 21, 2020, https://jacobin.com/2020/08/george-jackson-black-guerilla-family-san-quentin.
23. George L. Jackson, *Soledad Brother: The Prison Letters of George Jackson* (Chicago: Lawrence Hill Books, 1970).
24. Dennis O'Hearn points to the development of solidary cultures among populations who share similar grievances and, most importantly, who experience, survive, and resist together episodes of repression perpetrated by a common oppressor. See Dennis O'Hearn, "Repression and Solidarity Cultures of Resistance: Irish Political Prisoners on Protest," *American Journal of Sociology* 115, no. 2 (September 2009): 491–526.
25. According to the defense, there was no escape plot per se; if there was a plot and conspiracy, it was conducted by the state to kill Jackson (a plot that also involved the framing of Jackson's defense attorney). See Wallace Turner, "Two Desperate Hours: How George Jackson Died," *New York Times*, September 3, 1971, www.nytimes.com/1971/09/03/archives/two-desperate-hours-how-george-jackson-died-two-desperate-hours-how.html; "Stephen Bingham '64 interviewed by Marin Magazine," *Yale University Class News*, January 2014, www.yale64.org/news/bingham1.htm; "The San Quentin Six," Freedom Archives, accessed February 3, 2015, www.freedomarchives.org/Documents/Finder/DOC510_scans/SQ_Six/510.The_San_Quentin_Six.pdf; James Queally and Paige St. John, "The San Quentin Six: How a Wig and a Handgun Sent

a Prison into Chaos 44 Years Ago," *Los Angeles Times*, August 13, 2015, www.latimes.com/local/crime/la-me-san-quentin-six-retro-20150813-htmlstory.html; Paige St. John, "Hugo Pinell, Infamous 'San Quentin Six' Member, Killed in Prison Riot," *Los Angeles Times*, August 13, 2015, www.latimes.com/local/la-me-ff-inmate-killed-in-california-riot-20150812-story.html; Sharon Bernstein, "Inmate Who Participated in 'San Quentin Six' 1971 Escape Attempt Killed in California Prison Riot," *Reuters*, August 12, 2015, www.reuters.com/article/us-usa-california-prison/inmate-who-participated-in-san-quentin-six-1971-escape-attempt-killed-in-california-prison-riot-idUKKCN0QH2NT20150813/; *Corrections: Prisons, Prison Reform, and Prisoners' Rights: California: Hearings before H.R. Subcommittee No. 3 of the Committee on the Judiciary*, 92nd Cong. (1971), 329, www.google.com/books/edition/Corrections_Prisons_prison_reform_and_pr/YFlFAQAAMAAJ?hl=en&gbpv=1; Tom Hayden, *Long Sixties: From 1960 to Barack Obama* (New York: Taylor and Francis, 2015).

Based on my interview data, there was, in fact, an escape plan to save Jackson. Interviewees describe how the plan was to prevent the fatal success of an undercover plot by law enforcement to kill Jackson. There was indeed a conspiracy by the state to frame Jackson's defense attorney as participating in this plan, but he was not actually involved in the plan to prevent Jackson's murder at the hands of correctional officers and their aligned white supremacists. The state's framing of Jackson's attorney was a distraction designed to dissuade formal discussion about a law enforcement conspiracy and alliance with incarcerated white supremacists to kill Jackson inside San Quentin.

26. Nancy Ann Nichols, *San Quentin Inside the Walls* (San Quentin, CA: San Quentin Museum Press, 1991).
27. Direct quote from Hugo Pinell, "Quotes from Hugo Yogi Pinell," Fair Chance Project, January 30, 2013, http://fairchanceproject.com/campaigns/yogi-quotes. In 2018 I met with the coordinator of the nonprofit Fair Chance Project and confirmed the quotes are valid.
28. Pinell, "Quotes from Hugo Yogi Pinell."
29. According to a member of Hugo's family, whom I interviewed, Hugo identified as *moreno*. See note 10 of this chapter.
30. Associated Press, "2 Suspects Charged in Slaying of San Quentin 6 Inmate," KRCA, December 9, 2015, www.kcra.com/article/2-suspects-charged-in-slaying-of-san-quentin-6-inmate/6426177; "Aryan Brotherhood Leaders Attempted to Rule over All White California Prison Gangs," *Daily Democrat*, September 1, 2019, www.dailydemocrat.com/2019/09/01/build-an-army-aryan-brotherhood-leaders-attempted-to-rule-over-all-white-california-prison-gangs/; Don Thompson, "Lawsuit Says California Could Have Stopped Prison Slaying," *Orange County Register*, October 6, 2016, www.ocregister.com/2016/10/06/lawsuit-says-california-could-have-stopped-prison-slaying/; "2 Charged with Killing San Quentin 6 Inmate," *Houston Chronicle*, December 9, 2015, www.houstonchronicle.com/news/article/2-charged-with-killing-San-Quentin-6-inmate-6687528.php.
31. Interview with Rose.
32. Vernell Devon Bush, "I Was One of the Last Ones to See Our Beloved Brotha Yogi Alive," *San Francisco Bay View: National Black Newspaper*, letter to the

editor, January 30, 2016, http://sfbayview.com/2016/01/i-was-one-of-the-last-ones-to-see-our-beloved-brotha-yogi-alive/.
33. *Allegra Casimir-Taylor v. State of California, California Department of Corrections and Rehabilitation, Scott Kernan and Ron Rackey*, 2:2016cv02309, US District Court for the Eastern District of California (September 23 2016), https://dockets.justia.com/docket/california/caedce/2:2016cv02309/303284.
34. "Hugo Pinell—Rest in Power," August 2015, mp3, 20 minutes, San Quentin Six Collection, Freedom Archives, http://freedomarchives.org/Hugo_Pinell.html; *Allegra Casimir-Taylor v. State of California*.
35. Bush, "I Was One of the Last Ones."
36. See Kathleen Blee, *Women of the Klan: Racism and Gender in the 1920s* (Oakland: University of California Press, 2008); Sara Bullard, *The Ku Klux Klan: A History of Racism and Violence* (Collingdale, PA: Diane Publishing, 1998); David Cunningham, *Klansville, U.S.A.: The Rise and Fall of the Civil Rights-Era Ku Klux Klan* (Oxford: Oxford University Press, 2013); Rory McVeigh, *The Rise of the Ku Klux Klan: Right-Wing Movements and National Politics* (Minneapolis: University of Minnesota Press, 2009); Monica Muñoz Martinez, *The Injustice Never Leaves You: Anti-Mexican Violence in Texas* (Cambridge, MA: Harvard University Press, 2018); Michael Newton, *The FBI and the KKK: A Critical History* (Jefferson, NC: McFarland, 2005); Geoff Ward, "Living Histories of White Supremacist Policing: Towards Transformative Justice," *Du Bois Review* 15, no. 1 (2018): 167–84. For more scholarship investigating these connections, see The Civil Rights and Restorative Justice Project at Northeastern University School of Law, https://crrj.northeastern.edu/.
37. Don Thompson, "San Quentin 6 Prisoner Hugo Pinell's Slaying Triggers Wrongful Death Suit against California," *Marin Independent Journal*, October 6, 2016, www.marinij.com/2016/10/06/san-quentin-6-prisoner-hugo-pinells-slaying-triggers-wrongful-death-suit-against-california/.
38. Francesca Trianni, "Flags, Hate Symbols and QAnon Shirts: Decoding the Capitol Riot," *Time*, January 11, 2021, https://time.com/5928627/symbols-capitol/; Ellis Champion, "120 House GOP Members Share Incendiary Social Media Content Leading Up to Capitol Attack," *Democracy Docket*, March 5, 2021, www.democracydocket.com/2021/03/120-gop-house-members-share-incendiary-social-media-content-leading-up-to-capitol-attack/; Nicholas Wu, "Capitol Police Investigating 35 Officers for Jan. 6 Riots as Union Denounces 'Witch Hunt,'" *USA Today*, February 19, 2021, www.usatoday.com/story/news/politics/2021/02/19/capitol-police-investigating-35-officers-after-jan-6-riot/4506770001/.
39. Federal Bureau of Investigation, "United States Capitol Violence and Related Events of January 6, 2021, Part 16," FBI Records: The Vault, January 13–15, 2021, https://vault.fbi.gov/united-states-capitol-violence-and-related-events-of-january-6-2021/united-states-capitol-violence-and-related-events-of-january-6-2021-part-16/view; Mary Papenfuss, "Chilling Memo to FBI Official Warned of Sympathy in Bureau for Jan. 6 Rioters," *Huffington Post*, October 15, 2022, www.huffpost.com/entry/fbi-email-jan-6-rioter-sympathy_n_634ad223e4b03e8038d495d7.
40. Euro-Med Human Rights Monitor, "Israel-Palestinian Territory," accessed January 25, 2024, https://euromedmonitor.org/en/country/1/Israel-Palestinian-Territory.
41. "Journalist Casualties in the Israel-Gaza War," Committee to Protect Journal-

ists, February 5, 2024, https://cpj.org/2024/02/journalist-casualties-in-the-israel-gaza-conflict/.
42. "Application Instituting Proceedings," International Court of Justice, December 28, 2023, www.icj-cij.org/sites/default/files/case-related/192/192-20231228-app-01-00-en.pdf.
43. International Court of Justice, "Order of 26 January 2024," www.icj-cij.org/node/203447.
44. W. E. B. Du Bois, *The World and Africa and Color and Democracy*, ed. Henry Louis Gates Jr. (Oxford: Oxford University Press, 2014) 17; W. E. B. Du Bois, "Africa, Colonialism, and Zionism," in *The Oxford W. E. B. Du Bois Reader*, ed. Eric J. Sundquist (1919; New York: Oxford University Press, 1996), 650; W. E. B. Du Bois, *Dusk of Dawn: An Essay toward an Autobiography of a Race Concept* (New York: Harcourt Brace, 1940), 623–24. For a discussion of Du Bois's contribution as a founder of the discipline of sociology, see Aldon Morris, *The Scholar Denied: W. E. B. Du Bois and the Birth of Modern Sociology* (Oakland: University of California Press, 2015).
45. Morris, *Scholar Denied*.
46. Du Bois, *Dusk of Dawn*. For more on Du Bois's analysis of empire, see George Steinmetz. "Présentation de W. E. B. Du Bois," *Actes de la recherche en sciences sociales*, no. 171–72 (March 2008): 75–77.
47. W. E. B. Du Bois, "The Ethics of the Problem of Palestine" (draft of article published in the *Chicago Star* as "A Case for the Jews," ca. 1948), https://credo.library.umass.edu/view/full/mums312-b209-i090.
48. For a detailed discussion of the term "rebel archive," see Kelly Lytle Hernández, *City of Inmates: Conquest, Rebellion, and the Rise of Human Caging in Los Angeles, 1771–1965* (Chapel Hill: University of North Carolina Press, 2017).
49. Audie Cornish, "Rebel Historian Who Reframes History Wins MacArthur 'Genius' Grant," *National Public Radio*, September 25, 2019, www.npr.org/2019/09/25/764364172/rebel-historian-who-reframes-history-receives-macarthur-genius-grant.
50. Email anonymized, correspondence to author, September 24, 2018.
51. I thoroughly document the rise of the Adjustment Center in chapter 2.
52. To see an example of the literature I am referencing, see Keramet Reiter, *23/7: Pelican Bay Prison and the Rise of Long-Term Solitary Confinement* (New Haven, CT: Yale University Press, 2016).
53. Based on my interviews and archival sources, about nine to ten men founded the Black Guerilla Family in 1970 in San Quentin.
54. See the appendix of this volume.

Chapter 1

1. Thomas Pakenham, *The Scramble for Africa: White Man's Conquest of the Dark Continent from 1876 to 1912* (New York: Avon Books, 1992).
2. For a discussion of racial identity and property rights, see Chery L. Harris, "Whiteness as Property," *Harvard Law Review*, June 10, 1993, https://harvardlawreview.org/print/no-volume/whiteness-as-property/.
3. South African Truth and Reconciliation Commission (TRC), accessed March 22, 2022, www.justice.gov.za/trc/index.html.
4. Natacha Filippi, "Deviance, Punishment and Logics of Subjectification during

Apartheid: Insane, Political and Common-Law Prisoners in a South African Gaol," *Journal of Southern African Studies* 37, no. 3 (2011): 629.
5. Nelson Mandela, *Long Walk to Freedom: The Autobiography of Nelson Mandela* (New York: Little, Brown, 1995). President Mandela was elected in 1994 after the end of apartheid in the 1990s and following decades of Black resistance, international and regional support, and economic sanctions against the ruling Nationalist Party by former allies who came to condemn apartheid as unsustainable for broader global capitalism, given South Africa's failure to quelch the rise of Black resistance (the sanctions brought on by former allies were hardly due to a moral stance). See "Trials and Prisons Chronology," Nelson Mandela Foundation, accessed March 22, 2022, www.nelsonmandela.org/content/page/trials-and-prison-chronology.
6. Nelson Mandela, *The Prison Letters of Nelson Mandela*, ed. Sahm Venter (Auckland, NZ: Blackwell and Ruth, 2018).
7. Mandela, *Prison Letters*.
8. I ascribe to the practice of "concept-driven sociology," as put forth by Eviatar Zerubavel, which suggests that theorists can decipher often hidden, fundamental social patterns if we think and sample across diverse empirical contexts, which after close examination, allows for the discovery of analogous considerations and "generic" social facts. See Eviatar Zerubavel, *Generally Speaking: An Invitation to Concept-Driven Sociology* (New York: Oxford University Press, 2021).
9. See Catherine Besteman, *Militarized Global Apartheid* (Durham, NC: Duke University Press, 2020).
10. To learn more about these cases, see the following books: Andy Clarno, *Neoliberal Apartheid: Palestine/Israel and South Africa after 1994* (Chicago: University of Chicago Press, 2017); Vahakn N. Dadrian, *The History of the Armenian Genocide: Ethnic Conflict from the Balkans to Anatolia to the Caucasus*, 6th ed. (New York: Berghahn Books, 1995); Martin Gilbert, *The Holocaust: A History of the Jews of Europe during the Second World War* (New York: Henry Holt and Company, 1985); Azeem Ibrahim, *The Rohingyas: Inside Myanmar's Hidden Genocide* (London, UK: Hurst and Company, 2016); Jasbir K. Puar, *The Right to Maim: Debility, Capacity, Disability* (Durham, NC: Duke University Press, 2017).
11. "De jure" is segregation by law, and "de facto" is segregation, which is often enduring once de jure segregation is repealed because it has become official custom still policed by institutions of formal control and white civilians as a racial and spatial boundary.
12. Douglas S. Massey and Nancy A. Denton, *American Apartheid: Segregation and the Making of the Underclass* (Cambridge, MA: Harvard University Press, 1993). Yet, the authors' emphasis on a resulting "culture of segregation" among Black communities that produces antisocial attitudes and behaviors as a partial explanation for continued socioeconomic exclusion is not necessarily as far from a "culture of poverty" thesis as the authors might have hoped. The authors point to the rise of a "dysfunctional" culture in what they refer to as "Black ghettos," which is a racist interpretation of their evidence and likely not the interpretation taken up by Black feminist and other critical scholars. Also, Massey and Denton do little to interrogate the violence required to maintain

apartheid as governance, as seen across all cases of apartheid around the world, including in the United States.
13. *Merriam-Webster's Dictionary*, s.v. "governance" (noun), accessed March 18, 2021, www.merriam-webster.com/dictionary/governance.
14. James C. Scott, *Seeing Like a State: How Certain Schemes to Improve the Human Condition Have Failed* (New Haven, CT: Yale University Press, 1998).
15. Michel Foucault, *Discipline and Punish: The Birth of the Prison*, trans. Alan Sheridan (New York: Vintage Books, 1975). Foucault describes the fundamental role of the state as one of disciplining and punishing undesirables through social institutions such as schools, hospitals, and prisons, creating a carceral archipelago that extends well beyond institutions tasked with formal control (I would surmise these social institutions he is talking about exist at the meso level, though he does not clarify this in his work). The consequences of Foucault's carceral archipelago is the production of carceral subjects who become accustomed to surveillance and different forms of violence that extend to all in the population, to create a docile class in service to an alleged higher good for all. Issues with his analysis, however, are that race and gender are essentially absent from his articulation of how different forms and levels of violence, in terms of severity and intentionality, are enacted upon populations deemed racially inferior and subordinate to racially superior men.
16. Melissa Mejia, "The U.S. History of Native American Boarding Schools," The Indigenous Foundation, www.theindigenousfoundation.org/articles/us-residential-schools.
17. Frantz Fanon, *Black Skin, White Masks*, trans. Charles Lam Markmann (New York: Grove Press, 1967).
18. Fanon, *Black Skin, White Masks*.
19. Lawrence Bobo, James R. Kuegel, and Ryan A. Smith, "Laissez-Faire Racism: The Crystallization of a Kinder, Gentler, Antiblack Ideology," in *Racial Attitudes in the 1990s: Continuity and Change*, ed. Steven A. Tuch and Jack K. Martin (Westport, CT: Praeger, 1997); Eduardo Bonilla-Silva, "Rethinking Racism: Toward a Structural Interpretation," *American Sociological Review* 62, no. 3 (1997): 465–80; Eduardo Bonilla-Silva, *Racism without Racists: Color-Blind Racism and Racial Inequality in Contemporary America*, 3rd ed. (New York: Rowman and Littlefield, 2010); Victor Ray, "A Theory of Racialized Organizations," *American Sociological Review* 84, no. 1 (2019): 26–53.
20. See W. E. B. Du Bois, *Dusk of Dawn: An Essay toward an Autobiography of a Race Concept* (New York: Harcourt Brace, 1940); Charisse Burden-Stelly and Jodi Dean, *Organize, Fight, Win: Black Communist Women's Political Writing* (New York: Verso Books, 2022); Orisanmi Burton, *Tip of the Spear: Black Radicalism, Prison Repression, and the Long Attica Revolt* (Oakland: University of California Press, 2023); Patricia Hill Collins, *Black Feminist Thought: Knowledge, Consciousness, and the Politics of Empowerment* (New York: Routledge, 1990); Joy James, *Resisting State Violence: Radicalism, Gender, and Race in U.S. Culture* (Minneapolis: University of Minnesota Press, 1996); Walter Rodney, *Decolonial Marxism: Essays from the Pan-African Revolution* (New York: Verso Books, 2022); Kwame Ture and Charles V. Hamilton, *Black Power: The Politics of Liberation*

(New York: Vintage Books, 1992); Angela Davis, *Freedom Is a Constant Struggle: Ferguson, Palestine, and the Foundations of a Movement* (Chicago: Haymarket Books, 2016); Marcus Garvey, *The Tragedy of White Injustice* (Mansfield, CT: Martino Fine Books, 2017); Malcolm X and George Breitman, *Malcolm X Speaks: Selected Speeches and Statements* (New York: Grove Press, 1994).

21. William L. Patterson, ed., *We Charge Genocide: The Crime of Government Against the Negro People* (New York: Civil Rights Congress, 1951).
22. Julian Go, *Policing Empires: Militarization, Race, and the Imperial Boomerang in Britain and the US* (New York: Oxford University Press, 2024); Stuart Schrader, *Badges without Borders: How Global Counterinsurgency Transformed American Policing* (Oakland: University of California Press, 2019).
23. Table 1.1 draws from the headings (i.e., levels of analysis, analytic frames, representative features, conflict over) and the types of levels of analysis (i.e., institutional, organizational, and individual) in Ray's table 1, from "A Theory of Racialized Organizations," which outlines different levels of analysis in the study of race and ethnicity, as a model for how to show analytical distinction between levels and to showcase how each level influences each other. Other adapted features from Ray include the analytic categories such as racial segregation, the racial state, group membership, and so on, though this table necessarily places some of these categories in different arrangements according to my own theoretical framework.
24. "Race and Ethnicity," Prison Policy Initiative, accessed October 5, 2022, www.prisonpolicy.org/research/race_and_ethnicity/#:~:text=You%20can%20also%20see%20a,who%20are%20Black%3A%2037%25%20%2B.
25. Ida B. Wells, "Lynch Law in All Its Phases," *Our Day: A Record and Review of Current Reform* 11 (1893): 333–47.
26. *Merriam-Webster's Dictionary*, s.v. "clandestine," accessed March 18, 2021, www.merriam-webster.com/dictionary/clandestine.
27. In his theory of prison order, political economist David Skarbek focuses on official and extralegal governance institutions, providing a foundational theoretical starting point in the literature; his work is also significant in terms of analyzing prisons as political organizations, as he makes a strong case supporting the need for scholars to center governance frameworks in our research on prisons. See David Skarbek, *The Social Order of the Underworld: How Prison Gangs Govern the American Penal System* (Oxford: Oxford University Press, 2014).

    Importantly, however, given our different disciplinary distinctions (political science and economics vs. sociology and critical race theory) and my emphasis on racist intent, our conceptualization of official and extralegal differs in four key ways. First, he and I differ in that Skarbek centers the penal organization as the provider of official controls versus the incarcerated individuals as the creators of extralegal controls. As a result, he concentrates on when and how incarcerated individuals govern themselves by supplementing official controls with extralegal controls. Second, he does not recognize the penal organization as the initial perpetrator of racist intent and thus deliberate white supremacist violence, meted out as both punishment and social control, which in turn shapes the social organization of prison life at the micro level. Third, unlike Skarbek, I argue that racialization and racism are the defining structural forces organizing penal life, and I suggest that penal organizations are inherently illegitimate governance providers, given they are the product of social construction at the state level, embodying white power and cultivating conflict, and thus one of the most prominent sources of instrumental white supremacist violence throughout history. And finally, the use of secrecy and clandestine motives as a fundamental mode of governance by penal organizations is something I offer as a revision to how official and extralegal controls function.

28. Nicole Gonzalez Van Cleve, *Crook County: Racism and Injustice in America's Largest Criminal Court* (Palo Alto, CA: Stanford University Press, 2016).
29. Erving Goffman, *Asylums: Essays on the Condition of the Social Situation of Mental Patients and Other Inmates* (New York: Anchor Books, 1961).
30. Phillip Goodman, "'It's Just Black, White, or Hispanic': An Observational Study of Racializing Moves in California's Segregated Prison Reception Centers," *Law and Society Review* 42, no. 4 (2008): 735–70.
31. Gresham Sykes, *The Society of Captives: A Study of a Maximum Security Prison* (Princeton, NJ: Princeton University Press, 1958).
32. Joshua Page and Phillip Goodman define "carceral habitus" as a "reconceptualization of prisonization," meaning "a unique set of dispositions that shape conscious and preconscious practice within and beyond carceral institutions" (223). See Joshua Page and Phillip Goodman, "Creative Disruption: Edward Bunker, Carceral Habitus, and the Criminological Value of Fiction," *Theoretical Criminology* 24, no. 2 (2018): 222–40.
33. See Michael L. Walker, "Race Making in a Penal Institution," *American Journal of Sociology* 121, no. 4 (2016): 1051–78.
34. Michael Omi and Howard Winant, *Racial Formation in the United States* (New York: Routledge Press, 1994), 56, as cited in Walker, "Race Making," 1053.
35. Walker, "Race Making," 1053.
36. Patrick Lopez-Aguado, *Stick Together and Come Back Home: Racial Sorting and the Spillover of Carceral Identity* (Oakland: University of California Press, 2018).
37. Jesse Vasquez, "One Prison Taught Me Racism. Another Taught Me Acceptance: I Didn't Think of Myself as a Racist. I Had to Conform to Survive," *Washington Post*, October 1, 2018, www.washingtonpost.com/outlook/2018/10/01/one-prison-taught-me-racism-another-taught-me-acceptance/.
38. These consequences are collectively supported in what sociologist Joshua Page describes as the penal field, such as special interest groups, bipartisan legislative initiatives, officer unions, and often the public. The supportive feedback loop within the larger penal field should be no surprise. According to Page, the penal field consists of "the social space in which agents struggle to accumulate and employ penal capital—that is, the legitimate authority to determine penal policies and priorities." See Joshua Page, *The Toughest Beat: Politics, Punishment, and the Prison Officers Union of California* (Oxford: University of Oxford Press, 2011), 10. For a discussion of the rise of supermax confinement in California, see Keramet Reiter, *23/7: Pelican Bay Prison and the Rise of Long-Term Solitary Confinement* (New Haven, CT: Yale University Press, 2016).
39. Definition of social problems comes from Herbert Blumer, "Social Problems as Collective Behavior," *Social Problems* 18, no. 3 (1971): 326–30, quote on 298.
40. For thorough conceptualizations of the evolving historical culture of crime

control and social order in the United States, see the work of David Garland, *The Culture of Control: Crime and Social Order in Contemporary Society* (Chicago: University of Chicago Press, 2001); Elizabeth Hinton, *From the War on Poverty to the War on Crime: The Making of Mass Incarceration in America* (Cambridge, MA: Harvard University Press, 2016); Ashley Rubin, *The Deviant Prison: Philadelphia's Eastern State Penitentiary and the Origins of America's Modern Penal System, 1829–1913* (Cambridge, MA: Cambridge University Press, 2021); and Jonathan Simon, *Governing Through Crime: How the War on Crime Transformed American Democracy and Created a Culture of Fear* (Oxford: Oxford University Press, 2007).

Chapter 2

1. Leo L. Stanley, *Men at Their Worst* (New York: D. Appleton-Century Company, 1940), 1. First edition signed by Dr. Stanley, personal copy of the author.
2. Stanley, *Men at Their Worst*, 1.
3. Stanley, *Men at Their Worst*, 62–63.
4. Howard Becker, *Outsiders: Studies in the Sociology of Deviance* (New York: Free Press, 1963), 9.
5. The early modern era is widely dated as beginning in 1500 CE, following the post-classical era of the Middle Ages.
6. For an excellent book on the global exportation of US policing and military tactics, see Stuart Schrader, *Badges without Borders: How Global Counterinsurgency Transformed American Policing* (Berkeley: University of California Press, 2019).
7. Beginning in the late 1960s, critical criminology rose as a discipline to combat state-centered versions of criminality that ignored the state, institutions, and corporations as the main producers of crime and harm to society, see William J. Chambliss, *Power, Politics, and Crime* (New York: Basic Books, 1999). This view is later taken up to argue that the state engages in organized race crime, see Geoff Ward, "The Slow Violence of State Organized Race Crime," *Theoretical Criminology* 19, no. 3 (2015): 299–314. However, in *Black Reconstruction in America: An Essay toward a History of the Part Which Black Folk Played in the Attempt to Reconstruct Democracy in America, 1860–1880* (New York: Harcourt, Brace and Company, 1935), W. E. B. Du Bois's scholarship on the Reconstruction era makes him the first to jointly argue these overall points. This fact removes much of the novelty from the rise of critical criminology, particularly from the subfields that claim to be the first to privilege race, class, and a focus on state crime. Du Bois is one the first scholars to argue for a racialized strain theory of criminality that centers societal institutions and the broader state as the intentional perpetrator of racist violence that creates the conditions Black communities must survive.

However, Du Bois remains absent from mainstream criminology. For a discussion of Du Bois's absence from most of the critical and mainstream criminological canon, see Nicole Gonzalez Van Cleve, "How Does It Feel to Be the Problem: A Call for Du Boisian Criminology," in *The Oxford Handbook of W. E. B. Du Bois*, ed. Aldon D. Morris, Michael Schwartz, Cheryl Johnson-Odim, Walter R. Allen, Marcus Anthony Hunter, Karida L. Brown, and Dan S. Green (New York:

Oxford University Press, 2023). See also Ida B. Wells, "Lynch Law in All Its Phases," *Our Day: A Record and Review of Current Reform* 11 (1893): 333–47. Wells is also an early pioneer in this area, and she remains left out of the critical and mainstream criminological canon as well.

8. John Hagan, *Who Are the Criminals?: The Politics of Crime Policy from the Age of Roosevelt to the Age of Reagan* (Princeton, NJ: Princeton University Press, 2012).
9. Michel Foucault, *Discipline and Punish: The Birth of the Prison*, trans. Alan Sheridan (New York: Vintage Books, 1975). However, Foucault's analysis of race and gender is lacking.
10. Foucault, *Discipline and Punish*.
11. Foucault, *Discipline and Punish*; Frank E. Hagan and Leah E. Daigle, *Introduction to Criminology: Theories, Methods, and Criminal Behavior*, 10th ed. (New York: Sage Publications, 2019).
12. David Garland, *Punishment and Modern Society: A Study in Social Theory* (Chicago: University of Chicago Press, 1990).
13. Valerie Wright, "Deterrence in Criminal Justice: Evaluating Certainty vs. Severity of Punishment," *Sentencing Project*, 2010, www.sentencingproject.org/wp-content/uploads/2016/01/Deterrence-in-Criminal-Justice.pdf; National Institute of Justice, "Five Things about Deterrence," accessed July 20, 2020, www.ojp.gov/pdffiles1/nij/247350.pdf.
14. Marcello Maestro, *Cesare Beccaria and the Origins of Penal Reform* (Philadelphia: Temple University Press, 1973); Frank E. Hagan and Leah E. Daigle, *Introduction to Criminology: Theories, Methods, and Criminal Behavior*, 10th ed. (Thousand Oaks, CA: Sage Publications, 2019).
15. Cesare Beccaria, *On Crimes and Punishments* (n.p., 1764); Hagan and Daigle, *Introduction to Criminology*.
16. Jeremy Bentham, *Panopticon: Or the Inspection House* (n.p., 1791); Hagan and Daigle, *Introduction to Criminology*.
17. Ashley T. Rubin, *The Deviant Prison: Philadelphia's Eastern State Penitentiary* (Cambridge: Cambridge University Press, 2021).
18. Garland, *Punishment and Modern Society*.
19. Garland, *Punishment and Modern Society*.
20. Francis A. Allen, "Criminal Justice, Legal Values and the Rehabilitative Ideal," *Journal of Criminal Law, Criminology, and Police Science* 50, no. 3 (1959): 226–32; Stanley, *Men at Their Worst*.
21. Stanley, *Men at Their Worst*.
22. Ethan Blue, "The Strange Career of Leo Stanley: Remaking Manhood and Medicine at San Quentin State Penitentiary, 1913–1951," *Pacific Historical Review* 78, no. 2 (2009): 210–41.
23. Cesare Lombroso, *Criminal Man*, 1836, trans. and with a new introduction by Mary Gibson and Nicole Hanh Rafter (Durham, NC: Duke University Press, 2006).
24. Stanley, *Men at Their Worst*.
25. Katie Dowd, "The San Quentin Prison Doctor Who Performed over 10,000 Human Experiments," *San Francisco Gate*, 2019, updated May 2, 2022, www.sfgate.com/sfhistory/article/leo-stanley-gland-rejuvenation-surgery-14298920.php.
26. Alliance for Human Research Protection, "1913–1951: Dr. Leo Stanley," accessed March 5, 2021, https://ahrp.org/1913-1951-dr-leo-stanley/.

27. Stanley, *Men at Their Worst*, 62–63.
28. Stanley, *Men at Their Worst*, 62–63.
29. Foucault, *Discipline and Punish*.
30. Quoted from Stanley, *Men at Their Worst*, 98. See also the work on the history of Viagra, where Dr. Leo Stanley's experiments had a major impact on the development of this now widely popular pharmaceutical.
31. "Early San Quentin Doctor Pushes Prison Medicine into 20th Century," California Department of Corrections and Rehabilitation, November 8, 2018, www.cdcr.ca.gov/insidecdcr/2018/11/08/early-san-quentin-doctor-pushes-prison-medicine-into-20th-century/.
32. *Merriam-Webster's Dictionary*, s.v. "adjust" (transitive verb), accessed March 18, 2021, www.merriam-webster.com/dictionary/adjusting.
33. Richard A. McGee, *Treatment of Constitutional Psychopaths* (October 2, 1953), 1, Institutions—Adjustment Centers, Director's Subject Files, Department of Corrections Records, California State Archives, Sacramento (hereafter DOCR, CSAS).
34. Norman Fenton, *A Preliminary Statement of Policies and Procedures for an Adjustment Center in a Correctional Institution* (November 1953), 3, Institutions—Adjustment Centers, Director's Subject Files, DOCR, CSAS.
35. Fenton, *Preliminary Statement*, 2.
36. Fenton, *Preliminary Statement*, 3.
37. Norman Fenton, Justin K. Fuller, and Henry W. Rogers, *Policies and Procedures for Adjustment Centers in the Department of Corrections of California* (October 1954), 3–4, Institutions—Adjustment Centers, Director's Subject Files, DOCR, CSAS.
38. Fenton, *Preliminary Statement*, 6.
39. Fenton, Fuller, and Rogers, *Policies and Procedures*, 16.
40. Fenton, Fuller, and Rogers, *Policies and Procedures*, 12.
41. Fenton, Fuller, and Rogers, *Policies and Procedures*, 17.
42. Fenton, *Preliminary Statement*, 7.
43. Fenton, Fuller, and Rogers, *Policies and Procedures*, 17–18.
44. California Department of Corrections, *Review of Adjustment Centers* (June 1958), 4, Institutions—Adjustment Centers, Director's Subject Files, DOCR, CSAS.
45. California Department of Corrections, *Review of Adjustment Centers*, 8.
46. Significantly, this chapter documents how this was happening in the 1950s, decades before the 1980s, which scholars have otherwise identified as the onset of long-term, curated isolation in California.
47. California Department of Corrections, *Review of Adjustment Centers*, 8.
48. California Department of Corrections, *Administrative Bulletin No. 58/16: Special Procedures for Muslim Inmates* (February 25, 1958), Muslim correspondence, 1961–68, Investigation Files: 1960–68, Records of the Assistant Director, DOCR, CSAS.
49. Federal Bureau of Investigation, "Counterintelligence Program (COINTELPRO) Black Extremist, Parts 1–23," 1967, FBI Records: The Vault, https://vault.fbi.gov/cointel-pro/cointel-pro-black-extremists.
50. Milton Burdman, "Adjustment Center Staffing, 1959–1960 Budget Proposal," August 8, 1958, pp. 1–4, Institutions-Adjustment Centers, Director's Subject Files, DOCR, CSAS.

51. California Department of Corrections, "The Problem: What Should Be P&CS Policy as It Relates to Parolees Belonging to or Working for the Muslim Organization?," March 22, 1963, Parole and Community Services Division. Inter-office Communication. DOCR, CSAS.
52. California Department of Corrections, *Administrative Bulletin No. 58/16: Special Procedures for Muslim Inmates*, first revision (May 18, 1961), Muslim correspondence, 1961–68, Investigation Files: 1960–68, Records of the Assistant Director, DOCR, CSAS.
53. California Department of Corrections, *Administrative Bulletin No. 58/16* (1961).
54. California Department of Corrections, Inter-office Communication, CWLA Adult Parole Division Office, October 1, 1962, Muslim correspondence, 1961–68, Investigation Files: 1960–68, Records of the Assistant Director, DOCR, CSAS.
55. Fenton, Fuller, and Rogers, *Policies and Procedures*.
56. California Department of Corrections and Rehabilitation, 1851–2010, California Prisoners & Parolees Reports.
57. Erik Olin Wright, *The Politics of Punishment: A Critical Analysis of Prisons in America* (New York: Harper and Row, 1973).
58. California Department of Corrections, "Inter-office Communication, Parole and Community Services Division," March 22, 1963, Muslim correspondence, 1961–68, Investigation Files: 1960–68, Records of the Assistant Director, DOCR, CSAS.
59. California Department of Corrections, Letter to Arkansas State Police, October 26, 1962, Muslim correspondence, 1961–68, Investigation Files: 1960–68, Records of the Assistant Director, DOCR, CSAS.
60. California Department of Corrections, Confidential Internal Memo, March 29, 1966, Muslim correspondence, 1961–68, Investigation Files: 1960–68, Records of the Assistant Director, DOCR, CSAS.
61. California Department of Corrections, Letter to Nevada State Prison, January 9, 1963, Muslim correspondence, 1961–68, Investigation Files: 1960–68, Records of the Assistant Director, DOCR, CSAS.
62. California Department of Corrections, Confidential Internal Memo, October 16, 1961, Muslim correspondence, 1961–68, Investigation Files: 1960–68, Records of the Assistant Director, DOCR, CSAS.
63. See Dan Berger, *Captive Nation: Black Prison Organizing in the Civil Rights Era* (Chapel Hill: University of North Carolina Press, 2014).
64. California Department of Corrections, Letter to My Attorney, August 10, 1962, Muslim correspondence, 1961–68, Investigation Files: 1960–68, Records of the Assistant Director, DOCR, CSAS. Richard is a pseudonym.
65. California Department of Corrections, Inmate Depositions: Shooting Incident at San Quentin State Prison, deposition no. 1, February 25, 1963, Muslim correspondence, 1961–68, Investigation Files: 1960–68, Records of the Assistant Director, DOCR, CSAS.
66. California Department of Corrections, Inmate Depositions, deposition no. 2.
67. California Department of Corrections, Inmate Depositions, deposition no. 3.
68. California Department of Corrections, Letter to My Attorney, August 10, 1962.
69. Freedom Archives, "George Lester Jackson," accessed November 12, 2016, www.freedomarchives.org/George%20Jackson.html.

70. George L. Jackson, *Soledad Brother: The Prison Letters of George Jackson* (Chicago: Lawrence Hill Books, 1970).
71. Jackson, *Soledad Brother*, 34.
72. California Department of Corrections, Confidential Internal Memo, March 29, 1966, Muslim correspondence, 1961–68, Investigation Files: 1960–68, Records of the Assistant Director, DOCR, CSAS.
73. California Department of Corrections, Confidential Internal Memo, March 29, 1966.
74. For example, *Lee v. Crouse*, 284 F. Supp. 541 (D. Kan. 1967).
75. In re Jesse L. Ferguson et al., 55 CAL.2D 663 (Cal. 1961), available at https://scocal.stanford.edu/opinion/re-ferguson-24309.
76. In re Jesse L. Ferguson et al.
77. In re Jesse L. Ferguson et al.
78. In re Jesse L. Ferguson et al.
79. *Siegel v. Ragen*, 180 F.2d 785 (7th Cir. 1950).
80. *People v. Ford*, 175 Cal.App.2d 37, 345 P.2d 354 (Cal. Ct. App. 1959).
81. *Roberts v. Department of Corrections*, 183 F.2d 580 (9th Cir. 1950).
82. *Roberts v. U.S. District Court for the Northern District of California*, 339 U.S. 844, 70 S. Ct. 954 (1950).
83. California Department of Corrections, Correspondence with California Assistant Attorney General, April 26, 1966, Justice Attorney General, Division of Criminal Law Subject Files—Muslims, 1965–67, DOCR, CSAS.
84. See Garrett Felber, *Those Who Know Don't Say: The Nation of Islam, the Black Freedom Movement, and the Carceral State* (Chapel Hill: University of North Carolina Press, 2019).
85. *Williford v. People of California*, 352 F.2d 474 (9th Cir. 1965).
86. Eldridge Cleaver, Letter to San Quentin Warden, April 10, 1961, Muslim correspondence, 1961–68, Investigation Files: 1960–68, Records of the Assistant Director, DOCR, CSAS.
87. I use "master's tools" in the same way outlined by the work of Audre Lorde. For full examination of this phrase see Audre Lorde, *The Master's Tools will Never Dismantle the Master's House* (London, UK: Penguin Books, 2018); or Audre Lorde, "The Master's Tools Will Never Dismantle the Master's House" (1984), in *Sister Outsider: Essays and Speeches* (Berkeley: Crossing Press, 2007), 11–14, https://collectiveliberation.org/wp-content/uploads/2013/01/Lorde_The_Masters_Tools.pdf.

Chapter 3

1. Interview with Andrew. All the names in this chapter—including those in interview quotes listing Andrew's family members—are pseudonyms.
2. Interview with Andrew.
3. Interview with Andrew.
4. Interview with Andrew.
5. Interview with Andrew.
6. Interview with Andrew.
7. Interview with Andrew.

8. Interview with Andrew.
9. Interview with Andrew.
10. Interview with Andrew.
11. Interview with Andrew.
12. Interview with Andrew.
13. W. E. B. Du Bois, "Jefferson Davis as a Representative of Civilization," 1890, W. E. B. Du Bois Papers, Special Collections and University Archives, University of Massachusetts Amherst Libraries, Amherst.
14. On emotional attachment to racial identity, see Janine Young Kim, "Racial Emotions and the Feeling of Equality," *Colorado Law Review* 87 (2016): 437–500; Susan Smith, "Race and Trust," *Annual Review of Sociology* 36 (2010): 453–75. On emotional attachment to status benefits, see Corinne Bendersky and Jieun Pai, "Status Dynamics," *Annual Review of Organizational Psychology and Organizational Behavior* 5 (2018): 183–99. On emotional attachment to political claims, see Aldon Morris, *The Origins of the Civil Rights Movement: Black Communities Organizing for Change* (New York: Free Press, 1984); Pamela Oliver, "The Ethnic Dimensions in Social Movements," *Mobilization: An International Quarterly* 22, no. 4 (2017): 395–416. On emotional attachment to network and community ties, see Mary Pattillo, *Black Picket Fences: Privilege and Peril among the Black Middle Class* (Chicago: University of Chicago Press, 1999); Mary Pattillo, *Black on the Block* (Chicago: University of Chicago Press, 2007). On emotional attachment to state formation, see Howard Winant, "Race and Race Theory," *Annual Review of Sociology* 26 (2000): 169–85.
15. W. E. B. Du Bois, *Darkwater: Voices from Within the Veil* (New York: Harcourt Brace, 1920).
16. Brittany Friedman, "White Unity and Prisoner-Officer Alliances," *Contexts* 21, no. 3 (2022): 28–33.
17. John Irwin and Donald Cressey, "Thieves, Convicts, and the Inmate Culture," *Social Problems* 10 (1962): 142–55; S. Wheeler, "Socialization in Correctional Communities," *American Sociological Review* 26 (1961): 697–712.
18. See Karen Lahm, "Inmate-on-Inmate Assault: A Multilevel Examination of Prison Violence," *Criminal Justice and Behavior* 35 (2008): 120–37; David C. Pyrooz and Scott H. Decker, *Competing for Control: Gangs and the Social Order of Prisons* (Cambridge: Cambridge University Press, 2019). The level of group polarization and conflict also depends on deprivation variables such as the prison's security level, the use of isolation as punishment, the number of programs, and overcrowding.
19. *Nichols v. McGee*, 169 F. Supp. 721 (N.D. Cal. 1959).
20. In society, white aversion to residential integration is a well-known example of the power of physical space and racial aversion.
21. California Department of Corrections, "California Prisoners and Parolees Reports," 1851–2010.
22. California Department of Corrections, "Internal Memo," May 15, 1962, Muslim correspondence, 1961–68, Investigation Files: 1960–68, Records of the Assistant Director, Department of Corrections Records, California State Archives, Sacramento.
23. California Department of Corrections, "Internal Memo," May 15, 1962.

24. Erik Olin Wright, *The Politics of Punishment: A Critical Analysis of Prisons in America* (New York: Harper and Row, 1973), 98–99.
25. Wright, *Politics of Punishment*, 98.
26. Wright, *Politics of Punishment*, 95.
27. Wright, *Politics of Punishment*, 110.
28. Wright, *Politics of Punishment*.
29. Street weapons are items brought into the prison versus shanks, which are prison-made weapons out of everyday items (filed-down toothbrush, deconstructed razor, etc.).
30. Wright, *Politics of Punishment*, 110.
31. Wright, *Politics of Punishment*, 112.
32. See the 2002 indictment: *USA v. Mills et al.*, 2:02-CR-00938, US District Court for the Central District of California (August 28, 2002).
33. Wright, *Politics of Punishment*, 120.
34. Wright, *Politics of Punishment*, 121.
35. Southern Poverty Law Center, *Intelligence Report: Aryan Prison Gangs. A Violent Movement Spreads from the Prisons to the Streets* (Montgomery, AL: SPLC Intelligence Project, 2005), www.splcenter.org/sites/default/files/d6_legacy_files/ir_aryan_prison_gangs_special_report_web.pdf.
36. Regarding drug trafficking, see the full case *USA v. Mills et al.*, 2002.
37. As the number of Chicanos behind bars steadily increased, street and neighborhood conflicts between Chicanos and Blacks seeped into the prison, moving Chicanos to form alliances with white prisoners. Similar to Blacks, Chicanos faced discrimination and excessive violence from white guards, necessitating the formation of the Mexican Mafia in 1957 in the Deuel Vocational Institution (Tracy, CA). However, disagreements frequently occurred between Chicanos from Southern California (Sureños), thought to be more cultured because of their urban roots, and those from Northern California (Norteños), believed to be simple and impressionable because of their rural, farming origins. These fights ranged from accusations of physical abuse and intimidation to interpersonal disputes over disrespect. In 1968, the ongoing animosity erupted in Soledad State Prison after an alleged dispute involving a Mexican Mafia member stealing a pair of shoes from a Norteño. A riot ensued, prompting Northern Chicanos to form their own organization in 1965; it was officially named La Nuestra Familia in 1968. Nuestra Familia members quickly sought an alliance between Norteños and Black militant leaders who in 1970 would form the Black Guerilla Family. These alliances still stand in the contemporary United States in 2024.
38. Interview with Dean.
39. Interview with John. John was sentenced to life with the possibility of parole.
40. Interview with John.
41. Wright, *Politics of Punishment*, 120.
42. Interview with John.
43. Interview with Andrew. The example he gave occurred in Nevada; however, he explained that similar incidents occurred in the California system. He felt like his incarceration in Nevada prepared him for entering a similar environment once he was transferred to California.

44. Interview with Andrew.
45. Interview with Andrew.

Chapter 4

1. Interview with Anthony.
2. A claim that is consistent across interview data.
3. Loic Wacquant, "The New 'Peculiar Institution': On the Prison as Surrogate Ghetto," *Theoretical Criminology* 4, no. 3 (2000): 377–89.
4. Thomas Foster, "The Sexual Abuse of Black Men under American Slavery," *Journal of the History of Sexuality* 20, no. 3 (2011): 445–64; Karen A. Getman, "Sexual Control in the Slaveholding South: the Implementation and Maintenance of a Racial Caste System," *Harvard Women's and Law Journal* 7 (1984): 115–52; Deborah Gray White, Mia Bay, and Waldo E. Martin Jr., *Freedom On My Mind: A History of African Americans* (New York: Bedford/St. Martin's, 2012).
5. Jeff Forret, *Slave against Slave: Plantation Violence in the Old South* (Baton Rouge: Louisiana State University Press, 2015).
6. Charles M. Christian, *Black Saga: The African American Experience, a Chronology* (New York: Houghton Mifflin, 1995), 144.
7. Herbert Aptheker, *American Negro Slave Revolts* (New York: Columbia University Press, 1943).
8. Sarah Bullard, *The Klu Klux Klan: A History of Racism & Violence* (Montgomery, AL: Southern Poverty Law Center, 1998); David Mark Chalmers, *Hooded Americanism: The History of the Klu Klux Klan* (Durham, NC: Duke University Press, 1987).
9. Equal Justice Initiative, *Lynching in America: Confronting the Legacy of Racial Terror*, 3rd ed., 2017, https://lynchinginamerica.eji.org/report/.
10. Alma F. Taeuber and Karl E. Taeuber, "The Negro Population in the United States," in *The American Negro Reference Book*, edited by John P. Davis (Englewood Cliffs, NJ: Prentice-Hall, 1966), 96–160.
11. National Archives, "The Great Migration (1910–1970)," last reviewed June 28, 2021, www.archives.gov/research/african-americans/migrations/great-migration#:~:text=The%20Great%20Migration%20was%20one,the%201910s%20until%20the%201970s.
12. Hilary Herbold, "Never a Level Playing Field: Blacks and the GI Bill, "*Journal of Blacks in Higher Education* 6 (1994): 104–8; Edward Humes, "How the G.I. Bill Shunted Blacks into Vocational Training," *Journal of Blacks in Higher Education* 53 (2006): 92–104; Ira Katznelson, *When Affirmative Action Was White: An Untold History of Racial Inequality in Twentieth-Century America* (New York: W. W. Norton, 2005); David H. Onkst, "First a Negro . . . Incidentally a Veteran: Black World War II Veterans and the G.I. Bill of Rights in the Deep South, 1944–1948," *Journal of Social History* 31, no. 3 (1998): 517–43.
13. Albert S. Broussard, *Black San Francisco: The Struggle for Racial Equality in the West* (Lawrence: University of Kansas Press, 1993).
14. Douglas S. Massey and Nancy A. Denton, *American Apartheid: Segregation and the Making of the Underclass* (Cambridge, MA: Harvard University Press, 1993).
15. Alex Alonso, "Racialized Identities and the Formation of Black Gangs in Los Angeles," *Urban Geography* 25, no. 7 (2004): 658–74.

16. James Baldwin, *The Fire Next Time* (New York: Penguin Random House, 1963).
17. Interview with Avery.
18. Aldon D. Morris, *The Origins of the Civil Rights Movement: Black Movements Organizing for Change* (New York: Free Press, 1984).
19. "FAQs," *King Center*, accessed January 13, 2024, https://thekingcenter.org/about-tkc/faqs/#toggle-id-3.
20. Equal Justice Initiative, "Persecution of Civil Rights Activists," January 1, 2014, https://eji.org/news/history-racial-injustice-persecution-of-civil-rights-activists/.
21. Federal Bureau of Investigation, "COINTELPRO, Black Extremist, Parts 1–23," 1967, FBI Records: The Vault, https://vault.fbi.gov/cointel-pro/cointel-pro-black-extremists.
22. Ward Churchill and Jim Vander Wall, *Agents of Repression: The FBI's Secret Wars against the Black Panther Party and the American Indian Movement* (Cambridge, MA: South End Press, 1990); Ward Churchill and Jim Vander Wall, *The COINTELPRO Papers: Documents from the FBI's Secret Wars against Dissent in the United States* (Cambridge, MA: South End Press, 2002).
23. Mumia Abu-Jamal and Johana Fernandez, "Locking Up Black Dissidents and Punishing the Poor: The Roots of Mass Incarceration in the US," *Socialism and Democracy* 48, no. 3 (2014): 1–14.
24. Khalil Gibran Muhammad, *The Condemnation of Blackness: Race, Crime, and the Making of Modern Urban America* (Cambridge, MA: Harvard University Press, 2010).
25. Wacquant, "The New 'Peculiar Institution.'"
26. Dan Baum, "Legalize It All: How to Win the War on Drugs," *Harper's Magazine*, April 2016.
27. Elizabeth Hinton, *From the War on Poverty to the War on Crime: The Making of Mass Incarceration in America* (Cambridge, MA: Harvard University Press, 2017).
28. Bruce Drake, "Incarceration Gap Widens between Whites and Blacks," Pew Research Center, September 6, 2013, www.pewresearch.org/fact-tank/2013/09/06/incarceration-gap-between-whites-and-blacks-widens/.
29. Interview with Anthony.
30. Interview with Anthony.
31. Interview with Benjamin.
32. Interview with Benjamin.
33. Interview with Benjamin.
34. Much of the research on cynicism about the law and legal institutions investigates this phenomenon and its effect on violence within neighborhoods and communities. See David S. Kirk and Mauri Matsuda, "Legal Cynicism, Collective Efficacy, and the Ecology of Arrest," *Criminology* 49, no. 2 (May 2011): 443–72; David S. Kirk and Andrew V. Papachristos, "Cultural Mechanisms and the Persistence of Neighborhood Violence," *American Journal of Sociology* 116, no. 4 (2011): 1190–233.
35. Derrick Franke, David Bierie, and Doris Layton Mackenzie, "Legitimacy in Corrections: A Randomized Experiment Comparing a Boot Camp with a Prison," *Criminology and Public Policy* 9, no. 1 (2010): 89–117.

36. Kitty Calavita and Valerie Jenness, *Appealing to Justice: Prisoner Grievances, Rights and Carceral Logic* (Oakland: University of California Press, 2014).
37. Interview with Benjamin.
38. Interview with Kendrick.
39. Interview with Anthony.
40. Interview with Benjamin.
41. George L. Jackson, *Soledad Brother: The Prison Letters of George Jackson* (Chicago: Lawrence Hill Books, 1970), 21.
42. Interview with Anthony.

Chapter 5

1. Interview with Anthony.
2. Dan Berger, *Captive Nation: Black Prison Organizing in the Civil Rights Era* (Chapel Hill: University of North Carolina Press, 2014); Joy James, *Imprisoned Intellectuals: America's Political Prisoners Write* (New York: Roman and Littlefield, 2003); Joy James, "George Jackson: Dragon Philosopher and Revolutionary Abolitionist," *Black Perspectives*, August 21, 2018, www.aaihs.org/george-jackson-dragon-philosopher-and-revolutionary-abolitionist/.
3. *W. L. Nolen, et al. v. Cletus Fitzharris*, 1969.
4. James, "George Jackson."
5. "Underground News," *Ramparts Magazine*, April 2, 1973.
6. "Underground News."
7. A conclusion represented across all the interview data from my study with founders of the Black Guerilla Family.
8. "Underground News."
9. "Underground News."
10. "Underground News."
11. "Underground News," 37.
12. Hugo Pinell, "Letter from Soledad Prison," 1970, Fair Chance Project, accessed March 2019, https://sites.google.com/site/factsfairchance.
13. "Negro Prisoners Begin Hunger Strike in Bid for Investigation," *The Bulletin*, January 15, 1970.
14. Eric Cummins, *The Rise and Fall of California's Radical Prison Movement* (Stanford, CA: Stanford University Press, 1994).
15. "Underground News," 39.
16. Bettina Aptheker, *The Morning Breaks: The Trial of Angela Davis* (Ithaca, NY: Cornell University Press, 1999).
17. Berger, *Captive Nation*.
18. James, "George Jackson."
19. Interview with Eliza.
20. See introduction, note 22.
21. Interview with Anthony.
22. Interview with Anthony.
23. Berger, *Captive Nation*.
24. James, "George Jackson."

25. Cummins, *Rise and Fall*.
26. Aptheker, *Morning Breaks*.
27. George L. Jackson, *Soledad Brother: The Prison Letters of George Jackson* (Chicago: Lawrence Hill Books, 1970).
28. Interview with Eliza.
29. Jackson, *Soledad Brother*, 330.
30. James, "George Jackson"; George L. Jackson, *Blood in My Eye* (New York: Random House, 1972).
31. Interview with Anthony.
32. Interview with Anthony.
33. Interview with Anthony.
34. Interview with Anthony.
35. Interview with Sean.
36. "Statement to the People from Black Prisoners inside San Quentin," *Breakthrough: Political Journal of Prairie Fire Organizing Committee* 1, no. 3–4 (October–December 1977): 45, Breakthrough Collection, Freedom Archives, www.freedomarchives.org/Documents/Finder/DOC501_scans/Break/501.break.3.oct.1977.pdf.
37. Interview with Anthony.
38. Part III, Black Guerilla Family Constitution. A version of this constitution was disclosed to me by an interviewee. An almost identical version is available in Cummins, *Rise and Fall*.
39. Modeled after the Mau Mau oaths. The Mau Mau Rebellion (1952–60) was an independence movement to free Kenya from British colonial rule.
40. "George Jackson: P.S. on Ulysses," *The Black Panther Intercommunal News Service*, August 28, 1971, 5, www.marxists.org/history/usa/pubs/black-panther/07%20no%201%201-10%20aug%2028%201971.pdf. After George Jackson was killed in 1971, an additional line was added: *"Long live the spirit of George Jackson, long live the spirit of the Black Guerilla Family!"*
41. Interview with Anthony.
42. Interview with Jerome.
43. Interview with Carl.
44. Interview with Sean.
45. Interview with Benjamin.
46. California Prisoners Union, "The Folsom Prisoners Manifesto of Demands and Anti-oppression Platform," November 3, 1970, Folson Prison Strike Collection, Freedom Archives, www.freedomarchives.org/Documents/Finder/DOC510_scans/Folsom_Manifesto/510.folsom.manifesto.11.3.1970.pdf.
47. Interview with Carl.
48. Interview with Sean.
49. Interview with Jerome.
50. Consistent across my interview data.
51. Interview with Benjamin.
52. Interview with Anthony.
53. Jackson, *Soledad Brother*.
54. Interview with Eliza.
55. Interview with Lionel.

56. Interview with Lionel.
57. Interview with Lionel.
58. For an example of the state narrative, see *Spain v. Rushen*, 543 F. Supp. 757 (N.D. Cal. 1982).
59. Interview with Lionel; and interview with Frank.
60. Interview with Lionel.
61. Interview with Lionel.
62. Interview with Lionel. According to the official account by the Department of Corrections, the Black Guerilla Family took three officers and two prisoners hostage and executed them, leaving them dead in Jackson's cell. Three other officers were shot and stabbed when attempting to confront the escapees but later survived. See Cummins, *Rise and Fall*; Lori Andrews, *Black Power, White Blood: The Life and Times of Johnny Spain* (Philadelphia, PA: Temple University Press, 1999). Eyewitnesses tell a completely different story, adamantly arguing the main goal of the escape was to simply get Jackson out, not to take hostages. The officers and white prisoners were violently attacked because they tried to stop the escape, not because the Black Guerilla Family wanted to use them as "bargaining chips" (interview with Lionel). Official accounts argue that Jackson had met with his attorney Stephen Bingham earlier that day and that Bingham had smuggled the gun into the prison by stuffing it inside a tape recorder. The California Department of Corrections claimed at the time that Jackson was wearing a wig that had been smuggled into the prison weeks prior and in which he hid the gun. Though this account was later proven false, prison officials continue to maintain it as fact, and many media sources continue to cite it. Jo Durden-Smith, *Who Killed George Jackson? Fantasies, Paranoia and the Revolution* (New York: Alfred A. Knopf, 1976); Karen Wald, "The San Quentin Six Case: Perspective and Analysis," in "40th Anniversary Issue: Legacies of Radical Criminology in the United States," ed. Tony Platt, special issue, *Social Justice* 40, no. 1/2 (2013): 231–51. Academic sources also recount this tale. See Cummins, *Rise and Fall*; Andrews, *Black Power, White Blood*.

  The gun used during the attempt was actually smuggled into the prison by corrupt correctional officers some weeks prior. These were the same officers responsible for secretly supplying the Black Guerilla Family with the faulty C4. Little did the Black Guerilla Family know that the gun was a setup and would later be used to justify the officers shooting Jackson in the courtyard. Diligent members of the Black Panther Party eventually alleged that they proved the gun was a setup by tracing its original location to the FBI, Northern District of California, by way of the Oakland Police Department (interview with Lionel; interview with Frank).
63. N. B. Snellgrove to L. S. Nelson, "Books Taken from Cell of George Jackson," September 3, 1971, George Jackson Collection, Freedom Archives, https://freedomarchives.org/Documents/Finder/DOC513_scans/George_Jackson/513.George.Jackson.books.pdf.
64. Heather Ann Thompson, *Blood in the Water: The Attica Prison Uprising of 1971 and Its Legacy* (New York: Pantheon, 2016); Orisanmi Burton, *Tip of the Spear: Black Radicalism, Prison Repression, and the Long Attica Revolt* (Oakland: University of California Press, 2023).

65. "The Attica Liberation Faction Manifesto of Demands and Anti-depression Platform," 1971, Attica Prison Rebellion Collection, Freedom Archives, https://freedomarchives.org/Documents/Finder/DOC510_scans/Attica/510.Prisons.AtticaManifesto.pdf.
66. See Thompson, *Blood in the Water*, and Burton, *Tip of the Spear*, for a description of the historical events and the vicious level of brutality on the part of state troopers.

Chapter 6

1. Dan Berger, *Captive Nation: Black Prison Organizing in the Civil Rights Era* (Chapel Hill: University of North Carolina Press, 2014).
2. Interview with Benjamin.
3. Interview with Benjamin.
4. Interview with Jerome.
5. Interview with Jerome.
6. *Spain v. Procunier*, 408 F. Supp. 534 (N.D. Cal. 1976).
7. *Spain v. Procunier*.
8. *Spain v. Rushen*, 883 F.2d 712 (9th Cir. 1989).
9. *Spain v. Rushen*.
10. The FBI estimated Black Guerilla Family membership at about 1,000 in 1974. FBI, "Black Guerilla Family," Parts 1–3, 1974–1980, FBI Records: The Vault, https://vault.fbi.gov/black-guerilla-family/black-guerilla-family-part-1-of-3/view; https://vault.fbi.gov/black-guerilla-family/black-guerilla-family-part-2-of-3/view; https://vault.fbi.gov/black-guerilla-family/black-guerilla-family-part-3-of-3/view.
11. Federal Bureau of Investigation, "Black Guerilla Family," Part 1, 1974, p. 2, FBI Records: The Vault, https://vault.fbi.gov/black-guerilla-family/black-guerilla-family-part-1-of-3/view.
12. Interview with Anthony.
13. Interview with Anthony.
14. Interview with Anthony.
15. DEMONSTRATE flyer posted during the six-year anniversary of George Jackson's murder: "6th Anniversary of the Assassination of George Jackson," flyer, August 21, 1977, George Jackson Collection, Freedom Archives, https://freedomarchives.org/Documents/Finder/DOC513_scans/George_Jackson/513.George.Jackson.George.Jackson.San.Quentin.Demonstration.pdf.
16. DEMONSTRATE flyer.
17. Interview with Carl.
18. Interview with Carl.
19. *People v. Masters*, S016883 (Cal. Feb. 22, 2016), available at https://law.justia.com/cases/california/supreme-court/2016/s016883.html.

Chapter 7

1. Peter Collier and David Horowitz, "Requiem for a Radical," *New West Magazine*, March 1981; Diana Russell, "Fay Stender and the Politics of Murder," *On the Issues Magazine*, May 27, 1991, https://ontheissuesmagazine.com/feminism/fay-stender-and-the-politics-of-murder/.

2. Interview with Anthony.
3. Interview with Lionel.
4. Keramet Reiter, *23/7: Pelican Bay Prison and the Rise of Long-term Solitary Confinement* (New Haven, CT: Yale University Press, 2016).
5. Interview with Aaron.
6. Interview with Aaron.
7. Interview with Bill.
8. Erik Olin Wright, *The Politics of Punishment: A Critical Analysis of Prisons in America* (New York: Harper and Row, 1973), 96.
9. Interview with Bill.
10. Interview with Bill.
11. Interview with Bill.
12. Reiter, *23/7*.
13. Fareed Nassor Hayat, "Killing Due Process: Double Jeopardy, White Supremacy and Gang Prosecutions," *UCLA Law Review* 69, no. 18 (2021), www.uclalawreview.org/killing-due-process-double-jeopardy-white-supremacy-and-gang-prosecutions/.
14. See Patrick Lopez-Aguado, *Stick Together and Come Back Home: Racial Sorting and the Spillover of Carceral Identity* (Oakland: University of California Press, 2018).
15. See Reiter, *23/7*.
16. Abdul Olugbala Shakur, "90 Days of Darkness, No Running Water, Naked, No Blankets," *Daily Outrage* (blog), Center for Constitutional Rights, May 23, 2017, https://ccrjustice.org/home/blog/2017/05/23/90-days-darkness-no-running-water-naked-no-blankets.
17. Interview with Andrew.
18. Center for Constitutional Rights, "After Decades in Solitary They Joined Forces. Here's What Happened," uploaded September 1, 2015, YouTube video, 7:21, www.youtube.com/watch?v=xDyOBOnAQUI.
19. Center for Constitutional Rights, "After Decades in Solitary."
20. Center for Constitutional Rights, "After Decades in Solitary."
21. Center for Constitutional Rights, "Agreement to End Hostilities," August 12, 2012, https://ccrjustice.org/sites/default/files/attach/2015/07/Agreement%20to%20End%20Hostilities.pdf.
22. See introduction, note 4.
23. *Ashker v. Governor of State of California*, No. C 09-05796 CW (N.D. Cal. Sep. 6, 2016).
24. The Ashker case timeline can be tracked here: Center for Constitutional Rights, "Ashker v. Governor for California," last modified September 8, 2023, https://ccrjustice.org/home/what-we-do/our-cases/ashker-v-brown. See also "Impact of CDCR's STG/SDP: Proposed Permanent Regulations Fact Sheet," Prisoner Hunger Striker Solidarity, accessed January 12, 2024, https://prisonerhungerstrikesolidarity.files.wordpress.com/2014/03/fact-sheet-impact-of-cdcr-security-threat-groupstep-down-program.pdf.

Conclusion

1. Robin D. G. Kelley, *Freedom Dreams: The Black Radical Imagination* (New York: Beacon Press, 2002).
2. Malcolm X, *The Autobiography of Malcolm X (As Told to Alex Haley)* (New York: Ballantine Books, 1992).

3. Ruth Wilson Gilmore, *Change Everything: Racial Capitalism and the Case for Abolition* (Chicago: Haymarket Books, 2021).
4. Rachel Kushner, "Is Prison Necessary? Ruth Wilson Gilmore Might Change Your Mind," *New York Times*, April 17, 2019, www.nytimes.com/2019/04/17/magazine/prison-abolition-ruth-wilson-gilmore.html.

Appendix

1. John Hagan, Bill McCarthy, and Daniel Herda, *Chicago's Reckoning: Racism, Politics, and the Deep History of Policing in an American City* (New York: Oxford University Press, 2022); John Hagan and Wenona Rymond-Richmond, *Darfur and the Crime of Genocide* (Cambridge: Cambridge University Press, 2008).
2. Aldon Morris, *The Scholar Denied: W. E. B. Du Bois and the Birth of Modern Sociology* (Berkeley: University of California Press, 2017).
3. Nicole Conzalez Van Cleve, *Crook County: Racism and Injustice in America's Largest Criminal Court* (Palo Alto: Stanford University Press, 2016).
4. Michael Sierra-Arévalo, *The Danger Imperative: Violence, Death, and the Soul of Policing* (New York: Columbia University Press, 2024).
5. Shaonta' E. Allen, "The Black Feminist Roots of Scholar Activism: Lessons from Ida B. Wells-Barnett," in *Black Feminist Sociology: Perspectives and Praxis*, ed. Zakiya Luna and Whiteney Pirtle (New York: Routledge, 2022), 32.
6. Armando Lara-Millán, Brian Sargent, and Sunmin Kim, "Where Is the Archive in Historical Sociology? The Case for Ethnographic Dispositions," *Comparative and Historical Sociology*, June 20, 2019, http://chs.asa-comparative-historical.org/where-is-the-archive-in-historical-sociology-the-case-for-ethnographic-dispositions/.
7. Marcus Anthony Hunter, "Black Logics, Black Methods: Indigenous Timelines, Race, and Ethnography," Sociological Perspectives 61, no. 2 (2018), https://doi.org/10.1177/0731121418758646.
8. Brittany Friedman and Michael L. Walker, "Creating Intuitively: The Art and Flow of Intuitive Social Science," in *Disciplinary Futures: Sociology in Conversation with American, Ethnic, and Indigenous Studies*, ed. Nadia Y. Kim and Pawan Dhingra (New York: Oxford University Press, 2023), 303.
9. Kelly Lytle Hernández, *City of Inmates: Conquest, Rebellion, and the Rise of Human Caging in Los Angeles, 1771–1965* (Chapel Hill: University of North Carolina Press, 2017).

INDEX

Page numbers in italics refer to illustrations.

Aaron (Crips), 150–52
Abbate, Paul, 11
Abernathy, Ralph, xviii
abolition, 14, 163–64
abuse, childhood, 69, 71–75
Adjustment Centers: archives of, 167, 170; Black militants in, 51–61, 65, 80, 105, 107–8, 153, 155; creation of, xviii, 15, 46–51, 76, 154; lawsuits against, 64–65, 76, 110; as official control, 29; at San Quentin, 4, 135–36, 141–42; at Soledad, 113, 119. *See also* Secure Housing Units (SHUs); supermax confinement
administrative maximum (ADX). *See* supermax confinement
Afghanistan, xxii
Agreement to End Hostilities, xx, 160–61
Allegra Casimir-Taylor v. State of California, 171n4
Allen, E. Shaonta', 166
American Communist Party, 101
Andrew (Aryan Warriors/Brotherhood), 67–74, 86–90, 156–58, 186n1, 188n43
Anthony (Black Guerilla Family), xix, 93–95, 99, 103–9, 119, 121–22, 124, 126, 135, 143–45, 150
Anti-Drug Abuse Act, xx
apartheid, definition of, 19–22. *See also* carceral apartheid, definition of
Arab Spring, xxii
Arbery, Ahmaud, 10–11
archives, 14–16, 165–66
Arkansas National Guard, 101
Arkansas State Police, 55
Armstrong, Gregory, 118, 169
Aryan Brotherhood: alliances with correctional officers, 8, 106, 130–32, 143, 146–47; alliance with Mexican Mafia, xix, 83; and carceral apartheid, 27; founding of, xviii, 69, 81–82, 89; murder of Hugo Pinell, xx, 7–8, 138, 160, 171n4; and the Soledad Incident, 110–12; and supermax, 156; war with Black Guerilla Family, xix, 90, 144, 149–53; and "white above all," 84–86, 88, 154
Aryan Warriors, 69, 87–89
Ashker v. Governor of California, xx, 159–61
Atlanta, GA, xx
Attica Prison Uprising (1971), xix, 132
Avery (Black Panther Party), 99–101
Avery, Early Ida Marie Coffee Wilderness, xi, *xii*

Baldwin, James, xi, 1, 100
Baltimore, MD, 99, 100
Beccaria, Cesare, 40
Becker, Howard, 38
Benjamin (Black Guerilla Family), 104–7, 109, 126–27, 129, 135–38, 144
Bentham, Jeremy, 40–41
Berlin Conference, xxi
Biden, Joe, 12
Bill (Department of Corrections), 152–54
Bingham, Gary, 171n1
Bingham, Stephen, 193n62
biological determinism, 41
Black feminism, 23, 165–66, 178n12
Black Freedom Movement, 5–6, 16, 29, 59, 77–78, 102, 106, 118, 169. *See also* Black Guerilla Family
Black Guerilla Family: archives of, 167–70; and *Ashker* lawsuit (2012), 159–61; and carceral apartheid, 10, 27; and escape attempt (1971), xix, 129–32, 155, 193n62;

Black Guerilla Family (*continued*)
expansion and adaptation of (post-1971), 142–44, 149–55; founding of, xix, 5–6, 83, 94–95, 106–9; ideology and structure of, 124–27; interviews with, 16, 174n22; members of, 59, 69, 93, 100, 103–4; prison strike (1970), 127–28; and San Quentin Six, 135, 137–42; and Soledad Incident, 109, 111, 119–20, 121–23; split with United Guerilla Front, xix, 145–47; war with Aryan Brotherhood/Mexican Mafia, xix, 90, 144, 149–53
Black Liberation Army, 16, 94, 121, 124, 130, 132
Black Lives Matter, xx, 10–11
Black militants: alliances with other groups, xix, 83, 123, 188n37; archives of, 167–68; and escape attempt (1971), 130, 135; and founding of Black Guerilla Family, 94, 105–8, 121–22; incarceration of, 15–16, 29, 77; murders of, 5–7, 160; in Pelican Bay supermax, 155–57; as problem inmates, 51–66; and Soledad Incident, 109–12, 117–19; targeting by prison officials of, 28, 33, 79–82, 102–3, 138–41, 146–47, 153–54, 159. *See also* Black Guerilla Family; *and names of individual groups and organizations*
Black Muslims, xviii, 51, 53–55, 61–65, 78, 103, 106, 121. *See also* Nation of Islam
Black Panther Party: archives of, 167–69; founding of, xviii; interviews with, 16; George Jackson and, 59, 118, 193n62; members of, 64, 79, 99; and other Black militant groups, 94, 100, 102, 103, 121–25; shootouts with police, xix
Black Power Movement, 94, 130, 151
Black Vanguard, 94, 109. *See also* Black Guerilla Family
Bloods, 86, 98, 150–52
Bloody Sunday, 97
Bonfils, Maison, *18*
Braly, Malcolm: *False Starts*, 169
Brando, Marlon, 118
Brexit, xxii
Brook, John Lee: *Blood In, Blood Out*, 169
Brown v. Board of Education, xi, xviii, 101

Burdman, Milton, 52
Burge, John, 165
Bush, George H. W., xx

California: Los Angeles, xix, xviii, 16, 55, 60, 62, 98, 100, 121, 152; Los Angeles County, 70; Monterey County, 117; Northern, 70–71, 147, 188n37; Oakland, xviii, 16, 98–99, 146, 193n62; Sacramento, 15, 52, 55, 57, 115–16, 166; San Francisco, 65, 141; Southern, 67, 70, 83, 146–47, 152, 188n37; Tracy, xviii
California Department of Corrections: and Adjustment Centers, xviii, 46, 49; Administrative Bulletin 58/16, xviii, 15, 51–53, 60; archives of, 15, 167, 170; and the Black Guerilla Family, 94, 108, 147, 149–50, 152–53, 160; and Black militants, 54–55, 57–57, 63–64, 65, 107; and carceral apartheid, 10; lawsuits against, xx, 60–64, 109–10, 140–42, 159; and Hugo Pinell, 4–8, 160, 173n17; and prisoner resistance, 127–30, 132, 193n62; Leo Stanley at, 44–46; and white supremacists, 69, 152, 154, 156
California Department of Corrections and Rehabilitation (CDCR), xx, 34, 45
California Institution for Men (Chino), xvii
California Institution for Women, xvii
California Institution for Women (Chino), xvii
California Prisoners Union, 127
California State Archives, 14–16, 166–67
California State Prison–Sacramento, xx, 7, 171n4
Calipatria State Prison, 32
Capitol riot (January 6, 2021), xx, 11–12
carceral apartheid, definition of, 5–6, 10, 13–14, 21–22
carceral archipelago, 179n15
Carl (Black Guerilla Family), 126, 146–47
Carlisle Indian Industrial School, 22
Carter, Bunchy, xix
CDCR, xx, 34, 45
chattel slavery. *See* slavery
Chicago, IL, xix, 67, 69, 99–100, 122, 165

Chicanos, 68, 111, 188n37. *See also* Mexican Mafia
China, xxi, 124
Christianity, 39–40
citizenship, 63–64
Civilization Fund Act, xvii
Civil Rights Act, 63–64
Civil Rights Congress: "We Charge Genocide" document, xvii, 23
civil rights movement, 6, 29, 59, 101, 121–22, 169
Civil War, xvii
clandestine controls: and Black militants, 56, 58–59, 65, 103, 111, 147, 155; and carceral apartheid, 6, 9, 12, 25–29, 32, 34; and COINTELPRO, 101; and "white above all," 80
Clayton, John: *Pelican Bay*, 169
Cleaver, Eldridge, 64–65, 167; *Soul on Ice*, 169
COINTELPRO, xviii, 101–3, 143, 168; COINTELPRO-BLACKHATE, xviii, 102
Cold War, 98
Colston, Alex, 170
communism, 124–25
Confederate symbols, 11
Congo, xxi–xxii, xxii, 20
contraband market, 61–62, 82–83, 143–44, 147, 149
controls. *See* clandestine controls; extralegal controls; official controls
Cornelius (petitioner in lawsuit), 76–77
correctional officers: alliances with white supremacists of, 5, 8, 29, 77, 83, 106; archives of, 169; and gladiator fights, 90, 156–58; and Hugo Pinell, 2, 4–5, 7, 171n4; as plants in the Black Guerilla Family, 130–32, 143, 147, 193n62; sexual assaults by, 137–40; stoking racial tensions, 80–82, 105–6; treatment of Black inmates by, 49, 58–59, 60–61, 62–63, 76, 104, 111–15, 129, 175n25; unions of, 26; white supremacy and, 11, 75, 86, 88, 107, 154–55
counterterrorism, 10, 27

Crimea, xxii
criminality, 37–43, 47, 102, 173n12, 182n7
criminology, 38–39, 42, 182n7
Crips, 86, 98, 150–52
critical race theory, 75, 180n27
cross-racial mobilization, xi, 159–60
Cuba, 132; Guantánamo Bay detention camp, 24

Daley, Richard M., 165
D.A.R.E. program, xix
Davis, Angela, xix, 118, 120
Dean (white inmate), 83–84, 86
death, physical, social, and psychic, 44–45
death work, 1, 9
DeLeon, Frank, 8
Democratic Party, 103
demographics: of prisoners in California, xviii, 77, 150, 167; of prisoners in the United States, 26, 103
Denton, Nancy A., 178n12
Detroit, MI, 100
Deuel Vocational Institution (Tracy, CA), xviii–xix, 50–52, 104–5, 129, 142, 188n37
deviance, 37–38, 40–42, 173n12
Douglass, Frederick, xvii
Du Bois, W. E. B., 13, 17, 75, 165, 172n12, 182n7
Duffy, Clinton T., 36; *The San Quentin Story*, 169
Durkheim, Emile, 125, 173n12

Eastern State Penitentiary, 41
Edwards, Cleveland, 5, 111, 114–18
Ehrlichman, John, 102
Eliza (Soledad Brothers Defense Committee), 118
Emancipation Proclamation, 97
England, 24. *See also* Great Britain
Enlightenment, 40–41
escape attempts, xix, 7–8, 33, 120–21, 129–32, 135, 137–38, 140, 142, 155, 174n25, 193n62
eugenics, 42, 45
Europe, xxi, 13, 22, 39–40, 42, 96

Index

extralegal controls: and Black militants, 56, 58–59, 60–61, 65–66, 103, 110–11, 147, 155–57, 160; and carceral apartheid, 6, 9–10, 12, 25–29, 32, 34, 180n27; and COINTELPRO, 143; sexual assault as, 137–39; and "white above all," 80–82

Fair Chance Project, 172n9
Fanon, Frantz, 22, 125; *Black Skin, White Masks*, 22–23
Faubus, Orval, 101
FBI. *See* Federal Bureau of Investigation
Federal Bureau of Investigation: and the Black Guerilla Family, 130, 132, 143; and Black militants, 51, 60, 79, 100–103; and Angela Davis, xix, 120; founding of, xvii; the Vault, 168; white supremacist sympathies of, 11. *See also* COINTELPRO; Ghetto Informant Program
feminism, Black, 23, 165–66, 178n12
Ferguson v. California, xviii, 62–63
Filippi, Natacha, 20
First Step Act, xx
Flint, MI, 165
Floyd, George, xx, 10–11
Folsom Manifesto, 127–28, 132
Folsom State Prison: Adjustment Center in, 50–52, 57; Black Guerilla Family at, 142; Black Muslim inmates in, 62, 65; opening of, xvii; Hugo Pinell at, 113; prison strike at, 127–29, 132; segregation in, 76; white supremacists in, 89
Fonda, Jane, 118
Foucault, Michel, 179n15
Freedom Archives, 166, 168
freedom dreams, 163
Friedman, Brittany, 133, 163, 172n11

Garvey, Marcus, xvii, 102
genocide: and apartheid, 20; Armenian, 20; and carceral apartheid, 24–26, 57; in Congo, xxii; in Darfur, 165; in Palestine, xxii, 12–13, *18*, 24; and racist intent, 10; in Rwanda, xxii; in South Africa, 19; in the United States, xiii–xiv, 23, 43, 161

Georgia, 10
Georgia State Patrol, xx
Germany, xxi, 20, 118
Ghetto Informant Program, 102
GI Bill, xvii, 98
Gilmore, Ruth Wilson, 164
gladiator fights, 6, 25, 28–29, 69, 89–90, 96, 156–58
Golden State University Law School Digital Commons, 167–68
Gonzalez Van Cleve, Nicole, 30, 165
Goodman, Philip, 30
governance: and Adjustment Centers, 49; apartheid as, 19–21, 178n12; carceral apartheid as, 9–11, 24–29, *25–26*, 33–34, 39, 45, 56, 59, 94, 108; and prison order, 180n27; racialized, xiii–xiv, 6, 30, 66, 84
Graham, Jere P., 8
Great Britain, 124, 192n39. *See also* England
Great Depression, xvii, 98
Great Migration, 97–100
Guantánamo Bay detention camp, xxii, 24

Hagan, John, 165
Haiti: earthquake in (2010), xxii; Haitian Revolution, 96
Haley, Harold, 120
Hall, Cynthia, 142
Hampton, Fred, xix, 122, 135
Harris (Aryan Brotherhood), 112, 118
Hayat, Fareed Nassor, 154–55
Hayti Negro School, xi
Hell's Angels, 81
Hispanic people, 30–32, 83. *See also* Chicanos
Hitler, Adolf, xxi, 11, 82
Hobbes, Thomas, 40
Holocaust, xxi
Holohan, James B., 45
Hoover, J. Edgar, xvii, 101–2
Huggins, John, xix
hunger strikes, xx, 65, 117, 159–60
Hunter, Marcus, 166

imperialism, xxi, 9, 13. *See also* settler colonialism
incarceration, 5, 19, 24, 96, 102, 149
Indian boarding schools, xvii
Indian Reorganization Act, xvii
Indigenous peoples, xvii, 12, 22, 24, 83
Internal Revenue Service, 102
International Court of Justice, xxii, 13
intuitive social science, 166
Ireland, xxi, 24, 82; War of Independence, xxi
Islam. *See* Black Muslims; Nation of Islam
Israel, xxi–xii, 12–13, *18*, 20, 24. *See also* Palestine

Jackson, George: and the Black Guerilla Family, 100, 146–47, 150; *Blood in My Eye*, 121, 169; escape attempts, xix, 8, 120, 130, 132, 174n25; letters of, 167–69; murder of, xix, 7, 132, 142, 152, 193n62; sentencing of, xviii; *Soledad Brother*, 118, 120, 169; in solitary confinement, 59–60
Jackson, Jonathan, xix, 120–21
Jackson, Lester, 120
Jennings, Dean: *The San Quentin Story*, 169
Jerome (Black Guerilla Family), 125–26, 138–40
Jim Crow, 24, 75, 96–97, 101
John (white San Quentin inmate), 84–86
Johnson (petitioner in lawsuit), 62

Kaiser, Henry, 99
Kane, Ronald L., 8
Kelley, Robin D. G., 163
Kendrick (Nation of Islam), 106–7
Kennedy, John F., xviii
Kennedy, Robert F., xviii
Kenya, 124, 192n39
Kerner Commission, 102
Kim, Sunmin, 166
King, Martin Luther, Jr., xviii, 101–2, 122
"Klansville," xii
Kozinski, Alex, 142

Krasenes, Paul E., 8
Ku Klux Klan, 8–10, 29–30, *68*, 97, 99, 146

Lamott, Kenneth: *Chronicles of San Quentin*, 169
Lara-Millán, Armando, 166
Latinx people, 12, 76, 98. *See also* Chicanos; Hispanic people
law enforcement. *See* correctional officers; police officers
lawsuits, from prisoners, xix–xx, 60–66, 76, 108–10, 112, 140, 159–61. *See also* names of individual lawsuits
Levison, Stanley, 102
Lincoln, Abraham, xvii
Little Rock, AR, 101
Little Rock Integration Crisis (1957), 101
Locke, John, 40
Lombroso, Cesare, 42
Lopez-Aguado, Patrick, 31, 155
Lorde, Audre, 186n87; master's tools, 66
Los Angeles, xix, xviii, 16, 55, 60, 62, 98, 100, 121, 152
Los Angeles County, CA, 70
Los Angeles Police Department, xix
lynching, 6, 23, 25, 97, 146, 172n12
Lynn, John, 8
Lytle Hernández, Kelly, 14, 166

Malcolm X, xviii, 109, 122, 164
Mandela, Nelson, xxii, 19–20, 178n5
Mao Zedong, 124–25
March on Washington, xviii, *95*
Marin County Courthouse, xix, 120–21
Martin, Trayvon, xx
Marx, Karl, 125
Marxism-Leninism, 124
Massey, Douglas S., 178n12
mass incarceration, 5, 19, 24, 96, 102, 149
master's tools, 66, 186n67
Mau Mau Rebellion, xxi, 192n39
McGee, Richard, 46, 76
McNamara, Richard: *Pelican Bay*, 169
medical experiments, 42–43, 45, 49, 184n30
Meneweather (Soledad inmate), 114–15
Merton, Robert, 173n12

Mexican Mafia, xviii–xix, 69, 83, 111, 143–44, 146, 150, 152–53, 156, 160, 188n37
Michigan State University, Gerald M. Kline Digital and Multimedia Center, 167
migrant detention, 10, 12
Miller, Alvin, 5, 111, 115–18
Miller, Opie G., xix, 5, 111–12, 118, 129
Million Man March, xx
Mills, John V., xix, 117–19, 129
Minnesota, 10
Mississippi Delta, xiii
Missouri, xi–xii
Mitchell (petitioner in lawsuit), 62
Monterey County, CA, 117
Montgomery, AL, xviii, 101
Montgomery Bus Boycott, xviii, 101
morenos, 2, 172n10, 175n29
Morris, Aldon, 165
Morrison, Toni, 19
Muslim people. *See* Black Muslims
Myanmar, 20

Namibia, xxii
National Advisory Commission on Civil Disorders (Kerner Commission), 102
National Security Council, xix
Nation of Islam, 27, 51–56, 62–65, 78, 102–4, 106, 121–22. *See also* Black Muslims
Nazis: in Germany, xxi, 20, 82; neo-Nazis, 123; swastikas, 10, 67–68, 82, 84; in the United States, 11, 26, 28, 81–82, 105, 146
Nevada State Prison System, 55–56, 87–89, 188n43
New Folsom Prison, xx, 7, 171n4
New Jersey, 11; Newark, 100
New Madrid County, MO, xi
Newton, Huey P., xviii, 100, 118, 168; *Revolutionary Suicide*, 169
New York, xix, 16
New York City, xix, 23, 99–100, 130, 132
New York City Conspiracy (1741), 96
Nicaragua, 3, 174n19
Nigeria, xxi
9/11 attacks, xx

Nixon, Richard, xix, 102
Nolen, W. L., 5, 109–11, 114–19, 129, 138
Noonan, John T., Jr., 142
Northern California, 70–71, 147, 188n37
Northern Ireland, xxi
Northwestern University, 165–66
Nuestra Familia, xix, 69, 83, 144, 153, 156–57, 160, 188n37

Oakland, CA, xviii, 16, 98–99, 146, 193n62
Oath Keepers, 8
Observance Committee of the National Emancipation Proclamation Centennial, 78–79
Occupy Wall Street, xx
official controls: and Black militants, 56, 58, 60–61, 64–65, 103, 110–11, 147, 155–56, 160; and carceral apartheid, 5–6, 9, 12, 25–29, 32, 34, 40, 45, 180n27; and "white above all," 80
O'Hearn, Dennis, 174n24

Page, Joshua, 180n32, 180n38
Palestine, xx, 20, 24; Gaza, xxii, 12–13, *18*; Nakba, xxi, 12. *See also* Israel
Pan-African Liberation, 96
Panama Canal, xxi
Paris, France, 23
Parks, Rosa, xviii
parole, xx, 4, 7, 25, 53–55, 79–80, 167, 173n17
Patterson, William L., 23
Pattillo, Mary, 165
Pelican Bay State Prison, xx, 15–16, 69, 90, 153, 155–59, 169
penal field, 181n38
Philadelphia, PA, 99–100
Pinell, Hugo "Yogi Bear": early life of, 2–3; and escape plot (1971), 6–7, 130, 135; founding of Black Guerilla Family by, 5, 51, 104; murder of, xx, 7–8, 160–61, 171n4; at Pelican Bay, 155–56; at San Quentin, xix, 137–38, 171n3; sentencing of, 1, 3–5, 173n17; and Soledad Incident, 109–17, 174n19
Pitchford, Waylon, 7–8
Plessy v. Ferguson, 97

police officers: alliances with white supremacists, 9–10, 29–30, 97, 107; Black interactions with, xii–xiv; and Black militants, 103, 147; and carceral apartheid, 5, 12; murder of Black people by, xviii–xix, 10–11, 121–22; and protesters, xx, xxii, 95, 101; and settler colonialism, 23; violence by, xi, 3, 20, 98, 114, 119–20, 165
Portland, OR, 11
positivism, 41–42
Pratt, Geronimo, xix–xx
Pratt, Richard Henry, 22
prisoner class, 6, 127–28, 159
prisoners, as category, 30
prisoner strikes, xx, 127–29
prisons. *See names of individual prisons*
problem inmates, 42, 44, 46–54, 58, 59
problem populations, 28, 34, 38–39, 41, 44–45, 62–63
Prohibition, xvii
Proposition 36 (2000, California), xx. *See also* Three Strikes Law (1994, California)
Proud Boys, 8, 10
Puerto Rico, xxi, 67; nationalist movement in, xvii, 24

race riots (1967), xviii, 99–100
racial capitalism, 3, 9, 19, 24–25, 172n11
racial degradation, 30
racialization, xiv, 10, 21, 24, 27, 30–34, 96, 99, 123
racial projects, 25, 30–32, 34
racial segregation: and apartheid, 19–21; and carceral apartheid, 24–25, 180n23; de jure vs de facto, 178n11; in education, xi; and organizational racial projects, 31, 172n12; in prisons, 54–55, 76–77, 83, 115, 118, 145, 153, 155, 167; in US neighborhoods, 96–99, 101. *See also* Jim Crow
racial sorting, 31–34
racial tribalism, 128
racism, definition of, 22–23
racist intent, xiv, 8–10, 14, 22–26, 32, 60, 95–97, 131, 165, 180n27

rape, xiii, 3–4, 6, 12, 20, 25, 87–88, 96, 137–40, 173n17, 188n43
Ray, Victor, 26, 180n23
rebel archives, 14–16, 166
Reconstruction, xvii, 172n12, 182n7
Red Cross, 36
rehabilitative ideal, 37–38, 41–42, 44, 47, 49
reparations, 78–79
Republican Party, 11, 103
Republic of New Afrika, 121, 125
Revolutionary Action Movement, 102
Richard (Black militant at Folsom), 57–59
RICO Act, xix
Roberts v. Department of Corrections, 63–64
Robeson, Paul, 23
Robinson, Cedric J., 172n11
Rodney, Walter, 91
Rohingya, 20
Rousseau, Jean-Jacques, 40
Rubin, Ashley, 41
Russia, xxi–xxii
Rustin, Bayard, 102
Rwanda, xxii, 20

Sacramento, CA, 15, 52, 55, 57, 115–16, 166
Sacramento County Jail, 115–16
San Francisco, 65, 141
San Francisco Bay View, 8
San Francisco Examiner: "San Quentin's Valuable Work for Science Should Continue," 45
San Quentin Museum, 7
San Quentin Six, xix, 135, 137, 140–41
San Quentin State Prison, *xxiv, 36, 43, 56, 110, 136*; Adjustment Center at, 52, 135, 140–41; archives of, 167–69; Aryan Brotherhood at, xviii, 82, 89, 109; Black Guerilla Family at, xix, 6, 94, 104, 119–20, 143–44, 146; Black militants at, 58, 64–65, 106, 138, 147, 153; Crips and Bloods at, 150, 152; escape attempt (1971) at, xix, 6–8, 129–32, 135; Hugo Pinell at, xix, 1, 4–6; Leo Stanley at, 37, 42–45; and "white above all," 79–81, 84

Sargent, Brian, 166
SB 394 (2017, California), xx
Seale, Bobby, 100
Sean (Black Panthers/Black Guerilla Family), 122–23, 126
Secure Housing Units (SHUs), xx, 147, 151, 153–57, 159–61. *See also* Adjustment Centers; supermax confinement
segregation. *See* racial segregation
Selma, AL, xviii, 95
Sentencing Reform Act, xix
Servicemen's Readjustment Act, xvii, 98
settler colonialism, xiii, xxi, 21–23, 25–27, 42, 96
sexual violence, xiii, 3–4, 6, 12, 20, 25, 87–88, 96, 137–40, 173n17, 188n43
Shakur, Abdul Olugbala, 155–56
Shakur, Assata, xix
sharecroppers, xi–xii
Shedd, Carla, 166
Sierra-Arévalo, Michael, 166
16th Street Baptist Church bombing, xviii
Skarbek, David, 180n27
slavery, 6, 96–97; in prisons, xx; in the United States, 20
social problems, 34, 52, 58–60
sociology, concept-driven, 178n8
Soledad Brothers, xix, 118, 120, 135
Soledad Brothers Defense Committee, 118, 120, 140, 150
Soledad State Prison: Adjustment Center in, 50–52; Black militants in, 78, 129, 138, 142; Chicanos in, 188n37; opening of, xvii; Soledad Incident at, xix, 5–6, 109–21, 174n19
solidary cultures, 6, 174n24
solitary confinement. *See* Adjustment Centers; Secure Housing Units (SHUs); supermax confinement
South Africa, xxi–xxii, 13, 19–20, 178n5
Southern California, 67, 70, 83, 146–47, 152, 188n37
Southern Christian Leadership Conference, 102
Southern Tenant Farmers' Union, xi
Soviet Union, 98

Spain, Johnny, 131–32, 135, 141–42
Spain v. Procunier, xix
Spain v. Rushen, xix
Stanford University, Green Library, 167–68
Stanley, Leo L., 37–38, 42, 45–46, 184n30; *Men at Their Worst*, 43–44, 169
Stender, Fay, xix, 118, 150
sterilization, 42–43
Stono Rebellion, 97
strain theory, 172n12
strategic racialization, 32–33
strikes: hunger, xx, 65, 117, 159–60; prison-wide, xx, 127–29
summer racial uprisings (2020), xx
supermax confinement, xx, 15, 29, 34, 69, 90, 155–56, 160. *See also* Adjustment Centers; Secure Housing Units (SHUs)
Supreme Court of California, 60–65

Taylor, Breonna, xx, 11
tear gas, 140–41
Tehachapi State Prison, xvii
Terán, Manuel "Tortuguita," xx
Three Strikes Law (1994, California), xx. *See also* Proposition 36 (2000, California)
Tigel (incarcerated Black man), 79–80
Till, Emmett, xiii, 97
Tracy, CA, xviii
Tracy state prison. *See* Deuel Vocational Institution (Tracy, CA)
Treaty of Paris, xxi
Trump, Donald, xx, 11
truth-telling, as method, 165–70
Tubman, Harriet, xvii, 93, 100
Tulsa race massacre (1921), 9–10
Tuskegee Syphilis Study, 165

Ukraine, xxii
United Guerilla Front, xix, 145–46
United Kingdom. *See* England; Great Britain
United Nations, xvii, xxii, 23
Universal Negro Improvement Association, 102

Index

University of California, Los Angeles, xix
University of California–Berkeley, Bancroft Library, 166–67
USA Patriot Act, xx
US Congress, 11, 64, 98, 123
US Constitution: Eighth Amendment, 160; Fourteenth Amendment, 76; Thirteenth Amendment, xvii, 97
US Court for the Northern District of California, 77
US Court of Appeals for the Ninth Circuit, 142
US Department of Justice, 51, 102
US District Court for the Eastern District of California, 171n4
US Foundation, 16, 104, 121–22
US Supreme Court. *See names of individual lawsuits*

Vargas, Robert, 166
Vietnam War, xxi–xxii, 70, 118, 123
Violent Crime Control and Law Enforcement Act, xx
Virgin Islands, xxi

Walker, Michael L., 30–31, 166
warfare, 13, 22–23

War on Drugs, 102–3, 150
Washington, DC, xviii, xx, 10, *68*
Watergate scandal, xix, 102
Watts riots (1965), xviii, 60, 100
Wayne, John, 67
Weaver, Jayson, 7–8
Wells, Ida B., xvii, 28, 37, 183n7
West Virginia, 11
Wheatley, Phillis, 149
"white above all," 67, 69, 74–75, 80, 82–87, 112, 127, 131, 154
whiteness, xiii, 10, 17, 19, 25, 30, 32, 74–75, 82, 87, 107
white solidarity, xiii, xiv, 7, 30, 32–33, 75, 88, 131
white supremacists. *See* Aryan Brotherhood; *and names of individual groups and organizations*
Wilkinson, William Richard: *Prison Work*, 169
Women Against Rape, 139
World War I, xxi, 41
World War II, xxi, *36*, 98

Youth Authority, 103–4, 126

Zerubavel, Eviatar, 178n8
Zionism, xxi, 12–13

www.ingramcontent.com/pod-product-compliance
Lightning Source LLC
LaVergne TN
LVHW092349010825
817679LV00030B/584